MERCY IN ACTION

The Social Teachings of Pope Francis

Thomas Massaro, SJ
Santa Clara University

ROWMAN & LITTLEFIELD
Lanham • Boulder • New York • London

Executive Editor: Sarah Stanton
Assistant Editor: Carli Hansen
Senior Marketing Manager: Kim Lyons

Credits and acknowledgments for material borrowed from other sources, and reproduced with permission, appear on the appropriate page within the text.

Published by Rowman & Littlefield
A wholly owned subsidiary of
The Rowman & Littlefield Publishing Group, Inc.
4501 Forbes Boulevard, Suite 200, Lanham, Maryland 20706
https://rowman.com

Unit A, Whitacre Mews, 26-34 Stannary Street, London SE11 4AB, United Kingdom

British Library Cataloguing in Publication Information Available

Library of Congress Cataloging-in-Publication Data
Names: Massaro, Thomas, 1961– author.
Title: Mercy in action : the social teachings of Pope Francis / Thomas Massaro, SJ, Santa Clara University.
Description: Lanham : Rowman & Littlefield, 2018. | Includes bibliographical references and index.
Identifiers: LCCN 2017059081 (print) | LCCN 2018001617 (ebook) | ISBN 9781442271753 (electronic) | ISBN 9781442271739 (cloth : alk. paper) | ISBN 9781442271746 (pbk. : alk. paper)
Subjects: LCSH: Francis, Pope, 1936– | Social justice—Religious aspects—Catholic Church. | Christian sociology—Catholic Church.
Classification: LCC BX1795.S62 (ebook) | LCC BX1795.S62 M37 2018 (print) | DDC 261.8088/282--dc23
LC record available athttps://lccn.loc.gov/2017059081

♾ ™ The paper used in this publication meets the minimum requirements of American National Standard for Information Sciences Permanence of Paper for Printed Library Materials, ANSI/NISO Z39.48-1992.

Printed in the United States of America

CONTENTS

PREFACE

Few figures have ever burst upon the world stage as suddenly and dramatically as Pope Francis. Before his election as pope early in 2013, few outside his homeland of Argentina had even heard of Jorge Mario Bergoglio, a Jesuit priest who had served for over a decade as cardinal archbishop of Buenos Aires and was in the process of planning his retirement. Defying the predictions of Vatican watchers, his fellow cardinals elected him pope on the fifth ballot of the papal conclave to replace the retiring Pope Benedict XVI. In selecting the first pope ever to come from the Southern or Western Hemisphere, not to mention the first Jesuit to sit on the Chair of Peter, the electors set off something of a revolution in the Roman Catholic Church. The unlikely election of Francis would be just the first unpredictable development for the man who would soon earn the nickname "the pope of surprises."

From the moment he stepped onto the balcony overlooking Vatican City's Saint Peter's Square to be introduced to the enormous crowd drawn by the white smoke, Pope Francis captivated the attention of millions. His evident humility, genuine simplicity of style, and spontaneous joy struck many as extremely refreshing—a sharp break from the monarchical model of the papacy. He immediately relinquished the lavish private papal apartments for modest accommodations in a Vatican guesthouse, where he shared meals and casual conversations with travelers passing through. He replaced the papal limousine with a humble Ford Focus for local travel and opted for greatly simplified papal garments. He upended hidebound papal protocols and astonished the

world with his bold words and symbolic actions. His very choice of the
name Francis (inspired by Saint Francis of Assisi, a beloved saint associated with closeness to the poor, passion for peacemaking, and love of
nature) was itself a powerful gesture, one that telegraphed a healthy
slice of the papal agenda described in this book. The opening acts of the
Francis papacy provided vivid proof that actions speak louder than
words, and this book examines not only the bold words of Pope Francis
but also the great impact of the symbolic actions the pontiff employs to
communicate his message.

CHURCH SOCIAL TEACHINGS: CHANGE AND CONTINUITY

The focus of this volume is not on the personality of Pope Francis or his
impact on the internal life of the Catholic Church—the budding industry of Pope Francis literature already covers those topics quite amply.
Rather, this book examines the social teachings of Pope Francis—the
positions he stakes out and the commitments he makes regarding the
wider world of politics, culture, and the economy.

For well over a hundred years, popes have addressed deep concerns
about injustice and disorder in modern society and have developed a
large and sophisticated body of documents to express the values and
principles that should govern public life and the economy. Catholic
social teaching documents address such topics as the protection of human dignity, the rights of workers, family life, respect for the natural
environment, solidarity with the poorest members of society, and the
duty to promote peace and reconciliation. On each of these items and
more, Francis has not just embraced the existing teachings of previous
popes and church councils but significantly advanced them—updating
the message and putting his own distinctive spin on the tradition of
social justice advocacy he inherited. He has renewed these teachings by
adding certain new perspectives and an enhanced sense of urgency for
social change that enlivens the church's ministry to the marginalized.

The story of Catholic social teaching is a mix of continuity and
change. On one hand, the values and principles governing proper human relations in society remain consistent over time, so church pronouncements display a solid core of commitments from one pope to the

next. While many welcome the contributions of Pope Francis as a breath of fresh air in a stuffy church, even an innovative pope would hardly ever engineer major departures from church teachings on the basics of human social relations. On the other hand, rapid changes in culture, technology, and social organization do require church teaching to adjust to new conditions and challenges, applying established principles in creative ways. This book shows how Pope Francis retains core commitments that he inherited from previous church teachings on social and economic matters but has added many new elements that reflect the novel demands of our times. Each chapter shows what is old and what is new in Francis's social teachings—the mix of continuity and change that grounds him solidly in a rich tradition but still allows ample room for growth.

PLAN AND PERILS OF THIS BOOK

The introduction provides a brief biography of Pope Francis and some description of his intellectual background—just enough to assist the reader in situating and appreciating his contributions to social teaching. After exploring very briefly the roots of the social thought of Pope Francis, we move on to six topics on which his words and actions have advanced Catholic social teaching.

Chapter 1 treats economic justice, with a focus on how Francis has challenged the phenomenon of sharply increased economic inequality. In his first major papal document, *Evangelii Gaudium* ("The Joy of the Gospel"), published in November 2013, and on many other occasions, Francis strongly denounces structural injustices within a warped economy that does not function well in service to genuine human needs. Chapter 2 delves a bit deeper into a key feature of the globalized economic order, highlighting Francis's deep concern for workers whose rights are routinely violated in the global economy. He proposes a vision of a "globalization of solidarity" that he at once inherits from the previous popes and advances in his own distinctive ways. Chapter 3 treats the commitment of Pope Francis to the crucial matter of "care for our common home," a phrase describing his dedication to the natural environment, which serves as the subtitle of his 2015 encyclical letter *Laudato Si'* ("Praise Be to You"). Chapter 4 describes the pope's promotion of healthy family life, the subject of the 2016 apostolic exhortation *Amoris Laetitia* ("The Joy of Love") as well as two momentous (and controversial) meetings of the worldwide Synod of Bishops in 2014 and 2015. Chapter 5 chronicles the fervent advocacy of Pope Francis for some of the most marginalized people in the world: refugees, migrants, and victims of human trafficking. Chapter 6 describes the strong efforts of the pope to advance the cause of peace and disarmament, with bold words and actions to promote diplomatic solutions to global conflicts and to commit to an agenda of peacemaking and nonviolence. A brief conclusion draws together the many strands developed throughout the book and assesses how Pope Francis has contributed to the renewal of Catholic social teaching.

Of course, Catholic social teaching covers many further topics, such as bioethical issues (e.g., reproductive and end-of-life decisions) and cultural challenges (e.g., consumerism). These too are an authentic part of the social concerns of the church—indeed, of all people of goodwill. But I have chosen these six topics because they are obviously of great importance to Pope Francis and are highly representative of his core commitments. On topics well beyond the six selected here, Francis boldly challenges all people to build a world that is more humane and ethical—a social order grounded in the common good and the well-being of the most vulnerable rather than selfish private interests. For Francis and the Roman Catholic faithful, this agenda is part of a whole-hearted commitment to the gospel of Jesus Christ. For those outside the Catholic community, Francis's teachings may serve as a powerful inspiration to follow a shared core of ethical principles stemming from common faith-based or humanitarian values. Emerging from this examination of the roots and implications of the teachings of Francis in these six areas is a coherent picture of social concern, a profound vision of social justice, and a compelling agenda for the future.

It is important to acknowledge the perils of writing about a pope who is still in office and likely to contribute even more to the social teachings of the church. This volume, completed in the summer of 2017, about four years into the papacy of Francis, cannot predict developments in the remainder of his time at the helm of the Catholic Church. Indeed, the most reliable accounts of the work of any historical figure have to wait for the passage of some decades, while commentators assess the legacy of a given world leader and form more definitive judgments informed by the added perspective of history. But even if writing about Francis while he is still pope is akin to attempting to hit a moving target, it is still a worthwhile endeavor. Whatever else he will accomplish in office, we can be confident that his fundamental teachings and the commitments behind them are unlikely to change very much.

Readers interested in the fascinating biography of Pope Francis and other aspects of his leadership and his broader theology will want to consult the bibliography, which will steer them to some of the best of the burgeoning Pope Francis literature already available in English. Further, practically everything Pope Francis has done and said is documented on the user-friendly websites of the Holy See (www.vatican.va), Vatican radio (www.radiovaticana.va), and the Vatican news service (www.vaticannews.va), each with full English-language content. Readers in search of full texts of the documents he has published as pope, the addresses he has given, and Francis's travels and other activities will be well served by these splendid sources. For the benefit of readers less familiar with church matters, I make every effort to define theological terms and explain relevant church practices in the course of the analysis to follow.

Finally, the goal of this book is to provide the reader with a balanced and unbiased account of the work of the current pope. Already, a number of published works on Pope Francis resemble hagiographies (uncritically adulatory accounts of saintly qualities) more than reliable descriptions and objective analyses of his contributions. While works of pious admiration have their place and laudable purpose, this tendency to heap words of unmixed praise upon the pope diminishes their usefulness to a general audience, much less an academic one. While I readily admit to being a wholehearted enthusiast for the first Jesuit pope, I attempt here to provide an objective and accurate account of his social teaching—one that is characterized by a sober analysis of his ambitious social agenda rather than unrestrained cheerleading. Indeed, the prudent observer readily acknowledges certain shortcomings regarding the scope, shape, and pace of the reforms pursued and enacted by Francis. There is certainly no shortage of vocal critics of this pope, who by his own open admission has committed many errors and indeed sometimes misses the mark in his leadership initiatives. The account to follow offers some assessment of Francis's shortcomings along with a generally appreciative description of how he has advanced Catholic social thought.

DEDICATION AND ACKNOWLEDGMENTS

In the chapters of this book, a number of social activists and organizations will be mentioned, most merely in passing, as practically oriented exemplars of the values and principles Pope Francis commends. As a teacher and Universal Pastor, a solitary man in the Vatican can effect global change only by inspiring and empowering others to carry out a mission of mercy and social justice. Most of the hard work of forging a world of greater fairness and mutual respect is accomplished at the grass roots, by millions of people of conscience working collectively in concert though the operations of agencies and organizations promoting social justice. It is to these hands-on activists and practitioners of social justice that this book is dedicated. Their ranks include advocates for peace and disarmament, environmentalists, labor activists, and those who contribute to interreligious dialogue and social outreach locally and at higher levels. Anticipating the content of chapter 5, I hasten to single out those who work with the Jesuit Refugee Service and the Catholic Relief Services and the thousands of brave volunteers (many of them women in religious congregations) who advocate for victims of human trafficking and provide direct services around the world. I dedicate my effort at research and writing to their amazing work.

Words of heartfelt gratitude are also in order to the institutions that have sponsored and assisted my writing, including the Jesuit School of Theology of Santa Clara University, the Joan and Ralph Lane Center for Catholic Studies and Social Thought at the University of San Francisco (which generously awarded me its John LoSchiavo, SJ, Chair in spring 2017), the Library of Congress, and the Jesuit communities of St. Aloysius Gonzaga in Washington, DC, and Loyola House at the University of San Francisco, which hosted me during my writing. Thanks also go out (as ever) to my loving parents and family members who have encouraged me in so many ways. My faithful friend Tom Harrison reviewed the first draft of this book with great editorial insight. May the social justice mission of Pope Francis, as well as his message of charity and mercy, continue to inspire all those mentioned here.

INTRODUCTION

The Roots of the Social Thought of Pope Francis

The Catholic Church pursues a mission that includes many dimensions. As a pastor of souls, it engages in a wide range of activities—from sacramental ministry and counseling to education and charitable social services—that attempt to spread the Christian gospel and heal a broken world in practical ways. As a large global institution, the church directs its energies both inward (to care for the spiritual needs of the 1.2 billion Catholics located in every country on earth) and outward (in missionary work, relief services, and social communications of all sorts).

Catholic social teaching has been described as the place where the church turns its face most deliberately to the wider world—in other words, the part of its theology where faithful Catholics receive moral guidance as they encounter complex worldly realities such as politics and the economy. This guidance is communicated not only by official teaching documents promulgated by top church leaders but also through such local and less formal vehicles as homilies at Sunday Mass, the policies of Catholic schools and hospitals, an active presence in the media, and even the routine activities of a parish church. In order for this message to be effective and credible, values and priorities of social justice and reconciliation must be not only proposed in eloquent terms but also enacted in the everyday life of large institutions. While no one person exercises complete control over the shape and operation of Catholic social teaching, it is accurate to say that nobody exerts more influence on the priorities adopted in these teachings than a pope. A pontiff who is highly motivated to publicize and address a social problem or great injustice has the power to provide effective leadership and make a real difference in how Catholics throughout the world pursue a commitment to social justice.

From his very first days in office, the Catholic world discovered such a pope in Francis. The earliest appearances of the 266th pontiff after his election on March 13, 2013, contained unmistakable clues signaling his intention to be a different kind of pope—one impatient with the trappings of the monarchical papacy, eager to mingle with common people, and ready to embrace a model of church that is less about maintaining staid protocols and preserving liturgical forms and more about practicing mercy and promoting social justice. It did not take long for people around the world to witness Francis turning his attention outward, beyond the limits of internal church concerns to social issues where the church meets the wider world. Within hours of taking office, the new Holy Father revealed this longing: "How I would like a poor church for the poor." Within weeks, Francis was using a round of routine meetings with diplomats and other world leaders as occasions to emphasize his deepest economic and political concerns. These include the urgency of global reforms to address the growing chasm between rich and poor, widespread indifference to the suffering of refugees and trafficked persons, and the need for mercy and reconciliation wherever conflicts create victims among the vulnerable.

After a few months spent almost exclusively in Rome, Francis signaled his priorities with two high-profile trips in July 2013, when he modeled the kind of pastoral outreach he had been proposing as a core part of the mission of the church. First, he traveled on short notice to the small Mediterranean island of Lampedusa, a stopover point for desperate refugees fleeing to Europe from Africa, to mourn the thousands of victims of shipwrecks near that "island of tears," where so many bodies of the drowned have washed ashore. The solemn Mass and other ceremonies Francis conducted there (to be described in detail in chapter 5) called attention to the deepening crisis of migration worldwide and amounted to an appeal for more humane public policies regarding immigrants in all lands. Second and far more joyful in tone was the papal trip later that month to Rio de Janeiro to celebrate World Youth Day. In a series of exuberant public masses and events, Francis inspired young people to renew their faith and take up the duty of service to humankind, incorporating conscious and sacrificial efforts to pursue social justice into their way of life. He urged the pilgrims to return home "to stir things up" (a loose rendering of the Spanish phrase *quiero lio*, which he used at the time[1]) and to engage in fervent activism for social change. While most accounts of the pope's week in his native South America focused on the popular frenzy and jubilant gatherings of 3 million youths on Copacabana Beach, more accurate headlines would have contained phrases like "practicing social responsibility" and "living a life of charity"—key obligations the pope placed before the international gathering of youth during those days.

This rapid succession of events left the staid Vatican press corps with a bad case of whiplash. The reporters covering Francis were just getting accustomed to a certain dominant storyline: outsider selected as pope hunkers down in the Vatican to hammer out strategies to address festering internal crises in the church and to plan badly needed church reforms. Now it was dawning on the press pool that Francis had a broader agenda in mind, one that at every turn would include attention to social justice within and beyond the walls of the church itself. As important and ambitious as were Francis's plans to introduce reforms in such internal church matters as the mishandling of the clergy sexual-abuse crisis and the Vatican Bank (also embroiled in scandals for decades), the true object of his passion remained the area of social justice. Francis was not discouraged by predictions that it would be a full-time job for an outsider pope like him to oversee long-delayed reforms in the operations of the Roman Curia (the central administrative offices of the church in Vatican City, where one thousand priests and four thousand other employees work); he persisted in looking outward beyond internal Vatican affairs. When Francis published his first major teaching document, *Evangelii Gaudium* ("The Joy of the Gospel"), in November 2013, it included not only the expected material laying out his program for internal church activity to advance the theme of evangelization but also unexpectedly abundant coverage of poverty, economic inequality, and the need for greater global solidarity. Francis continued to use every opportunity to turn the attention of the people of faith outward and to address deep social concerns.

We might ask, What motivates Francis to keep the struggle for social justice front and center? What factors have contributed to his drive to renew the church's advocacy for the poor and its contribution to peace-making and care for the environment? What formative influences led him to work so tirelessly on behalf of oppressed workers, refugees, and trafficked persons? In short, what in his background might account for the shape and depth of his social justice concerns?

This series of questions about Pope Francis and his leadership priorities raises the more general question of why any of us displays the qualities or chooses the goals we do. Now, even the most insightful psychologists have long despaired of identifying with pinpoint accuracy the origins of anyone's personal commitments or offering a definitive explanation of why a given person adopts certain values and not others in the course of a lifetime. Only a crass determinist with a low estimation of human freedom would expect to "explain" the actions of another person in terms of a few tightly defined causal factors. Obviously, no single factor accounts for why Pope Francis cares about particular aspects of social justice or chooses to highlight particular global issues the way he does.

But it will be useful to review some of the formative influences that surely shaped the worldview of the pope and contribute to his leadership on social issues like the six topics treated in this volume. Among the chief influences accounting for the social justice agenda of Francis are (1) his personal history and background, (2) his Jesuit identity, and (3) the inheritance of previous Catholic social teaching. While other elements surely come into play, these emerge as the major roots of the social thought of Pope Francis.

PERSONAL HISTORY AND BACKGROUND

Jorge Mario Bergoglio was born in 1936 in the Flores neighborhood of Buenos Aires. The future pope was the firstborn of what would eventually be four children in a family of recent immigrants from humble origins in northern Italy. Between the disruptions associated with adjusting to a new homeland and some unfortunate financial setbacks (a failed family business and repeated Depression-era job loss for Jorge's father), the Bergoglio family never rose above the level of modest means. Although there was always a sufficiency of the essentials of life, out of the question would be luxuries such as a family car or expensive vacations.

By all accounts, the future pope's family lived a frugal existence in a middle-class neighborhood where much of the social life was organized around the local Catholic parishes and their associated schools and social institutions. Since every bit of possible income was needed to support the family, Jorge held a variety of service jobs in his teen years (custodian, chemistry lab worker, even, briefly, bouncer at a nightclub) and eventually enrolled in a vocational course to train as a chemical technician. In his late teens, Jorge began to feel the pull of a religious vocation and came to spend more time reading works of theology than the science textbooks he was assigned in school. He enrolled in a diocesan seminary and, after surviving a life-threatening lung infection, delicate surgery, and months of recuperation, decided to enter the Society of Jesus (the Jesuits) in 1958.

Certain aspects of his early life likely contributed to the shape of the social justice commitments of the future Pope Francis. As a member of a family of slender means, he would always appreciate the struggles of low-wage workers to make ends meet. The proximity of his centrally located middle-class neighborhood to both the highly opulent and the desperately poor sections of the sprawling metropolis of Buenos Aires instilled in the young man an awareness of sharp stratifications of socioeconomic status. Buenos Aires has acquired the nickname "the Paris of Latin America," but many sections continue to be ravaged by deep poverty. Jorge Bergoglio grew up just a long walk or an easy bus ride away from places where he could encounter the great disparities in lifestyle generated by a modern economy. In one direction, he could easily observe affluent families living lives of privilege and luxury with few economic cares. In other directions lay the barrios and shantytowns (in Argentine parlance, the *villas miserias*, or misery dwellings) plagued by high unemployment, unsanitary conditions, endemic drug addiction, and gang-related violence that rocked the ramshackle neighborhoods. Slim indeed were hopes for upward mobility, even for enterprising residents of these slums who took advantage of whatever opportunities presented themselves for gainful employment, education, and personal development. Even if they worked long hours each day at a succession of low-wage jobs, those occupying the bottom rungs of the labor force faced grim prospects for achieving a better life for themselves or their children. When regular work was unavailable, many in the poorest precincts of Buenos Aires (both then and now) turned out of necessity to the informal economy of seasonal and contingent work, serving, for instance, as *cartoneros*, or garbage pickers who scour the dumps to salvage recyclable materials for cash. When all other doors to income were slammed shut, some resorted to black-market activities, such as prostitution and drug dealing, to feed their families or put off marriage and despaired of having children entirely because of their dire economic prospects.

It makes a great difference that Pope Francis grew up and lived a majority of his life in Buenos Aires. For one, it is a large port city, the principal commercial center and political capital of the second-largest nation in South America. As such, it attracts new arrivals from around the world, who rub shoulders and contribute to a rich mix of ideas and religious communities. As a young man, as a priest, and as a bishop, Bergoglio would encounter and minister to a variety of these communities. Many of the residents of the *villas miserias* were recent arrivals from poorer countries of Latin America, particularly the politically turbulent landlocked nations of Bolivia and Paraguay. His pastoral contact with these struggling immigrants would leave a mark on the future Pope Francis, sensitizing him to the needs of migrants (who were, after all, not so different from the Bergoglio family itself a generation or two earlier). Above all, it is easy to imagine how decades of this decidedly urban formative experience contributed to Francis's ethical formation. Witnessing such great economic inequality would lead any perceptive and morally serious person to ask hard questions regarding the fairness of our economic system, which rewards a lucky few but punishes millions despite their hard work and best efforts to build a better life. It is hard to sidestep such concerns in a multiethnic city of 13 million people such as Buenos Aires, and Francis stands apart as the first pope to come of age in this type of postmodern sprawling megalopolis.

What we might claim about city of origin shaping one's social commitments is also true about country of origin. It certainly makes a difference that Pope Francis is a son of Argentina. Its national identity is shaped by a rich colonial history (it achieved political independence from Spain in the nineteenth century), a fascinating culture (especially in dance, sports, and literature—all three featured in colorful interviews granted by Pope Francis over the years), and a distinctive experience of political conflict. When Bergoglio was a young man, the political life of the nation was dominated by Juan Perón, a populist reformer who ruled as president from 1946 to 1955 and again in the early 1970s, to be succeeded in office by his third wife, Isabel. The decades on either side of these Perón regimes witnessed a series of coups, military juntas, and dictatorships that placed great stress on the economy of Argentina and caused widespread suffering, especially for the poorer classes. Perhaps the deepest influence of all these national developments on the future Pope Francis was the phenomenon of Peronism, a populist approach to political life that at once promoted social reforms to benefit workers and the common people and capitalized on the charisma of the strong leader himself (not to mention his first wife, the cultural icon Evita Perón). Bergoglio admits that, like many Argentinian teens at the time, he was an enthusiast (though too young to be a true partisan) for the social reforms promised by Peronism, which displayed much resonance with the egalitarian ideals of Catholic social teaching. Peronism also included a unique (and potentially problematic) approach to the delicate relationship between church and state in Argentina, appealing to popular religiosity to bolster its political support but also provoking significant tensions with the Catholic establishment at the time, with which it vied for popular support.

It is beyond the scope of this book to offer a detailed account of the political history of Argentina or even to assess its ultimate influence on Pope Francis.[2] But there is much evidence to support the conjecture that the ongoing experience of political instability and social strife in the nation he loved sensitized Bergoglio to both the tragedy of political betrayal (which was too often accompanied by a resort to violence and corruption) and the potential of constructive civic leadership to work for the common good. The lessons of Argentina's recent history highlight the crucial role of trust building, deep commitments to principles of fairness even across social divisions, and a willingness to compromise and settle disagreements in peaceful ways. For keen observers of national history such as Bergoglio, these imperatives emerge as preconditions for the achievement of social justice.

These very lessons were on vivid display in the most traumatic era the future pope would witness in his homeland: the "Dirty War" of 1976 to 1983, a bloody era when a brutal military regime hunted down, "disappeared," and executed tens of thousands of its opponents. During part of these years, Bergoglio was serving a six-year term (1973–1979) as Jesuit provincial superior and then as rector of the theology faculty in Buenos Aires. These top positions afforded the future pope a front-row view of the violence and oppression ravaging his homeland. As an administrator charged with care and oversight of hundreds of Jesuits as well as the schools and parishes that they staffed, he was forced to walk a tense tightrope to keep his men safe from the brutal regime. The stressful situation was complicated by the fact that some Jesuits (especially those working among the poor) were repeatedly threatened and accused of fomenting subversive activities. Bergoglio was criticized for failure to protect all his charges (notably, in 1976 two Jesuits were arrested, tortured, and held captive for months before their eventual release) and for not roundly denouncing the dictatorship. While a consensus on the full truth of the matter is elusive, it appears that the agonized Bergoglio had deliberately chosen a prudent strategy of quiet work behind the scenes that allowed the Jesuits to shelter and assist those targeted and to protect as many lives as possible from the murderous regime. Although some questions remain unresolved, much evidence has surfaced of heroic actions on the part of Bergoglio and his fellow Jesuits in the depths of this national crisis.

For present purposes, it is sufficient to take note of how Bergoglio's leadership of the Jesuit province in those extremely difficult times tested him and honed his commitment to social justice and the peaceful resolution of conflicts. Similar things could be said about his leadership of the archdiocese of Buenos Aires, where he served as auxiliary bishop from 1992 to 1998 and then as archbishop until his election as pope in 2013. Though not nearly as dramatic as the national trauma he endured during the Dirty War, these two decades presented serious challenges to Bergoglio as the leader of the large and contentious Catholic community of the nation's capital. Not only did Argentina witness a sharp economic recession and employment crisis that left millions desperately poor in the early years of the new millennium, but the archdiocese itself labored under financial scandal and a deeply uneasy relationship with successive national leaders. Church-state relations were especially strained under two recent presidents of Argentina (Néstor Kirchner and his wife and successor, Cristina), who openly thwarted many initiatives of the Catholic Church to advocate for the disadvantaged and provoked Catholic ire on a range of public policy matters. To his credit,

Archbishop Bergoglio continued to work hard at forging common ground with the secularist government, never closing the door that could lead to constructive compromises, although the intersection of faith and politics in that nation remains fraught to this day.[3] The crucible of Argentinian politics not only prepared Bergoglio for the intricacies of global diplomacy involving contentious secular leaders but also tutored him on how to promote social justice in the face of fierce opposition.

THE JESUIT IDENTITY OF POPE FRANCIS

The second stream of influence that contributes to Pope Francis's social teachings pertains to his identity as a Jesuit priest. Without a doubt, his membership in the Society of Jesus shaped his entire approach to life, including his ardent commitment to social justice. From the ages of twenty-one (when he entered the Jesuit novitiate) to fifty-five (when he became an auxiliary bishop), Bergoglio shared living quarters with many other Jesuits, underwent fifteen years of Jesuit spiritual formation and graduate education in theology and philosophy, and held the most important leadership positions within his province (director of novices, provincial superior, and rector of the major house of studies in Buenos Aires, among others). When he was elected pope at age seventy-six, several interviewers posed questions about how deeply he identified with his Jesuit roots, since he had not lived in a Jesuit community or worked with many Jesuits for two decades.[4] His answer was unambiguous: "I feel I am a Jesuit in my spirituality, in the spirituality of the *Exercises*, the spirituality that I have in my heart. I have not changed my spirituality, no. Francis, Franciscan, no. I feel Jesuit and I still think like a Jesuit."[5]

This quotation requires some explanation. Here the pope makes passing reference to another religious congregation, the Franciscans, which features its own distinctive spirituality. On earlier occasions, the pope had explained that his selection of the papal name Francis was motivated by his admiration for Saint Francis of Assisi (1181–1226), founder of the order of mendicant friars that bears his name. Foremost in the mind of the pope are several themes associated with that great Italian saint, including his humility and closeness to the poor, his love of nature, and his dedication to peacemaking. But the pope repeats that hard-to-define word "spirituality" four times specifically in explaining his continuing identification with the Jesuits, a religious congregation founded in 1540 by another saint, Ignatius of Loyola (1491–1556). It was Saint Ignatius who wrote the *Spiritual Exercises* and the *Constitutions*, two key documents that provide the essentials of the spiritual practices and way of life that all Jesuits share. The following paragraphs sketch a few elements of this Ignatian spirituality that provide substantial insight regarding the personal commitments and the social teachings of Pope Francis.

First, the Jesuit is called to a spiritual orientation, an approach to life that is never primarily materialistic in emphasis. At the beginning of the text of the *Spiritual Exercises*, Saint Ignatius draws upon a principle of the Christian catechism he knew to identify the overall purpose of life: "Man was created to praise, reverence and serve God, and thereby to save his soul. And the other things on the face of the earth were created for man's sake, and to help him in following out the end for which he was created."[6] Notice how these key sentences prioritize spiritual life over material progress without in any way denigrating the physical needs and well-being of people (or, arguably, nonhuman creation). The Jesuit commitment to the virtue of spiritual detachment allows adherents to live *in* this world (with a serious resolve to improve earthly life for all, especially the poorest) without being completely *of* this world (in other words, a slave to material things). Ignatius exhorts his readers and followers to practice a healthy indifference to material things that do little to advance the state of one's soul or the spiritual welfare of others whom they seek to assist along their own way to God. If Pope Francis appears free of inordinate attachments to luxuries and able to measure progress with a healthy indifference to worldly standards, it is because he still draws deeply from his Jesuit roots.

This profound starting point evidently leads Pope Francis (as it does other sincere and faithful adherents of Ignatian spirituality) to the simplicity of lifestyle for which he has become famous, to a desire for humble service rather than ostentation, and to a close identification with the poor and outcast of the world. As a young Jesuit, Bergoglio would have meditated on this principle many times, including on annual eight-day retreats and occasional thirty-day silent retreats. The call to prioritize the spiritual over the material was reinforced by a requirement of frequent humble service among the poor and the marginalized from the days of his novitiate, throughout his formation and beyond. As novice director, Bergoglio was himself responsible for supervising the customary Jesuit practice of engaging in "humble experiments" for many of his young charges, assigning the young men to work as hospital orderlies or on cleaning crews for weeks at a time. The future pope developed a reputation for relishing this kind of direct pastoral work among struggling urban and occasionally rural communities in Argentina. Throughout his career, Bergoglio displayed a legendary personal generosity to families in special need of material assistance and spiritual support, reflecting the principle of "gratuity of ministries" to which Ignatius (author of the "Prayer for Generosity" and known for his personal kindnesses to the poor) exhorted his confreres.

Once he became pope, Bergoglio had to adjust his range of accustomed activities considerably. There are things that a pope, if only for reasons of security and tight scheduling, cannot do—such as mingling daily with the poor masses and common folks. But then again, this high office does offer certain advantages, affording a man dedicated to uplifting the poor unique opportunities to publicize key issues. The deep support of Pope Francis for the series of World Meetings of Popular Movements he has sponsored and convened reflects this commitment to embrace the way of humility and closeness to the poor whenever possible. And he still finds occasions to exhibit evident enthusiasm for mingling with people of humble estate both in Rome and during his travels abroad, as his itineraries often include visits to soup kitchens, homeless shelters, and hospitals for the indigent. Against the criticisms of certain detractors that his "popular touch" is somehow contrived and merely for cameras, the record shows that Francis exhibits a deep and genuine desire to be close to common folk and to know and share their humble condition, as he has done throughout his career as a seminarian and priest. While it may be difficult to demonstrate precisely how this orientation of Jesuit spirituality directly affects the content of the social teachings of Pope Francis or his daily activities in office, there is no question that a leader whose first instinct is to advance the spiritual as well as the material progress of underresourced people stands apart in many ways from ordinary leaders. His common touch even sets him apart from most of his papal predecessors, who have tended to come from privileged backgrounds that rarely include much direct pastoral work among the poor.

Second, the tradition of Jesuit spirituality consistently focuses one's energy outside oneself, toward other-directed service rather than self-aggrandizement of any sort. Indeed, the phrase perhaps most commonly associated with the Society of Jesus is the overarching purpose that Saint Ignatius repeats many times in the text of the Jesuit *Constitutions*: "for the greater glory of God." This signature marker of Jesuit identity and resolve leaves no room for unhealthy self-regard. The follower of Ignatius is called to put aside all personal ambition, self-concern, and greed ("riches, honor, pride" in the idiom of the *Spiritual Exercises*) in order to engage in collective efforts to serve others. At the level of large institutions, this principle has prompted the worldwide network of Jesuit schools to adopt the motto "men and women for others." The motto applies especially transparently to Pope Francis, both in his earlier work as a Jesuit and even today in his work as pope. The Jesuit vows of poverty, chastity, and obedience that Bergoglio pronounced and the prodigious efforts at asceticism and self-denial that he has long affirmed reflect an extraordinary self-mastery that Francis has practiced for decades. He rarely buys a new pair of shoes; he even more rarely takes a vacation from his duties. This Jesuit orientation toward service of others clearly affects the style of his papacy and the content of his social teachings. It provides a distinctive ethos and makes a tangible difference in the operations of the church as an institution and as a spiritual force in a world of fierce competition where the pursuit of raw self-interest is the norm.

Third, Jesuit spirituality includes the practice of deep and sincere discernment, a spiritual practice described in Jesuit founding documents with the Latin phrase *caritas discreta* (discerning love). Discernment involves a dedication to empathetic listening and open dialogue—deliberative processes that are required before anyone can make a wise, well-informed decision. A sincere commitment to discernment motivates us to look beyond our own personal desires of the moment and to pay attention both to the interior movements in the hearts of our interlocutors and to developments in the larger world. The Ignatian-style listener is not afraid to engage in the arduous process of prayerful listening that may reveal God's compassionate will for the world, with the hopeful expectation of discovering the best path forward. As a Jesuit in formation, Bergoglio developed distinctive methods for discernment within his own personal life: a dedication to daily prayer, regular examination of conscience, and other techniques to enhance self-awareness and foster sound decision making. As a Jesuit superior, he learned how to employ even more specific tools that assist Jesuit governance and corporate discernment and provide the raw material for prudent leadership decisions. More than mere token consultations, these Jesuit practices demand the hard work of conducting the decision-making process in a thoroughly dialogical way.

The discernment process thus emerges as the nexus between the life of prayer and the life of action; the Jesuit commitment to sound discernment is not surprisingly reflected in the signature Jesuit aspiration to remain *simul in actione, contemplativus*, or a contemplative in action. This dual regard for the interior life and external effectiveness so evidently characterizes the leadership of Pope Francis, accounting for the observation of many that he appears extremely genuine, sincere, and uniquely "comfortable in his own skin." If he projects confidence, boldness of purpose, and inner freedom in his demanding office, it is because this Jesuit pope trusts in the discernment process that brought him thus far. Turning his back on neither the inner nor the outer dimensions of his somewhat paradoxical role as a spiritual leader within a fierce global political landscape, Francis draws on the Ignatian heritage of deep spiritual discernment even as he faces many highly practical decisions.

Fourth, Jesuit spirituality includes a signature commitment to "finding God in all things," a phrase that has inspired Jesuit efforts to dialogue with culture and secular learning in many lands and social contexts over several centuries. Because of its confidence in the coherence of faith and reason, Ignatian spirituality has been described as world embracing, incarnational, and transformationalist. These labels accurately capture the Jesuit proclivity to emphasize the indwelling of God within creation and to trust that God's purposes can be achieved precisely by engaging secular institutions across all cultures—drawing out of them what is best and most coherent with gospel values. For example, this spiritual orientation provides the grounding for the characteristic Jesuit encouragement of faith-based political activism, since a privatized faith is incomplete until it commits itself to the social dimension of discipleship. While very few Jesuits have themselves been active in the political process itself (five-term U.S. congressman Robert Drinan, SJ, is a rare exception), the impetus to practice social responsibility by engaging political systems directly is frequently evident in the careers of graduates of Jesuit schools, who often become noteworthy political leaders. When Pope Francis goes out of his way on many occasions to affirm "a good Catholic meddles in politics," he is reflecting this aspect of his Jesuit heritage.[7]

"Finding God in all things" has led Jesuits to be pioneers and boundary crossers in many ways throughout the history of the Society of Jesus. Within the sixteenth-century European context of their founding, the earliest Jesuits made great efforts to break down the animosities unleashed by the Protestant Reformation and founded schools dedicated to principles of Christian humanism and broad toleration. Their creative work in the arts and sciences of the time displayed their eagerness to resist the temptation to feel in any way threatened by secular learning. Beyond Europe, their courageous participation in the age of exploration, colonization, and missionary expansion that forged a global Christianity reflected their keen desire to engage other cultures and religions with reverent appreciation. Starting with the great missionary Saint Francis Xavier, who paved the way for the creative evangelizing work of such luminaries as Matteo Ricci in China and Robert de Nobili in India, Jesuits have distinguished themselves as pioneers of inculturation—the project of adapting the message of European-based Christianity to new contexts in respectful and sensitive ways that welcome new dialogue partners into a mutual process of discovery. Although no religious group can boast a perfect record of practicing consistently sensitive methods of evangelization since the era of global missions began in early modern times, the Society of Jesus has operated on the commendable Ignatian premise that God is already actively present in those we encounter in new settings and to whom we owe great reverence.

As a son of Ignatius, Pope Francis displays a deep commitment to respectful interreligious dialogue, building creatively upon both his own previous work with various faith leaders in Argentina and the fine examples of his papal predecessors. If recent popes built bridges to other faith communities, it appears that Francis intends to cross boldly over those same bridges—for example, in encouraging interfaith efforts to protect the natural environment and combat climate change. As we shall see in chapter 3, his 2015 encyclical *Laudato Si'* draws explicitly upon insights of several world religions and eagerly invites future ecological collaboration with people of all faiths. Francis describes this priority for determined outreach as "the culture of encounter," and it applies to political and diplomatic spheres as surely as it does to interreligious dialogue.

From the Jesuit inheritance, then, Francis draws a profound openness to engagement in all areas of public life, displaying a willingness to approach anyone of goodwill and to reach out the hand of diplomacy in rather bold ways. Chapter 6 describes his diplomatic efforts to facilitate the breakthrough in Cuban-American relations in 2014 and his interventions on numerous occasions to ease regional hostilities in the Middle East. All these efforts at constructive dialogue spring from several sources and motivations: the personal qualities and priorities of Pope Francis himself, the long Jesuit heritage of interreligious dialogue that shaped him, and the unique position of the Holy See in the international community. Under the leadership of Francis, the Catholic Church definitively renounces any sort of defensive crouch and emerges as an especially promising partner in any coalition for constructive social change, such as for greater global social justice and conflict transformation.

We have examined four key spiritual qualities evident in the Petrine ministry of Pope Francis that spring from the core of his Jesuit identity. It would not be hard to compile an even longer list of elements of Jesuit spirituality that have evidently influenced the leadership of Pope Francis in general, and specifically his ethical values and social justice teachings and agenda. No examination of the Jesuit roots of the social teaching of Pope Francis would be complete without pointing out two further influences of a historical nature—one a few decades old, the other a few centuries old. First, it is helpful to note that social justice emerged as a particularly prominent priority of the Society of Jesus and its apostolates at a 1974–1975 meeting that the future Pope Francis attended. As provincial superior in the mid-1970s, Bergoglio represented the province of Argentina at the Thirty-Second General Congregation in Rome, a worldwide legislative meeting at which the Society of Jesus adopted a seminal document that recommitted all Jesuits and their works to "the service of faith and the promotion of justice."[8] Four decades later, the Society of Jesus continues to promote social justice and to produce impressive documents outlining agendas for global change.[9] While it is undoubtedly true that all recent popes have spoken eloquently and acted boldly to promote social justice, the approach of Francis reflects the distinctive Jesuit commitment to addressing questions of proper social order. He also brings to the table a wealth of administrative and direct pastoral experience, much of it in challenging social contexts, that has most evidently shaped his imagination for greater social justice.

The second historical note takes us back to the earliest generations of Jesuits in the sixteenth century. Lurking within the Jesuit background of Pope Francis is the potential influence of some well-articulated political theories pertaining to questions of power, legitimate authority, church and state relations, and the virtues associated with proper governance—key dimensions of social justice. No Jesuits have been more influential within the history of Christian political thought than the theologians Robert Bellarmine (1542–1621) and Francisco Suárez (1548–1617). Their writings on the origins of political power, their challenge to the legitimacy of absolutism and the divine right of kings, and their articulation of what would later be called popular sovereignty and social contract theory exerted great influence around the world, especially where Jesuits settled and worked. When the Jesuits reached South America and gradually set up the missionary ventures that came to be known as the Paraguay Reductions, some considered these settlements of the indigenous Guaraní peoples as miniature utopian experiments—communities modeled on the principles of participatory democracy and common good (albeit a paternalistic version) outlined by the Jesuit theorists Suárez and Bellarmine. An influential biography of Pope Francis by Austen Ivereigh[10] and a more recent monograph by political scientist Thomas Rourke[11] propose that some of the "Jesuit DNA" of the reductions (eventually destroyed amid violent colonial rivalry, as viewers of the motion picture *The Mission* will surely recall) not only lingered in Argentina's collective memory for centuries but came to form part of the country's intellectual patrimony. In this national context, the argument runs, they influenced not only contemporary Jesuit thought but also Peronism, which in turn influenced the political views of the young Jorge Mario Bergoglio (by his own admission, a onetime enthusiast for this populist social democracy movement).

Assessing these fascinating matters involving political theory, the intersection of spirituality and politics, and the shape of church social teaching deserves more space than is available here. This much is clear: Jesuit spirituality is key to understanding the stances Pope Francis assumes regarding life in human society and the meaning of true justice. While it would be an exaggeration to claim that Jesuit spirituality explains every position the pope takes on issues of social justice, it is safe to say that the "Jesuit stream" that contributes to his river of teachings and advocacy is extremely influential. If I may indulge in another water-based metaphor, the pope is fully aware that Jesuit spirituality is the well from which he has been drinking for most of his life, and this font of wisdom has influenced his social thought immensely.

THE INHERITANCE OF PREVIOUS CATHOLIC SOCIAL TEACHING

Since its founding two thousand years ago, the Christian Church has engaged in social teachings of all sorts. Church leaders and theologians have developed interpretations of scripture (both the Hebrew Bible and the New Testament) and applied the gift of human reason to reach conclusions on a wide range of social issues. When is it allowable to wage war? What principles should govern business enterprises and their profits? What forms of government are compatible with the gospel of Jesus Christ? Hard questions like these abound and take centuries to settle to the satisfaction of all Christians, if they ever are.

While there is nothing new about the daunting challenges to be faced regarding faith-based social teaching, the experiences of every age and generation do provide something new. Judgments that seemed sound in earlier centuries (the reasonableness of slavery, the prohibition on interest considered as usury, the exclusion of women from voting, various justifications of warfare) were called into question by new experiences and new perspectives on scripture and church tradition. The Industrial Revolution of the nineteenth century was one episode of especially rapid change that demanded profound updating of church thinking on social order. In response to the social upheaval associated with the introduction of the factory-based system of production and massive urbanization in Europe and elsewhere, the Catholic Church began to take on a new social mission. Sparked by a progressive European movement called Social Catholicism, a cadre of courageous bishops and bold lay pioneers of social concern, and a sincere desire to make life better for the oppressed new class of industrial workers, the Roman Catholic Church began to develop a body of modern social teachings to offer guidance on economic and political matters.

When in 1891 Pope Leo XIII issued the first social encyclical *Rerum Novarum* ("On the Condition of Labor"), the church had definitively embraced a new role as a public moral teacher and interpreter of momentous questions of social justice. Especially in the decade just after the Second Vatican Council (1962–1965), the profile of Catholic social teaching grew sharply, as a "justice orientation" increasingly supplemented the previously dominant "charity orientation." It would no longer suffice for church leaders to exhort the faithful to practice voluntary charity toward the less fortunate. Henceforth, the church would include in its social message the obligation to enact structural change to benefit the disenfranchised and empower the poor. Adding the imperative of working for justice to the existing theme of charity transformed the social mission of Catholics around the world. Worthy pastors preaching on the parable of the Good Samaritan, for example, now instructed the faithful not only to look for opportunities to bind the wounds of victims but also to work assiduously to change social structures in order to prevent victimhood in the first place.

The thirteen decades since *Rerum Novarum* have witnessed a succession of fourteen social encyclicals, as well as the promulgation of many social teaching documents from church councils, the worldwide Synod of Bishops, national episcopal conferences, regional groupings of bishops, and even individual bishops. Besides these official documents, unofficial teachings take the form of exemplary ideas and prophetic actions that spring from many sources, including prominent lay leaders, gospel-inspired social movements, activist religious congregations, and Catholic universities and think tanks. In many cases, the best ideas about social justice and proper order have a way of "trickling up" so that official documents reflect thinking that may have surfaced and found expression first at the grassroots level. The social encyclical *Laudato Si'*, published by Pope Francis in 2015, was especially frank in acknowledging its debt to a variety of sources (including non-Christians). It made explicit the sound insight that the best ideas rarely drop down from heaven onto the desk of the pope but more often bubble up as people at the front lines of economic and political life in society process their experiences and reflect on the challenges of doing justice in a world desperately in need of the light of gospel values.

If the social teachings of Pope Francis owe a debt of gratitude to many contemporary sources (a point to be illustrated in the chapters to follow), they also owe a debt to the sheer momentum of previous papal social teachings. The claim that papal social encyclicals build upon one another is easy to verify; a simple perusal of the footnotes of any encyclical demonstrates that the single greatest source of what a given pope will write is the previous writings of his predecessors on the Chair of Peter. Although the footnote citations in the documents he has published display an unprecedented variety of sources, Pope Francis shares this in common with previous popes who contributed to Catholic social teaching. He is wise in perceiving no need to "reinvent the wheel" in those instances when his predecessors have already "hit the nail on the head." To provide one example, both John Paul II and Benedict XVI (Francis's two immediate predecessors) made excellent use of the concepts "the globalization of indifference" and "the globalization of solidarity" in their social teaching documents. Since these phrases continue to capture precisely what needs to be said about the conceptual roots of and solutions to our contemporary social problems on a worldwide scale, Pope Francis has continued to employ these same terms to very good effect.

Similar claims could be made about how environmental concern has been treated by these three consecutive popes. The analysis of the ecological crisis (as well as proposals for a responsible Christian response to it) articulated by John Paul was handed seamlessly on to Benedict, who deepened the points and passed them on to Pope Francis so that he could add his own perspective, without in any way contradicting his predecessors. New global experiences (such as accumulating data confirming climate change) and distinctive personal commitments (the perspectives of Franciscan and Ignatian spirituality, as treated above) allowed Francis to expand on the message of his predecessors in substantial ways, but the Argentinian pope is consistently eager to express his debt to his Polish and German predecessors.

And yet, the election of the first non-European pope since the early centuries of the church is quite a game changer. Visualizing a truly and

thoroughly global church alters the landscape of the Christian imagination in many ways, not least in the area of social teachings. Recall that
modern Catholic social teachings were part of the church's response to
the plight of oppressed workers in a rapidly industrializing Europe over
a century ago. As the wave of advanced economic development spread
over the curve of the globe in recent decades, astute observers remarked that all our tools of social analysis—from the collection of quan-
titative economic data to cultural anthropology to religious social ethics—should be updated to account for the new social contexts. Profound questions remain about how adequately the concepts and measures that developed in Europe and North America apply to Latin America, Africa, and the rest of the Global South. Specifically regarding
matters within the Catholic Church, long after we have recognized that
Latin America is now the region of the world with the largest numbers
of Catholics, we continue to struggle to update our consciousness and to
realize the profound implications of this shift.

If anyone is fully aware of the ramifications of this new situation, it is
Pope Francis himself. In his very first appearance as pope on the balcony overlooking St. Peter's Square, he joked that his fellow cardinals had
"gone to the ends of the world to find a new Bishop of Rome." He
identifies himself repeatedly as a man from the global periphery, coming as he does from the Southern Cone of South America, the very
geographical margins of the earth. His eagerness to appoint cardinals
from unaccustomed places (such as Tonga, East Timor, Cape Verde,
Laos, Mali, Haiti, Burkina Faso, and Myanmar) and to convene a Council of Nine Cardinal Advisors with representatives from all six conti-
nents indicates something of the message he wishes to send. Only time
will tell precisely what this new consciousness will mean for his leadership and his legacy, but without doubt his election has broken Europe's
monopoly control over the papacy, the central institutional hub of a
church whose consciousness has at last caught up with its identity as a
world church. In this renewed context, the agenda for Catholic social
teaching can no longer be set exclusively by and for the Global North.

The six chapters to follow demonstrate how Pope Francis takes each
of the three streams of influence treated above (his personal background, his Jesuit identity, and the inheritance of previous Catholic
social teaching) and appropriates them in service to matters of social
justice particularly close to his heart. If social justice in general occupies

a place at the top of his agenda, then these six particular areas of focus in his papal ministry emerge as central to his sense of the church's mission in a world of great injustices and intense challenges.

I

ECONOMIC JUSTICE

Challenging Economic Inequality

This chapter and the next explore the contribution of Pope Francis to Catholic social teaching on economic justice, with special attention to people suffering the effects of inequality, poverty, unemployment, and low wages in the global economic system. As with each of the chapters to follow, a review of Francis's words and actions will demonstrate an abiding commitment to ethical principles, values, and (above all) flesh-and-blood people. It will be revealing to situate the work of Pope Francis (primarily in the first four years of his papacy) within the context of the previous century and a quarter of modern Catholic social teaching. This comparative perspective will bring to the surface both points of continuity and certain innovations and distinctive concerns that the Argentinian pontiff brings to each topic. From each of the six chapters will emerge a clearer picture of what is old and what is new in Catholic teaching on each topic, as well as some sense of what the future might hold as the church continues to grapple with the challenges of global justice issues.

In gauging the priorities of Pope Francis regarding economic justice, this chapter enjoys the advantage of an especially noteworthy source of information—one that requires a bit of initial explanation to appreciate its significance. Just eight months into his papacy, Francis published the apostolic exhortation *Evangelii Gaudium*, or "The Joy of the Gospel."[1] Released on November 24, 2013, the English version of the text runs

over 47,500 words—making it one of the longest documents any pope
has ever published. While some commentators criticized Pope Francis
for displaying a lack of writerly discipline, there are good reasons he
produced such a lengthy work. Like most recent popes, Francis used
this, his first major document as pope, to provide something of a road-
map for what he would attempt to achieve in his papacy. As might be
expected from the title and purpose, a majority of this extensive document consists of a program to reform and energize the inner life of the
church, including a series of instructions for pastoral workers (for example, proposals for improving the preaching heard at church liturgies and
for the spiritual formation of ministers). But a significant portion of
Evangelii Gaudium reaches beyond internal church matters to cover
social concerns beyond the boundaries of the church itself, such as
poverty, inequality, and threats to peace in the world.[2]

Documents in this genre of apostolic exhortation generally restrict
themselves to addressing audiences within the church itself. Those who
might initially be surprised by the outward-directed focus of "The Joy of
the Gospel" should consider several reasons why Francis used this opportunity to make a contribution to Catholic social teaching beyond
internal church matters. First, any pope describing his plans for the
years ahead is wise to consider the ways he will be called upon to reach
out to the wider world, since the duties of his office include not only
internal church management but the moral leadership embodied in the
broad concerns of Catholic social teaching—the aspect of church theology that focuses on the political, social, and especially economic life of
all people, not just Roman Catholics. Second, in light of the primary
motivation for Pope Francis to take up its writing, it makes especially
good sense for this particular document to include ample attention to
advancing social justice teaching. The primary purpose of the document
was to spark reflection on the topic of evangelization (or the spread of
the gospel, which had been the topic of the 2012 worldwide Synod of
Bishops that occasioned this exhortation in the first place).[3] No treatment of evangelization can be complete without considering the specific worldly circumstances—including the social and economic conditions
we all face—within which this missionary work of spreading the gospel
unfolds.

Consequently, Pope Francis devotes paragraphs 52 to 70 to a description of key economic and cultural challenges of today's world that

hinder evangelization and cause great suffering and disorder. These include economic exclusion, increasing inequality, and warped financial systems that victimize the poor, as well as an equally serious list of cultural concerns (individualism, consumerism, rampant urbanization, secularization, moral relativism, and the homogenizing effects of global-ization). The next section of this chapter summarizes and comments upon the major claims of Pope Francis here, focusing primarily upon his analysis of the economy rather than of culture or theology. Later parts of *Evangelii Gaudium* (especially the fourth chapter, "The Social Dimension of Evangelization") contain sections titled "The Inclusion of the Poor in Society" and "The Common Good and Peace in Society," and these themes and passages also come into play in the economic analysis to follow.

Before we examine the key social teaching paragraphs of *Evangelii Gaudium*, it is worth noting a few preliminary points. The paragraphs treating economic justice echo many points that Pope Francis has made on innumerable other occasions, both before and after the release of this document (indeed, even before he was elected pope).[4] This pattern of repetition confirms how deeply Francis holds these convictions; this document reflects far more than just a passing concern or analysis of the moment. Close attention to the content of this document reveals how Pope Francis perceives and judges the most important social injus-tices in the world today and what he is eager to add to received Catholic social teaching on the topic of this chapter: economic inequality and social exclusion.

Further, the analysis contained in *Evangelii Gaudium* will surely make many readers uncomfortable. Although its title ("The Joy of the Gospel") sounds upbeat and uncontroversial, the document turns out to contain serious words of warning about social injustices in our economic system that will be jarring to some. While millions of believers clearly prefer the cheery "gospel of prosperity," a feel-good version of Chris-tianity popularized by certain televangelists and preachers who deny any tension between gospel values and greatly accumulated wealth,[5] Francis calls us to look much deeper. The reality of sharply concentrat-ed economic power in our world reminds us that the message preached by Jesus includes a marked suspicion of riches and elitism and an abid-ing concern for those left out. The easier route is surely to avert our eyes from the realities of suffering and oppression that accompany our

economic system in its present form, but the duty of intellectual honesty demands that we examine and take seriously the observations, cri-
tiques, and suggestions offered by Pope Francis.

ECONOMIC JUSTICE AND INEQUALITY IN "THE JOY OF THE GOSPEL"

The final sentence of paragraph 202 of *Evangelii Gaudium* is an aphorism that Francis is famous for repeating in many contexts (even on his
Twitter feed) both before and after publication of this document. That
simple sentence runs, "Inequality is the root of social ills." If we appreciate the centrality of this claim, we gain an important window into the
social thought of Pope Francis. He clearly identifies the fight against
vast economic inequalities as a key priority in the quest for social justice. Indeed, six years earlier, in a speech at a historic meeting of bishops gathered from throughout Latin America in Aparecida, Brazil, he
expanded on this point with these words: "We live in the most unequal
part of the world, which has grown the most, yet reduced misery the
least. The unjust distribution of goods persists, creating a situation of
social sin that cries out to heaven and limits the possibilities of a fuller
life for so many of our brothers."[6] Clearly, this is a prophetic pope who
has prioritized the fight against inequality, a man of the church who is
eager to expose and address the sources of extreme inequality in society.

While most of the pope's lifelong experience of the ill effects of
inequality did unfold in Latin America (and a later section of this chapter considers the significance of that context), the insights into inequality in *Evangelii Gaudium* announce a universal concern. Paragraph 52
begins the analysis of inequality by noting that great advances in "health
care, education and communications" are not being shared fairly, since
"the majority of our contemporaries are barely living from day to day,
with dire consequences." He cites disease, fear, depression, and violence as symptoms of the unequal access to resources and notes that the
ill effects of inequality plague rich nations as well as less economically
advanced ones. Those who control the benefits of science and technology exert "new and often anonymous kinds of power" over the less fortunate, whose hopes for a better life are thwarted at every turn.

When "The Joy of the Gospel" was released, it was the next paragraph (53) that received the most attention, grabbing headlines in newspaper coverage and even inspiring the title of a book on the topic.[7] Here Pope Francis places a stark label on the core injustice he is eager to denounce and does not hesitate to employ prophetic language to spell out its most dire effects. He urges us to say no "to an economy of exclusion and inequality. Such an economy kills." While this may sound overly dramatic to some, Pope Francis supplies vivid examples to support his case and explain his denunciation. He cites the tragedies of "when an elderly homeless person dies of exposure" and "when food is thrown away while people are starving." Having already invoked the word "exclusion" several times in the paragraph, he raises the ante by introducing one of the signature phrases heard during his papacy: the "throw-away culture." Nowadays not only are food and consumer items thrown away lightly, but "human beings are themselves considered consumer goods to be used and then discarded." The famous paragraph concludes with a litany of terms describing the plight of those damaged by the effects of inequality: "exploitation," "oppression," "society's underside or its fringes or its disenfranchised," "the outcast, the leftovers."

The next four paragraphs (54–57) offer the pope's further analysis of the economic system that produces so many victims. How did society reach this point of allowing such vast inequalities and death-dealing exclusions? Paragraph 54 contains a spirited indictment of the "trickle-down theories which assume that economic growth, encouraged by a free market, will inevitably succeed in bringing about greater justice and inclusiveness in the world." Approaches such as this have been invoked for decades as rationalizations to defend an agenda of free markets and minimal regulation. Their proponents ask the nonaffluent to be patient for results and to place "naïve trust in the goodness of those wielding economic power and in the sacralized workings of the prevailing economic system. Meanwhile, the excluded are still waiting." With these stirring words, Pope Francis is challenging economic leaders to be more honest about the distributive consequences of how markets function.

These four paragraphs underline the urgency of these claims by reminding the reader of the disastrous financial crisis that shook the world's economy about five years earlier (its peak moment struck late in

2008).[8] Among other points raised here, Pope Francis attributes the
devastating effects of this debt crisis and resulting deep recession to the
greed-driven decisions and imbalances associated with excessive financial speculation. Avarice and shortsighted pursuit of immense profits for
those at the top of the economic pyramid were the cause of great
hardships (including home foreclosures, unemployment, and massive
loss of retirement savings) for many millions, especially for those at the
very bottom. As jolting as these traumatic events were, they were only
symptoms of a deeper crisis of values that constitutes a scandal perpetuated by financial elites at the expense of the less affluent.

The subsequent dozen paragraphs (58–70) launch an appeal for a
return to ethical ideals, for a "rejection of the idolatry of money" (58)
and the adoption of "authentic Christian values" (68), which can reverse
some of the effects of recent imbalances and disastrous collective
choices. Ongoing global economic dislocations are about more than just
money; behind the collapse of so many financial institutions lies a deeper crisis of values involving the denial of the human dignity of the
disenfranchised. In this section, Francis appeals to his readers to reverse the "globalization of indifference" (a phrase he borrows from
previous popes), which prevents us from feeling compassion for the
plight of the needy throughout the world and hinders works of solidarity. These points all obviously address the crucial changes in attitude
and culture (rather than in economic realities per se) that will lead to
social improvement. There is even a profound first-person plea for a
change of heart in paragraph 58 ("The Pope loves everyone, rich and
poor alike, but he is obliged in the name of Christ to remind all that the
rich must help, respect, and promote the poor. I exhort you to generous
solidarity"). But the most noteworthy remaining points of economic
analysis in this papal document—the message that constitutes a significant advance in Catholic social teaching—pertain to the notion of structural evil (sometimes referred to as structures of sin, or social sin).
Someone who views economic problems, their causes, and their potential solutions in terms of deep-seated structures is termed a structuralist, and the paragraphs below examine how and why Pope Francis engages in a structuralist analysis of inequality.

While the reader gets a glimpse of the pope's structural approach in
the paragraphs treated above (paragraph 59 contains the memorable
phrase "evil crystalized in unjust social structures"), it is only much later

in the document that we see its full flowering. The fourth chapter includes a subsection (it runs from paragraphs 186 to 216 and is labeled "The inclusion of the poor in society") that explicitly adopts a structural perspective on the causes and effects of inequality in human society today. For example, paragraph 188 mentions the importance of "working to eliminate the structural causes of poverty and to promote the integral development of the poor." The next paragraph similarly calls attention to the importance of "changing structures" and embracing an agenda of "structural transformations." One final citation from this part of the document returns us to the important paragraph 202, which ends with the papal aphorism with which the section began: "Inequality is the root of social ills." That paragraph opens with the admonition "The need to resolve the structural causes of poverty cannot be delayed" and along the way to its conclusion recalls words uttered by Pope Benedict XVI in 2007 about the consummate importance of "attacking the structural causes of poverty."

THE STRUCTURALIST APPROACH OF POPE FRANCIS: SIGNIFICANCE AND ORIGINS

What is the significance of a structural approach to social problems, particularly one that emphasizes structural evil, as Francis does here? At the heart of any structural approach to poverty or similar social dysfunctions is an abiding belief that the worst problems are neither caused nor resolved in simple, straightforward ways—for example, on the level of individual decisions and face-to-face interactions. A close study of history reveals that the accumulated weight of many discrete acts over the centuries establishes social patterns that are deeply ingrained and require diligent and prolonged efforts if we expect to reverse the effects of regrettable previous history. In other words, it was the accumulated sins of many generations that produced various deplorable patterns that still affect us today: racism, sexism, militarism, colonialism, and so forth.

A structural perspective on economic outcomes is an especially valuable tool, for it affords us valuable insight into the true nature and causes of poverty in today's world. Through a structural lens, we can recognize that the poor are not just people who encounter random misfortunes that leave them momentarily short of cash. Rather, they are victims of enduring forces and large institutions that operate beyond their control. Think, for example, of shifting trade patterns and corporate marketing policies that shift the demand for agricultural products and certain types of manufactured goods, rendering humble farmers and assembly-line workers jobless and placing their families in precarious positions. Even without any malevolence, the functioning of these forces and organizations limits the opportunities of many for a secure livelihood, robbing them of hope unless some countervailing forces implement systemic changes. Viewed in the aggregate and in terms of such a root cause analysis, poverty is not a mere misfortune but a structural injustice—one that needs to be addressed in deep and systematic ways.

The economic exclusion and disadvantaging of the poor highlighted by Pope Francis certainly reflect these core dynamics of structural evil. Several times in *Evangelii Gaudium*, he demonstrates the structuralist perspective he has adopted. For example, he reminds us that, as laudable as individual acts of charity and almsgiving (in paragraph 202 he refers to them as "welfare projects") might be in meeting urgent needs, small-scale efforts need to be supplemented by more ambitious and sustained efforts to change the underlying structures and dependencies that cause poverty in the first place and generate long-lasting social injustices. To cite an old Christian adage, charity is no substitute for justice withheld. Both the causes of the social problem of poverty and its potential solutions run deeper below the surface than we may have surmised.

But despite his keen awareness of the difficult path to the achievement of greater social justice, Pope Francis is never one to wallow in desolation or gloom. The burden of overcoming these obstacles to improvement is not a reason to despair but rather an incentive to sharpen our thinking and intensify our resolve for the struggle ahead. While he is generally averse to proposing detailed solutions (since any given courses of action is unlikely to apply in all parts of the world), he does on occasion venture to suggest constructive structural changes to address the most obvious human needs. For example, in paragraph 192 of "The Joy of the Gospel," he identifies public policies for broader access to education, health care, and employment as particularly promising paths to address social and economic exclusion in our increasingly segmented world. Because such investments in the well-being of people will protect human dignity, they emerge as structures of inclusion capable of offsetting the structural evils that cause widespread exclusion.

This awareness of structural evil is by no means entirely new in Catholic social thought. As far back as 1971, a brief but groundbreaking document from the worldwide Synod of Bishops (titled "Justice in the World") highlighted the reality of "social sin" and the need for structural transformation to overcome ingrained systemic injustices. By the 1980s, Pope John Paul II was regularly speaking about social sin and even included a dozen references to the notion of structures of evil (evident in the economic and political realities of the late Cold War era) in his 1987 social encyclical *Sollicitudo Rei Socialis* ("On Social Concern"). But Pope Francis takes the analysis to a new level, applying a structural perspective to the reality of economic exclusion in an original and comprehensive way, employing new rhetorical flourishes ("such an economy kills") and a style of prophetic denunciation that no pope had previously employed.

Without doubt, the skewed pattern of social and economic relations that Jorge Bergoglio had observed all his life in the distinctive context of Latin America contributed to his keen sensitivity to the human suffering that springs from poverty and marginalization. It makes a real difference that Francis is the first pope to bring to the Vatican a background in a colonized land of the Global South. Although Argentina displays some features of an advanced industrial nation, it still shares with its Latin American neighbors the heavy legacy of colonialism. The centuries of European political and economic control hindered its economic and human development, generating a lasting sharp division between the poor masses of low-paid workers and the landed elites who enjoyed great power and privilege. The fallout of colonial domination warped more than the economy; throughout Latin America, sharp social divisions meant that even the church was tragically split between poor and elite sectors.

Fortunately, the centuries-long divisions within Latin American church life have come to be addressed very constructively in the past fifty years or so, especially in the wake of the Second Vatican Council (1962–1965). That momentous worldwide council insisted that the church must always be understood as the people of God—that is, the entire people of God, excluding the concerns of none of its members, especially the poorest. Pope John XXIII (over whose canonization as a saint Francis enthusiastically presided in April 2014) called and planned the council proceedings. Shortly before convening the opening of one of the church's rare ecumenical councils, Pope John revived the programmatic phrase "a church of the poor,"[9] which indicated his own priorities for the direction of the council and its documents.[10] The bold leadership of the Conference of Latin American Bishops (in which Archbishop Bergoglio played multiple key roles) in the decades since has continued this momentum for the church to identify itself with the poor majority. Admiring John XXIII as he does, Pope Francis signaled to the world on only his third day in office that he would embrace this key priority of his predecessor. On March 16, 2013, in his first public conference with international journalists assigned to the Vatican, Francis declared before the world, "How I would love a church that is poor and for the poor!"

It is well worth rehearsing this bit of recent church history (especially as it pertains to Latin America), since it provides helpful perspective on Pope Francis's deep and distinctive concerns with inequality and poverty. Being from Latin America affords the pope a distinct advantage: an ability to discern clearly the realities of social division and the tragic consequences of economic exclusion. Because of the creative ferment of recent decades, this region of the world has sometimes been called "the laboratory for the church of the poor." It is also the birthplace of liberation theology—a half-century-old movement within the church that dedicates itself to fashioning an adequate Christian response to the realities of poverty, suffering, and the vast disparities of wealth that have been part of regional history since the days of colonialism. One of the core commitments of liberation theology is to strive to see social reality clearly; to have an accurate picture of structures of injustice is a precondition for right actions (i.e., orthopraxis) for improvement. From liberation theology arose the signature phrase "a preferential option for the poor," which found its way into documents of the Conference of Latin American Bishops and eventually came to be enshrined in universal social teaching through the encyclicals of John Paul II.

With the structuralist lens he employs, Pope Francis is able to see clearly that endemic poverty is not just an accident of history or bad luck on the part of a few. To paraphrase a sentiment he expresses frequently, directing a few dollars here or there to worthy causes is commendable, but it will not solve the underlying problems as long as patterns of economic exclusion remain. The deep poverty of so many is caused by a skewed economic system—one that provides great wealth for those who control the major institutions such as banks, stock markets, investment funds, and even public policy. These are some of the structures, on the national and international level as well, that require reform if progress toward greater equality is to come. Changing the distributive results in the direction of greater equality is not impossible, but it will require changing key elements of the overall system, as we are instructed in "The Joy of the Gospel."

PREVIOUS CATHOLIC SOCIAL TEACHING ON INEQUALITY

Now that we have examined the key texts within "The Joy of the Gospel" on economic justice and inequality and located them in the context of the structuralist perspective of Pope Francis, we are in a favorable position to assess what is new here and what is in continuity with previous Catholic social teaching on these topics. Somewhat amusingly, if we were to take the words of Pope Francis at face value, our focus in this section of the chapter would be somewhat different, as he has repeatedly suggested that, in publishing "The Joy of the Gospel," he is adding nothing new to Catholic social teaching. He intimates this in paragraph 184 of the document itself, where he (in a fit of modesty) downplays the social teaching content of his own document and steers the reader to another church publication (a reference work titled *The Compendium of the Social Doctrine of the Church*, published by the Holy See over a decade earlier) for the fuller account of what he is asserting. Further, less than a month after "The Joy of the Gospel" appeared, he granted an interview to the Italian daily newspaper *La Stampa* in which a question arose regarding the originality of the social teaching content in this new document. On that occasion, Francis somewhat coyly professed, "In the exhortation I did not say anything that is not already in the teachings of the social doctrine of the church."[11]

The remainder of this chapter does not, advisedly and with all due respect, take these claims of the pope at face value. Despite his humble demurral, Pope Francis has indeed advanced church social teaching on inequality. He does so primarily by bringing his own distinctive focus (which comes out of his personal history and Latin American background), as well as some novel and sharper rhetoric, to the topic of economic inequality. The review that follows of previous Catholic teachings on inequality sheds some light on how these innovations build upon the received church teachings on these vital matters of social justice. By examining the moral teachings Pope Francis inherited, we will be able to identify and appreciate the continuities and the innovations that the Argentinian pope brings to bear on the topic of economic inequality.

Recall that the entire endeavor of modern Catholic social teaching represents the church's response to deep problems arising from the new economic order that was bursting forth in the nineteenth century. If there were no morally objectionable aspects of the Industrial Revolution of that century, there would have been no impetus to develop papal social encyclicals or other teachings and innovative social ministries to care for the victims of the new economy. But there were indeed profound moral concerns that spurred the Catholic community to respond, and among them was an explosion of ruinous inequality and life-threatening poverty experienced by the new class of factory workers.

When Pope Leo XIII published *Rerum Novarum* ("On the Condition of Labor") in 1891, he had an opportunity to roundly condemn the entire capitalist system of production, trade, and consumption. But despite his outrage over the exploitation of workers, the judicious Leo did not follow this path. Rather than side with those calling for *revolution* (a resounding and categorical repudiation of capitalism), he opted for a stance of *evolution*. Pope Leo's prudent decision to issue a nuanced ethical assessment, one calling for deep but incremental reforms of capitalism's labor policies and distributive effects, was driven by deeply held theological values. The key principles at stake in our judgments about any economic reality relate to human dignity and the optimal way to protect it. All people should continue to enjoy the right to obtain and make good use of private property; citizens should retain the full range of civil liberties; families should continue to enjoy the ability to determine the course of their lives.

The major alternative to market-based economies that Leo considers, socialism in its various incipient varieties, emerged as a far worse alternative on these counts and others (for example, it tended to be hostile to religion). Even in those decades before there were any socialist or communist nations to observe (the Russian Revolution was over twenty-five years away), Catholic leaders were not persuaded by this particular vision of a utopia of enforced egalitarianism (a system of complete material equality). And so, Leo rejected the leveling agenda that was associated (at least in his mind) with socialism. Paragraph 14 of his encyclical shares a bit of Leo's own social theory and contains these strong claims: "Humanity must remain as it is. It is impossible to reduce human society to a level. The socialists may do their utmost, but all striving against nature is in vain. There naturally exist among mankind innumerable differences of the most important kind; people differ in capability, in diligence, in health and in strength; and unequal fortune is a necessary result of inequality in condition."

By stating a strong preference for a capitalist system that preserved inequality over a socialist alternative that would pursue an uncompromising leveling agenda, church leaders were by no means endorsing the oppressive treatment of workers. The church was eager to advocate for improvements in the status quo but had to be very deliberate about the task of recommending the proper means to that end. Pope Leo argues for a combination of moral conversion (a charity approach) and public policy reforms (a justice approach that includes interventions such as workplace regulations and the introduction of a "family wage") that would improve the condition of labor and restore some of the social unity that had been damaged by unregulated capitalism. Rejecting radical socialism and applying these remedies, which still protected the institution of private property, a pillar of Catholic social theory, would of course allow inequality to continue. Two key questions that Leo left to be worked out by subsequent church leaders are these: How much inequality is allowable? And what measures should Christians recommend to address excessive inequality?

It is fair to say that to this day nobody has answered these questions to the satisfaction of all. To be sure, successive church documents have repeatedly bemoaned the scandal of poverty and denounced structures of evil that allow (and even encourage) an ever-widening gap between rich and poor. For example, paragraph 29 of the Vatican II document *Gaudium et Spes* warns, "Although rightful differences exist between men, the equal dignity of persons demands that a more humane and just condition of life be brought about. For excessive economic and social differences between the members of the one human family or population groups cause scandal, and militate against social justice, equity, the dignity of the human person, as well as social and international peace." The sentiments expressed in this 1965 council document capture the mixed evaluations of equality found in the writings of popes both before and since. In sum, while it would be highly desirable to curb inequality and address the situation in which "luxury and misery rub shoulders" (a phrase from paragraph 63 of *Gaudium et Spes*), it is far from clear how to reorganize society to achieve these goals. The benefits of greater equality are clear, but the path to a more equal society remains murky.

The major sticking point is that the capitalist market system continues to be the only workable framework to preserve core human freedoms affirmed in both modern secular thought and Catholic social teaching. Not only are markets the most efficient and productive mechanisms for generating wealth and directing resources to their best ends, but the capitalist principles of free contract and free enterprise respond to authentic human desires for self-expression far better than centrally planned economies ever could. Courageous popes like Paul VI, in his prophetic 1967 encyclical *Populorum Progressio* ("On the Development of Peoples"), and John Paul II, author of three groundbreaking social encyclicals between 1981 and 1991, make strong recommendations for improving and regulating the market system so that it better protects human dignity and responds to genuine human needs.

But no pope has reversed the basic judgment of Leo XIII—namely, that inequality of outcomes generated by natural endowments and amplified by a market economy appear to be an inevitable part of the human condition. Unless society is willing to discourage constructive achievements and productive enterprises or to forcibly confiscate the accrued financial gains that reward enterprising individuals, inequality of income and accumulations of wealth are here to stay. The demise of Soviet communism over a quarter century ago, while not in itself constituting a vindication of capitalism, demonstrated the shortcomings of a state-sponsored socialism that was the most ambitious effort at an enforced system of material equality that the world has ever known. Even the few remaining nations that today profess allegiance to collectivist principles tend to make increasing concessions to social values (such as

free enterprise and consumer choice) that entail departures from radical egalitarianism.

By no means does this recognition of interminable material inequality amount to utter resignation regarding the cause of promoting human
dignity. Besides producing social teaching documents, Catholicism has
sponsored ambitious social ministries and inspired great efforts at advocacy for the poor and activism for social change to redress glaring disparities. As a perennial champion of those in need, the Catholic community has maintained a commitment to ethical principles that include
a certain social egalitarianism that is based on a core belief that all of us,
whether materially rich or poor, were created with equal dignity and
stand as equals before God. This basic human equality is ever in search
of being worked out amid the complexity of earthly existence, in ways
that affirm what humans share in common, despite material inequality.

So even if the Catholic tradition of reflection on human inequality
remains unable to resolve these complexities, at the very least we can
give it high marks for consistently treating great inequality as the deep
and troubling problem that it is. All too often, those who observe economic matters simply shrug their shoulders when confronted with data
on the persistence of vast inequality. For some, the large and expanding
gap between rich and poor is merely a background condition, an acceptable and perhaps inevitable outcome of human nature or the facts of
economic scarcity. Simply to make the ethical judgment that raises a
condition to a true problem is an ethical accomplishment—a first step
on the way to addressing the moral conundrum of inequality with the
seriousness it deserves. If Christians are more dedicated to this project
than others, it is because of the core Christian theological principle that
material creation is intended by God to benefit all, not just a fraction of
humanity. Nobody should be cut off from benefiting from our common
inheritance of nature, which includes the very land we inhabit and
which provides an abundance of essential food for everyone. All humans have a moral obligation to see that the common gift of creation
supplies the necessities of life for all God's children, since property,
however we might acquire it, possesses a social nature. So deep poverty
and abiding inequality are not just an offense against the victims of
scarcity due to the greedy appropriation of the commons and the hoarding of resources intended for all; they constitute an offense against the
Creator God as well. Technological advances have afforded our genera-

tion an unprecedented ability to provide for all a sufficiency of the basic goods of life, so there is no excuse for anybody to face severe poverty and even starvation.[12]

Ultimately, the premier Christian theological principle that helps us sort out all our claims and judgments regarding equality and inequality is the notion of the common good. All the Catholic social teaching documents cited above eventually come around to invoking the common good as the key criterion for justifying some measure of inequality in society and condemning its excess, and the documents of Pope Francis are no exception. Appealing to the common good opens up an entirely new perspective on economic life and the basic purpose of the production, trade, and consumption of goods and services. An appropriate regard for the common good of all shifts the focus off merely private benefits or crass self-interest and places it where fair-minded people will agree it belongs: on the promotion of mutual gains and the fostering of favorable conditions for a shared life together that allows all to thrive.[13] If the freedom to acquire more extensive private property promotes the common good (for example, by supplying incentives for innovation, as equitable patent and copyright systems do), then certain inequalities are beneficial. But if a heightened accumulation of wealth damages the common good by amplifying social disparities and further separating people into distinct classes, then remedial action is justified. Through policies such as progressive taxation, antitrust measures, prudent regulation of industries, and provision of a social safety net for low-income people, government fulfills its mandate to exercise its legitimate role as a key agent of the common good.

Three decades before Pope Francis wrote *Evangelii Gaudium*, another Jesuit took a stab at summarizing in a single sentence the gist of the Catholic tradition of reflection on economic inequality. In a seminal 1984 article, social ethicist Drew Christiansen, SJ, reviewed many documents and worldwide developments in Catholic thought up to that time regarding what levels and types of inequality are ethically allowable. He concludes his study, "There can be legitimate differences, but these must always be regulated to common sharing in a full human life."[14] The accurate and insightful summary of the inherited tradition in this article emphasizes the common good as the key regulative principle for justifying certain levels of inequality, but not an unrestricted level. It also joins several popes of the twentieth century in expressing deep concern that society had by then already exceeded the advisable or allowable level of accumulation of wealth. Paul VI said as much in 1967 when he conducted a survey of global economic trends in the opening paragraphs of *Populorum Progressio* and concluded that ever greater inequality is a key "sign of the times" that causes untold misery, hinders genuine human development, and shows no sign of improvement. "Left to itself, the economy works to widen these differences," noted Pope Paul.[15] The persistence and spread of deep inequality was also critiqued on many occasions by John Paul II, who lamented its acceleration due to the effects of greed, an "idolatry of the market," and weak governmental controls over private property and market forces.[16]

Now, in the twenty-first century, we have a pope who states this conclusion with an even greater sense of urgency. Francis clearly believes that we have exceeded the moral limits of allowable inequalities. He does not hesitate to identify the accelerating concentration of wealth and power into a few hands as a great injustice—one that threatens the livelihoods of many. Drawing upon his Latin American background (which provides social context no previous pope has experienced firsthand), he vividly portrays the effects of ever sharper disparities of wealth as potentially death dealing for the poor and marginalized victims. Unlike previous popes, Francis identifies exclusion as a force that kills. For him, a sharp accumulation of economic privilege and power crosses an ominous threshold and becomes a grave injustice when it begins to work against the common good. A key sign of such a transgression of Christian values is when inequality reaches such a high level that it begins frustrating the cause of solidarity and making a mockery of all talk of social unity. Following the logic of the warnings against inequality laid out by Pope Francis, unless we revive the virtue of deep solidarity and reverse this dysfunction in economic life, we will witness ever greater obstacles to establishing economic justice. In short, in an economy increasingly unequal and a society increasingly divided, it will be less and less possible to live in right relationships with God and others.

TOWARD A MORE HUMANE ECONOMY: THEOLOGICAL AND SOCIAL SCIENCE PERSPECTIVES

We have been using primarily theological language to situate Pope Francis within the context of previous social teachings on inequality and social justice. A helpful perspective is added when we supplement the religiously inspired values we have been citing (for example, solidarity and the common good) with recent insights and tools generated by the social sciences, especially the field of economics. Naturally, economists and sociologists employ different methodologies than popes and theologians. These secular experts are primarily interested in developing an accurate quantified analysis of a social phenomenon such as inequality rather than commenting on moral obligations pertaining to the distribution of wealth. Their goals and their methods are thus quite different from those of Pope Francis, who approaches economic realities as a religious and moral leader rather than a statistical analyst. But it is often fruitful to engage in an interdisciplinary dialogue by pairing the normative (that is, value-driven) and positive (that is, descriptive) aspects of a social reality such as inequality. By juxtaposing insights on the level of facts (what is the case) and values (what ought to be the case), we may gain insights that neither religious ethical leaders nor secular experts would reach in isolation from one another.

A fine example of the contribution of social sciences to theological claims is on display in paragraph 56 of "The Joy of the Gospel." It begins with this foreboding sentence: "While the earnings of a minority are growing exponentially, so too is the gap separating the majority from the prosperity enjoyed by those happy few." Pope Francis simply reports the existence of this economic trend and moves on quickly to an ethical analysis of why this growth of inequality is a cause of moral concern. Because he is writing an exhortation on the church's efforts at evangelization, he does not make the effort here to support the economic arguments contained in this document with any statistical evidence (despite the fact that he consults frequently with the Pontifical Academy of Social Science, a respected collection of distinguished scholars retained by the Holy See for purposes of advising the pope on such social matters). Those eager to follow up the ethical teaching of Pope Francis by verifying his claims and expanding on his treatment of these social concerns must look elsewhere for further guidance and analysis.

Fortunately, scholars have assembled a vast literature documenting the growth of economic inequality and tracing its damaging social effects. The tools of contemporary economics have grown increasingly sophisticated, allowing analysts to measure aggregate levels of inequality and to pinpoint changes in those levels over time. The best-known tool is the Gini index,[17] a ranking of the concentration of distributive shares on a scale from zero (for most concentrated) to one (for most widely dispersed), which captures the degree of inequality within a given nation or population group. Comparing the Gini coefficient assigned to a given nation allows an observer to conduct valuable cross-national comparisons, such as measuring the effects on income distribution of various fiscal or social policies over time. Another extraordinary tool within the United States is the data set called the Panel Study of Income Dynamics, which has been maintained by the University of Michigan for over half a century. By tracking the income of thousands of families over several decades, researchers have been able to answer important questions about the likelihood of social mobility (a household moving up or down the income scale over time) and the existence of equality of opportunity as well as equality of result.

Even without a discussion of further statistical tools, it is easy to conclude that the work of social scientists contributes a great deal to the theological and ethical analysis of inequality. For one thing, the data compiled by economists have considerable power to verify or falsify the value-laden claims of a religious leader like Pope Francis. Social science research also brings to the table a beneficial conceptual clarity that is often lacking in theological arguments. For example, theologians often confuse matters by conflating the terms "poverty" and "inequality," while economists (rightly) insist on tighter definitions. Another mistake is to speak of poverty exclusively in a broad sense (as nonspecialists tend to do), while economists are eager to remind us of the complexity of the phenomenon of poverty, including the important distinction between absolute and relative poverty. Our concern in this chapter with inequality hinges on the relative variety of poverty, which is a matter of interpersonal comparison (captured in the phrase "keeping up with the Joneses") and occasionally cross-national comparison (regarding industrialized and less developed nations). Further, while this chapter (following the lead of Pope Francis) has rarely distinguished between inequalities of wealth and income, economists are vigilant to maintain this distinction, since trends in annual household income are rarely fully correlated with inequality of wealth accrued over time (which is often much more concentrated).

For all these differences of emphasis and contribution between social scientists and theologians, there is one especially significant point of convergence between what both professional groupings have said in recent years on the topic of inequality and its social consequences. We have already seen how the social teachings of Pope Francis reflect the deep concerns of previous popes and Catholic thinkers (especially theologians from Latin America and the Global South) that an especially pernicious effect of increased inequality is a deepening social divide between rich and poor, a split that threatens the lives of the poor and erodes the common good that serves all. Might there be any economists and social scientists, drawing on their own data-driven fields, who perceive a similar threat and warn about similar disturbing consequences?

The answer is a resounding yes. In the past decade, there has been an explosion of economic research and publishing on the widening gap between the rich and poor, the affluent and the disinherited in many nations. Most impressive is the work of French economist Thomas Piketty, whose 2014 volume *Capital in the Twenty-First Century* has commanded broad cultural attention.[18] Piketty takes advantage of newly available national accounts data to discern trends in distributive shares that have accrued to citizens of several nations in the course of the past century or so. While he can identify certain eras of convergence of incomes in the past century in nations like Britain, France, and the United States, he reports that the past forty years have witnessed a marked divergence in incomes and wealth. He expresses his deep concern that the forces that have been channeling ever-larger shares of the economic pie to the superrich are growing stronger in recent years, exacerbating a trend toward plutocracy and utter domination of the political and economic system by a small group of the wealthy. As we might expect from the sharply divided profession, not all economists agree with the diagnosis or prescriptions of Thomas Piketty. Some analysts challenge his reading of the historical trends, and others take issue with his recommendation of an ambitious program of income redistribution.

Those who affirm Piketty's main argument identify the process of economic production itself as the key mechanism for this amplified concentration of wealth. Capital (supplied exclusively by the affluent) and labor (supplied primarily by those of modest means) are the two main components of production, and they are continually renegotiating the terms of their participation, including wage levels and returns on investment. The relative distribution of the benefits of production depends on trends in industrial relations, including the interactions of such institutions as labor unions, banks, and the stock market and public policies such as antitrust regulation. Piketty documents how a given equilibrium of distributive shares may be upended rather rapidly when certain key institutions grow weaker (as labor unions have in recent decades) and others evolve and adapt rapidly (as has the financial sector). Existing social contracts regarding fair distribution are endangered by changed circumstances; delicate balances in social expectations may collapse with little warning, producing alienation and social instability.

While workers contribute handsomely to continued productivity gains, they are receiving diminishing shares of the goods they produce and the services they deliver. Even without reading long technical works of economics, most people are aware that the share of national income going to the top stratum in the United States has increased sharply in recent years—and wealth holdings are becoming even further concentrated among the elite. This disturbing analysis of Thomas Piketty is echoed in similarly groundbreaking works on inequality by American Nobel Prize winner Joseph E. Stiglitz and late British economist Anthony B. Atkinson.[19] Each of the latter pays considerable attention to the social effects associated with the further divergence of life prospects in our increasingly divided society. If trends continue unabated, the fortunate few will enjoy access to ever further concentrated wealth and power, on one hand, while the vast majority in the lower and middle classes will face declining wages and compounded financial setbacks, on the other hand. Other social scientists have written eloquently about a range of deleterious consequences of this "Great Divergence," from decreasing political stability and crises of legitimacy in many nations to weakening public health indicators (more suicides, drug abuse, depression) that will accompany further inequality of wealth and income.[20]

These are secular voices that have affirmed a central message in the social teaching of Pope Francis—that there is something deeply objectionable and socially damaging about the growth of inequality. For economists and other social scientists, the proof is in the numbers; the data confirm that society grows weaker when economic stratification increases, as it has for decades throughout the world. For those who view the world through the lens of Christian theology, sharply increased inequality takes a severe toll on the achievement of solidarity—our vital sense of fellow feeling and the possibility of true human fellowship. This value is severely compromised when members of social classes are no longer traveling the same path but rather are alienated from one another. Those who are excluded from economic success are cast aside and face markedly different life experiences and prospects from their fortunate neighbors. Our economic situations belie the Christian belief that we are fellow children of God, equal in dignity and status before our Creator.

In this chapter, we have seen that Pope Francis weighs in very strongly against economic inequality that will further divide humanity, and the economists who rely upon their own data and methods to reach similar conclusions express similar concerns.

2

PROMOTING LABOR JUSTICE IN A GLOBALIZED ECONOMIC ORDER

The previous chapter explored the ethical call of Pope Francis for deep changes in economic structures to address the problems of poverty and inequality. Along the way, we identified many of the pope's key moral commitments in economic matters and noted the distinctive style by which he draws ethical judgments. It is hard to miss Francis's professed impatience for abstractions and ideologies. In line with his assertion in "The Joy of the Gospel" that "realities are more important than ideas,"[1] it turns out to be impossible to situate Pope Francis in any particular school of economic theory. For example, he rarely uses the terms "capitalism" and "socialism," as one might expect. None of the standard secular labels captures his positions, since his true focus in advocating for economic reforms is to improve the lives of real people, the actual flesh-and-blood victims of "an economy that kills."

Pursuing this priority of Francis's, the present chapter turns to the topic of labor justice. It will come as no surprise to observers of the long tradition of Catholic social teaching that the pope spends so much effort promoting the well-being of those who work for a living. Perhaps the most concrete way that people participate in the economy is through their labor—in the factories, farms, offices, and other workplaces where they typically spend about half or more of their waking hours. If a church leader plans to utter a word of hope for ordinary people facing harsh economic forces, then a message about alleviating labor-related injustices must be part of the message. Although Francis has yet to produce a full-length document devoted exclusively to this set of economic issues, the pursuit of worker justice is clearly something that lies close to his heart.

In numerous speeches and written documents, Pope Francis displays his constant awareness that the all-encompassing context in which our economic lives play out nowadays is a thoroughly globalized economic order. Even if globalization cannot be identified as the direct cause of particular hardships faced by specific workers he encounters, Francis nonetheless views the juggernaut of globalization as a powerful force to be reckoned with as the church shapes its social teachings and extends pastoral ministry to hard-pressed workers and their families. In order to appreciate his commentary fully, a few preliminary words about the phenomenon of economic globalization are in order. The job prospects we face, the investments we make, the markets for consumer goods in which we participate, the competitions we enter as individuals and through the activities of corporations—all are shaped by the forces of a globalized economic order. For better or worse, we are inextricably connected to people and events around the world, and our economic well-being is tied to these many rapidly changing interactions.

Recent decades have witnessed a quantum leap in the process of globalization, hastened by international trade agreements that have lowered tariffs and diminished other barriers to trade. With improvements in transportation and communication, it is easier and easier for all manner of things to cross national borders—not just traditional exports such as raw materials and finished products but also investment capital, technological innovations, and even people (that is, not only literally when they are migrants but also metaphorically in their capacities as workers and consumers). In often surprising ways, the production process for many goods is spread all over the world; workers in dozens of countries may have contributed to the automobiles and cellphones we use every day. In our digital age, increasingly complex patterns of production and consumption are making the world a much smaller and far more interdependent place than ever before.

As has been true throughout history, progress comes with a price—and those costs are rarely paid equally across socioeconomic lines and demographic groupings. While the economic advances associated with globalization might sound magnificent, there remain serious concerns about how ordinary people are being treated in this process—and the deepest concerns pertain to the fate of less skilled workers and the unemployed. Chief among the economic forces that guide the globalization process is a fierce international competition that motivates transnational firms to cut labor costs whenever possible, rendering millions of workers underpaid and highly insecure in their jobs. For centuries, labor markets around the world have undervalued and discounted the labor of women and ethnic minorities in particular; now vast categories of workers, regardless of gender and ethnicity, are finding it impossible to land jobs that feature job security and decent remuneration.[2]

One of the root causes of these severe pressures on the workforce is the freedom of corporations to move production offshore very rapidly, to whatever nations or jurisdictions promise fewer regulations, looser environmental protections, lower wages, and lucrative tax advantages. When jobs are shifted around this way, capital flight contributes to "a race to the bottom," resulting in the deterioration of acceptable working conditions and terms of employment across entire industries. With labor unions growing weaker in their ability to address power imbalances in contract negotiations with major employers, workers around the world need whatever allies they can find in the field of industrial relations.

Some voices come and go quickly on the national or world stage. Recall the Occupy Wall Street movement, which for several months in 2011 and 2012 grabbed world headlines by calling attention to the abuses of the "top one percent" and the injustices faced by the rest of society (with the resounding chant "We are the ninety-nine percent"). In dozens of cities in the United States and abroad, Occupy settlements took over parks and other public spaces to publicize these grievances, but this grassroots (and deliberately decentralized) movement soon faded from prominence. Other voices for worker justice command a more permanent base of support. Religious communities of all types, in often remarkably courageous advocacy for human rights over many decades, have supported measures to humanize the global economy, and the Roman Catholic Church has long been a prominent member of this faith-based coalition for global economic justice. The previous chapter sketched a few of the concerns of Catholic social thought since the Industrial Revolution of the nineteenth century.

Pope Francis is far from the first Catholic leader to express sincere concern for workers. How do his expressions of support for workers and objections to the unfair conditions they face build upon the inheritance of Catholic social teaching? How does his advocacy for worker justice reflect his own distinctive concerns and commitments? We begin our treatment of these questions by identifying a few key messages Pope Francis has offered on those occasions when he has dealt squarely with the plight of workers today. Later in the chapter we step back from his actual words to discern the underlying commitments and patterns of thought that inform his advocacy. Unlike the previous chapter, where the focus on economic inequality allowed us to rely primarily on a single long papal document ("The Joy of the Gospel"), the treatment of worker justice in this chapter draws from the shorter texts of various spoken addresses of Pope Francis. Each of them is readily available on the Vatican website, as indicated in the footnotes.

WORDS OF ADVOCACY AND ACTS OF SUPPORT FOR WORKER JUSTICE

The lack of a single, fully developed papal text from Francis exclusively on the topic of worker justice does not mean that advocating for workers is not close to his heart. Indeed, the highly deliberate way that the Holy Father spreads his expressions of concern for the rights and well-being of laborers over the entire sweep of his ministry is an indication of his enthusiasm—he seems eager to highlight these concerns in a wide variety of venues and symbolic activities that cannot be overlooked. Another factor contributing to the prominence of this papal message is the matter of timing. It is highly significant that some of the earliest travels of Pope Francis outside Rome brought him to locations that are associated with deep concerns regarding the labor force.

A stellar example is his September 22, 2013, pastoral visit to Sardinia, a Mediterranean island that suffers from Italy's highest rate of unemployment (about half of all young adults are jobless due to economic collapse in key local industries). Coming a mere six months into his papacy, this was just the third trip outside Rome for Francis. In choosing this economically distressed location and planning an itinerary that included ample time for mingling with local workers and listening to their concerns, Francis clearly intended to highlight work-related hardships. At one point, in an eloquent gesture of solidarity, he even ventured to don the customary helmet worn by bauxite ore miners on the island, where thousands have lost jobs in the mines in recent years, as large mining corporations have moved jobs to lower-cost sites. After listening most empathetically to the testimonies of laid-off workers, Francis tossed aside his prepared remarks and extemporized on the situation he was perceiving firsthand. First he highlighted his recognition that "it is a form of suffering, the shortage of work that leads you to feel that you are deprived of dignity. Where there is no work there is no dignity!" He then moved on to voice his belief that the root problem (whether in Sardinia or elsewhere) is not any shortcoming in the workers themselves but "an economic system which leads to this tragedy, an economic system centered on an idol called money." He offers his diagnosis of the problem—namely, that "this globalized economic system which does us so much harm" is "devoid of ethics" since "money is in command."[3]

Pope Francis is legendary for his attraction to visiting humble places such as soup kitchens, prisons, and hospitals for the indigent in his evident eagerness simply to spend time with forgotten people as he did so often in Argentina before becoming pope. But his genuine desire for proximity to poor individuals is paired with an equally keen desire to express solidarity with entire social groups experiencing financial hardship and exclusion due to global economic structures that shape contemporary labor markets. Specifically, besides the trip to Sardinia, he has made a point to visit other (relatively nearby) locations similarly distressed by unemployment, including the French island of Corsica and the country of Albania—a nation just across the Adriatic Sea from Italy where workers suffer under the weight of the lowest prevailing wages in Europe. On each occasion, he took pains to mention that, although in close proximity to centers of power like Rome, these places are very much "on the periphery" of Europe, generally forgotten by their more affluent neighbors where jobs are more plentiful and wages higher. While Sardinia, Corsica, and Albania each face particular problems generated by the vagaries of local histories, they share a common set of challenges in finding a favorable place in the global economic system. As Francis well knows, their future progress in generating job opportunities adequate for their citizens will depend on their ability to overcome disadvantages that are exacerbated by the forces of global competition.

In another local but high-profile visit to deliver a message about employment, Francis ventured a few hours south of Rome to Scampia, an economically struggling neighborhood within the port city of Naples. On the morning of March 21, 2015, his warm greetings to a mixed gathering of local residents included a reminder of what they already knew all too well: that even in the relatively poor region of southern Italy, Scampia is very much "on the periphery" due to its high unemployment rate and a variety of related social problems. Part of his brief address on that occasion repeated the off-the-cuff sentiments he had expressed in Sardinia eighteen months earlier, since youth unemployment in Scampia is nearly as high: "Think: over forty percent of young people aged 25 and under are unemployed! This is serious. What does a young person do without a job? What future does he or she have? This lack of work robs us of dignity."

But on such occasions, Francis has a further agenda item to discuss, and that involves lamenting not solely the lack of availability of work but the sometimes unacceptable terms of employment when it is offered. He calls this "partial-pay employment," which amounts to doing a full-time job for roughly half-time pay. In Scampia he cited the case of a young woman he had just met who agreed to work eleven hours a day for a mere fraction of ordinary pay, and the position offered (it was in the tourism industry) came with no health-care or retirement benefits. Francis mused aloud that someone would only accept such a job contract out of desperation and fear of persistent unemployment. The pope reached for the words that might describe such an arrangement. He chose "slavery," "exploitation," and "corruption" and expressed his judgment that "this is not human, this is not Christian."[4]

Citing such examples of violations of proper respect for labor allows Pope Francis to highlight bedrock social justice principles of the church, such as the inherent dignity of labor and the rightful ability of people who work hard to earn a decent livelihood for themselves and their families. It is not only unemployment that constitutes an affront to workers' rights but also unjust terms of employment itself. Labor exploitation and new forms of veritable wage slavery are part of the dark side of today's globalized economy. The pope's activities in 2014 and 2015 make clear that he was eager to drive home this point to many audiences over several months. For example, when he met in Rome with United Nations Secretary-General Ban Ki-moon ten months earlier, he included the goal of "providing dignified labor for all" among the key objectives that he solemnly recommended to all international agencies.[5]

Three months after that Rome meeting, when Francis addressed a large gathering of Christian youth gathered in Daejeon, South Korea, he again referred to abuses in the job market, where employers all too often prey on the insecurities of young job seekers. On that occasion, Francis identified "unbridled competition" and "selfishness" as vices that distort employment policies and force young people into untenable situations that create great stress and can even prompt suicide (perhaps not coincidentally, Korea has one of the highest suicide rates in the world). The pope summed up his ethical guidance about the need to reform exploitative employment policies: "May they [youths and world leaders alike] also reject inhuman economic models which create new forms of poverty and marginalize workers."[6]

Although he has not used the popular phrase "the gig economy," the incidents described above suggest that even as far back as 2014, Francis was aware of the ethical downside of this growing trend toward less secure and regular employment. While temp agencies and "day labor" exchanges are established institutions at the lower end of the labor market, the nature and extent of contingent or "on-demand" employment have taken a quantum leap in recent years. In a gig economy, digital technology allows workers, generally working from their homes or even out of their cars, to chase down a series of billable tasks without traditional supervision or assured reimbursement of job-related expenses. Working as freelancers or independent contractors rather than long-term employees to whom the employer is committed, such laborers enjoy few of the customary benefits and legal protections afforded to traditional salaried employees, including health, retirement, and disability benefits, overtime pay, minimum wage guarantees, and paid vacation days. Such gigs are not jobs at all in the traditional sense of the word, as there is often no centralized workplace, little training, and limited assurance of continued availability of work from week to week. In an economy of tight deadlines, high turnover, and small margins, gigs are temporary, contingent, and dependent upon the fluctuations of shifting markets and the whim of the boss.

Defenders of contingent employment arrangements (such as app-driven taxi services, courier dispatchers, cleaning service agencies, and telephone solicitors working within or outside traditional call centers) emphasize the flexibility that on-demand work scheduling affords entrepreneurial young people today. But by the ethical standards Pope Francis espouses, highly contingent work usually amounts to exploitative work. It gives employers the lion's share of the decision-making power and almost all the profits that come from the work done, allowing corporations to sidestep responsibility for the long-term well-being of these members of the workforce. Even relatively prestigious gig work, such as graphic design and computer coding performed on short-term contracts, remains highly contingent in nature and does not necessarily contribute to a stable career for short-term employees. Reliable data show declining per-hour earnings and rising corporate revenue in industries (such as ride services and data entry) where gig employment is most pronounced. Truly healthy workplace arrangements affirm the workers' sense of dignity, creativity, and human community; they should never leave laborers feeling exploited, objectified, underpaid, and insecure about their future. The ethical pronouncements of Pope Francis on the topic of labor highlight the increasing difficulty of seeing how the new variety of contingent work fulfills the long-held Catholic position that, in order for work to honor the dignity of each person and to meet its purpose, "work must be good for us as humans."[7] The repeated advocacy of Pope Francis to advance the goal of ensuring dignified labor for all challenges this trend and many recent developments in labor relations in our globalized economy.

THE WORLD MEETINGS OF POPULAR MOVEMENTS

One often hears the retort that certain apparent problems actually amount to luxuries, as in the quip "Those are very First World problems." For example, to people living in desperate poverty in the less developed nations, the prospect of holding even a contingent or exploitative low-paying job in the Global North might well seem infinitely preferable to the conditions of widespread joblessness and economic despair they face every day. With this point of comparison in mind, we turn to some special recent occasions when church leadership arranged an opportunity to address the economic plight of millions in the developing world. Pope Francis, coming as he does from the Global South, is highly aware of the potential benefit of organizing those impoverished by global economic forces so that they can leverage what little power they have to advocate for improvements. Drawing on his experience of successful pastoral planning work in Argentina, he has given his whole-hearted support to a novel Vatican initiative to establish a forum to address the concerns of landless peasants, unemployed workers, and a variety of marginalized peoples—all on an ambitious global scale.

Through the Pontifical Council for Justice and Peace, working in tandem with the Pontifical Academy of Social Sciences, Francis has sponsored a series of multiday gatherings called World Meetings of Popular Movements. At each gathering, the pope has offered a substantial address to the gathered delegates. The invited participants have been highly diverse, primarily grassroots personnel—farmers working for land reform, community organizers from all parts of the world, and leaders and rank-and-file members of trade unions and labor cooperatives of all sorts. The remarkable eagerness of the Holy See to take responsibility for organizing these large events, arranging the logistics, and assuming many of the travel and accommodation costs for participants of such modest means sends a clear signal. Without a doubt, engaging issues of labor justice and structural reform of the global economy is a prominent part of the agenda of this papacy. The following summarizes the first three such papal addresses to these novel global gatherings.

The first of the world meetings was hosted at the Vatican in October 2014. The opening sentences of the pope's comments on that occasion reveal his delight at being able to offer "in the first person" some words of welcome and appreciation to "you who suffer exclusion and inequality" and who struggle for justice at the grassroots level of the global economy. Francis next encourages his hearers not to be passive but to be "protagonists" in the ongoing project of "fighting against the structural causes of poverty and inequality." The overall theme of his talk is how to overcome the lack of land, housing, and work, captured well in the three alliterative words (at least in English translation) "land," "lodging," and "labor" that recur throughout the nearly one-hour address.[8] To set the desired tone, Francis reminds his hearers, "This meeting of ours is not shaped by an ideology. You do not work with abstract ideas. . . . You have your feet in the mud, you are up to your elbows in flesh-and-blood reality. You carry the smell of your neighbor-

hood, your people, your struggle! We want your voices to be heard."
Francis sprinkles his paragraphs with a litany of the problems yet to be
overcome: violations of "sacred rights" to pursue a better life, the "up-
rooting of people from their native land," the "global process of hunger," persistent "denial of housing to thousands of our neighbors," and
"poverty which deprives people of the dignity of work."⁹

In this address, Francis repeatedly signals his structural perspective
on the plight of the economically deprived. Nowhere is his awareness of
unjust structures at work in various dimensions of the global economy
more obvious than in this key paragraph, worth quoting in its entirely,
which treats a range of labor injustices:

> From now on, every worker, within the formal system of salaried
> employment or outside it, should have the right to decent remunera-
> tion, to social security and to a pension. Among you here are waste-
> collectors, recyclers, peddlers, seamstresses or tailors, artisans, fish-
> ermen, farmworkers, builders, miners, workers in previously aban-
> doned enterprises, members of all kinds of cooperatives and workers
> in grassroots jobs who are excluded from labor rights, who are de-
> nied the possibility of unionizing, whose income is neither adequate
> nor stable. Today I want to join my voice to yours and support you in
> your struggle.

This remarkable paragraph on worker rights displays the pope's conviction that providing adequate pay and benefits for all workers, however
humble their profession, is the responsibility of all who take part in the
economic system. As beneficiaries of the global system, we are all culpable for any continued failure to enact decent conditions and terms of
employment. Further, the list of professions describing the attendees
affords a glimpse not only at the diversity of the gathering but also at
the theme of "unity in diversity" that the pope is deliberately striking
here. A recurring motif of this powerful talk is that all deserve to participate in a democratic process to address the inequities in the global
economy. If Francis offers one top recommendation regarding the
strengthening of that process, it would be the development of solidarity
across all lines of demography, religion, and profession. Of course, solidarity does not materialize out of thin air; this great virtue of fellow
feeling and mutual support is the product of ongoing relationships that
must be nurtured quite deliberately amid constructive projects of mu-

tuality and genuine other-regard. By participating together in efforts to advance labor justice and forming coalitions to insist on respect for the rights of all workers, Francis is convinced, we will insure progress in the struggle for inclusion and human dignity.

The Second World Meeting of Popular Movements was held in Bolivia in July 2015, scheduled to coincide with the visit of Pope Francis to Santa Cruz, a city at a high altitude in that landlocked South American nation. Once again, a diverse assortment of about two thousand delegates from popular movements in many nations participated in the meeting, which was again opened with a substantive address by Pope Francis. The Holy Father's text is somewhat longer than the previous one from nine months earlier, and his remarks convey even greater feeling, rhetorical power, and urgency. Perhaps the heightened emotional tone can be attributed to the fact that Francis found himself on the soil of his native continent, where he instinctively invests much energy and concern in the plight of the struggling masses. One international journalist noted that on this trip (which included visits to Ecuador and Paraguay), the pope's "primary agenda was to begin renewing Catholicism in Latin America and repositioning it as the church of the poor."[10] Regardless of how we might characterize his underlying motive, Francis used this occasion to launch a withering critique of a global economic system that does far too little to protect the majority of poor workers and unemployed people from deprivation and suffering. Francis calls the system "intolerable" and asserts that "something is wrong in a world where there are so many farmworkers without land, so many families without a home, so many laborers without rights." To spark hope for the needed transformations, he repeats throughout the talk this sentiment: "We want change, real change, structural change."[11]

This address of Francis in Bolivia once again touches on substantial matters concerning labor justice. Early on, he reports that some of the participants had mentioned in previous correspondence and encounters "many forms of exclusion and injustice which you experience in the workplace, in neighborhoods, and throughout the land. . . . These are not isolated issues. I wonder whether we can see that these destructive realities are part of a system which has become global." While the pope is inviting his listeners to view their struggles as part of a larger pattern of systems and structures, he nevertheless resists the temptation to venture down a path cluttered with too many abstractions. Instead, he deliberately calls his audience back to the level of the concrete, which to him matters most. He implores, "Look into the eyes of the suffering, see the faces of the endangered *campesino*, the poor laborer . . . the unemployed young person, the exploited child. . . . We are moved because we have seen and heard not a cold statistic but the pain of a suffering humanity. . . . This is something quite different from abstract theorizing." Throughout the address, which some commentators have called a "little encyclical," Francis maintains a remarkable tension between an adherence to the concrete and an eye for larger structural dimensions. On one hand, he readily identifies the need to address large global patterns of activity, above all in order to change "an idolatrous system which excludes, debases and kills." But on the other hand, he simultaneously encourages his hearers to "never stop being rooted in local realities." A commitment to systemic change for justice does not replace attention to local and concrete needs. After all, "we do not love concepts or ideas, we love people."

The third worldwide meeting in this series was convened in Rome in November 2016. The pope's address on that occasion once again included ample treatment of issues related to labor in the global economy. Francis was especially attentive to placing the need for worker justice in the context of overcoming "the globalization of indifference," a recurring theme over the past three papacies. Advocating for change in the treatment of workers is part of the mandate of these worldwide gatherings and emerges as a central component of the key task Francis identifies early in this particular address: "to put the economy at the service of people." Among the labor-related goals Francis mentioned more prominently and specifically than in previous addresses are "finding fitting work for those excluded from labor markets," "the eradication of discrimination, of violence against women and new forms of slavery," and placing "technology at the service of peoples."[12]

In his address to the Third World Meeting of Popular Movements, Francis also works to bring more specificity to his treatment of the barriers to progress. In the middle section of this address, he mentions the problems of terrorism, intolerance, political tyranny, corruption, and the idolatry of money as powerful cultural forces arrayed against those who work for social and economic change. With his characteristic optimism, he urges his listeners to continue to develop the type of effective solidarity that allows agents for change to cross all borders (both literal and metaphorical in nature) and to further the cause of justice. Pledging the continued support of the Catholic Church at all levels to this important cause, he also poignantly repeats an encouraging assertion he had made in his address in Bolivia the previous year: "The future of humanity is not only in the hands of the great leaders, the great powers and the elites. It is essentially in the hands of the people, in their capacity to organize themselves."

History will judge the ultimate effectiveness of these and future world meetings of popular movements. Only time will tell whether the seeds sown in these church-sponsored gatherings—featuring deliberately broad participation and encouragement of networks of social concern across national boundaries—will yield a rich harvest of justice. One encouraging sign suggesting that they are a sound investment of energy is that they in no way replicate the other regular meetings on social justice issues convened by the Holy See: those of the Pontifical Academy of Social Sciences (which is primarily a gathering of scholars and researchers) and the Pontifical Council for Justice and Peace itself (a Vatican department established by Pope Paul VI half a century ago and recently reorganized and renamed the Dicastery for Promoting Integral Human Development[13]). In other words, the mission of these meetings is unique and without precedent in church circles.

Another encouraging sign is the way that a system of regional meetings of delegates on this same model has already started up, as Francis joyfully noted in his November 2016 address to the worldwide gathering. In the United States, for example, the Regional World Meeting of Popular Movements gathered in February 2017 in Modesto, California. This location in the enormously productive Central Valley of the nation's largest agricultural state is an especially fitting location for an assembly of social justice activists. Modesto is a hub of advocacy for the interests of farmworkers, recent immigrants, and low-income people struggling with the signature social and economic issues that prompted the formation of this group.[14] Deep concerns about the promotion of labor justice for hard-pressed workers remain at the very top of this agenda for change.

RESPONSES TO A CALLOUS ECONOMY

In setting up the World Meetings of Popular Movements, Vatican officials were creating a new category of built-in opportunities for Pope Francis to express his concern about injustices in the global economy and to communicate his support for hard-pressed workers and the unemployed—two groups routinely victimized by the negative effects of globalization. A previously existing opportunity for popes to weigh in on global challenges to economic justice is the regularly scheduled plenary assembly of the Pontifical Council for Justice and Peace (reorganized and renamed as of January 1, 2017, but still headed by Cardinal Peter Turkson of Ghana). On October 2, 2014, Francis gave a brief but powerful opening address to this gathering of Vatican officials in which he treated not only "the benefits, but also the dangers of globalization, when it is not oriented to the good of peoples. If globalization has notably increased the aggregate wealth of the whole and of numerous individual states, it has also exacerbated the gap among the various social groups, creating inequality and new poverty in the very countries considered the wealthiest."[15]

Although Francis chose to use more restrained language to address this more scholarly minded group (a sharp contrast to the frequent invocation of vivid images and folksy metaphors he employs with the audiences of social movement delegates), even on this occasion he did not hesitate to use the sharp word "exploitation." In expanding on his judgment that globalization exploits many categories of workers, he maintained, "This imbalance not only fails to respect the dignity of those who provide low-cost labor, but it destroys the sources of employment in those regions in which it is most protected." He recommends that the Pontifical Council look to identify ways "of overcoming the structural causes of inequality and poverty," such as his earlier recommendation (in paragraph 192 of "The Joy of the Gospel") to expand "three fundamental instruments for the social inclusion of the most needy: education, access to health care and employment for all."

Francis drives home his point by drawing a contrast between this constructive proposal and "views that claim to increase profitability, at the cost of restricting the labor market, thereby creating new exclusions [which] are not in conformity with an economy at the service of man and of the common good, with an inclusive and participatory democracy." With this brief but eloquent statement of his diagnosis of what is wrong with the global economy and his prescription for what types of measures might restore an equilibrium favorable to workers, Pope Francis accomplishes a great deal. He takes advantage of this scheduled opportunity, built into his ordinary duties as head of the Catholic Church, to address the structural cause of labor justice and to commission this Vatican office to advance this agenda of advocacy for workers.

But other opportunities to demonstrate papal support for workers have popped up on nobody's tidy schedule. In social justice advocacy, as in so many matters within the church and beyond, popes do not always get to set the agenda and time line. Very often, Pope Francis has responded to rapidly moving developments in the global economy (some of them utterly tragic in nature) in order to employ the "bully pulpit" of his high-profile office. For example, on April 24, 2013 (just six weeks after his election as pope), Francis learned of a horrific factory collapse in Dhaka, Bangladesh. Over eleven hundred people were killed and twice as many injured when an eight-story building collapsed due to catastrophic structural failure. Investigators discovered that the particularly high death toll among garment workers (whose workplace occupied the upper floors) was due to negligence on the part of factory owners who ignored advance warnings of serious cracks in the support beams of the building, dooming their employees to a horrible death. Pope Francis was only one of many world leaders to express deep sorrow for the victims of this industrial mishap, but as a moral leader he went further than most. On several public occasions that month, he called attention to the economic structures and mentality of "profit at any price" that contributed to the disaster. One Catholic bishop from nearby India offered this assessment of Francis's strong support for worker justice in the course of this incident: "The Pope's statement on the crash was widely acclaimed all over the world, particularly by economists and social activists. He called the job given to them 'modern-day slavery,' paying only a dollar or two a day. It was a hard-hitting critique of the management responsible for such practices."[16]

Disregard for the well-being of workers in the global economy is by no means confined to disastrous industrial accidents; it includes harsh treatment and callous disregard for their dignity in the routine operations of industrial relations. Here again, Pope Francis is on the lookout to respond to lamentable developments in a turbulent economy by expressing his deep concerns for mistreated workers. For example, in March 2017 he received wide media coverage when he spoke out in support of hundreds of threatened employees of the Italian telecommunications firm Sky Italy, which had just announced a round of particularly drastic layoffs and relocations. Citing the Catholic social principle that business is obliged to protect the dignity of workers and their families, Francis called upon the corporate managers handling the planned layoffs to reconsider how they were treating these stunned employees targeted for termination or reassignment. In a weekly general audience address, he warned, "He who shuts factories and closes companies as a result of economic operations and unclear negotiations, depriving men and women of work, commits a very grave sin."[17] In this verbal intervention, Francis is of course not presuming to dictate the details of business decisions to any particular company, but he is issuing a reminder that principles of social responsibility and ethical accountability must guide all business dealings. While he recognizes that restructuring is sometimes necessary for a business to survive, he insists that the desire to boost shareholder profits should not in itself justify the act of taking away the livelihood of a faithful worker. Respect for the rights of workers is a particularly compelling component of any decision to downsize a firm and move its operations.

We have seen Francis take maximum advantage of singular world economic events to demonstrate his support for worker justice, but there are many other ordinary occasions when he uses the platform of the papacy to spread this message as well. As one example, every May 1, Catholics throughout the world celebrate the Feast of Saint Joseph the Worker, and from his first year in office, Francis has used this occasion to preach forcefully about the dignity of labor and the rights of workers. Even primarily secular observances are fair game for Francis to publicize positions on sensitive labor justice matters on a regular basis. For example, on June 11, 2014, when his weekly general audience fell on the eve of the annual World Day against Child Labor, Francis offered a prayer intention in support of the "tens of millions who are forced to work in degrading conditions, exposed to forms of slavery and exploitation. . . . I strongly hope that the international community can extend its social protection over minors in order to weaken this scourge of child exploitation."[18]

The extensive travels of Pope Francis present further opportunities to express particularly pointed concerns about the state of worker justice. In planning international itineraries, Francis deliberately selects venues that highlight the dire need for economic reform to protect laborers. While in Brazil for the World Youth Day in July 2013, Francis visited the favela of Varghina, one of the poorest sections of Rio de Janeiro, a neighborhood racked by high unemployment and many social problems associated with low wages and unfavorable terms of employment. In that poignant setting, he struck a signature theme of his papacy: "We must never allow the throwaway culture to enter our hearts, because we are brothers and sisters. No one is disposable!"[19]

Similarly, the pontiff's six-day February 2016 trip to Mexico deliberately bypassed the customary meetings with elites in the corridors of power (previous visiting popes had spent time primarily in the central federal district of Mexico City) in favor of an itinerary featuring humbler locales such as the state of Chiapas (the far southern region where he met with struggling communities of indigenous peoples) and the northern city of Ciudad Juárez. In Juárez, just over the border from the United States, the economy is dominated by low-wage export-producing factories called maquiladoras. In those sweatshop settings, managers cavalierly take advantage of the desperate need for work of the assembly-line laborers who endure long hours and slave-like conditions to retain their jobs. One reporter who witnessed this historic visit to the factory town on the border described a pope who seemed to relish striking a prophetic pose as he addressed a mixed crowd of workers and employers. On that occasion, the journalist recalled, Francis posed three especially poignant questions: "What kind of Mexico do you want to leave your children? Do you want to leave them the memory of exploitation, of insufficient pay, of workplace harassment? Or do you want to leave them a culture that recalls dignified work, a proper roof, and land to be worked?"[20] Once again, a well-executed papal visit fit very well into Francis's program of advocating for greater protections for powerless workers in a global economy that is all too often callous to needs of the workforce.

PRESCRIPTIONS FOR ECONOMIC CHANGE

In this chapter, we have surveyed many of Pope Francis's words (both spoken and written) and actions (including travels and symbolic gestures) in his advocacy for workers. It is not uncommon for these initiatives to be misunderstood and sharply criticized. Conservative free market boosters (including radio host Rush Limbaugh, politician Sarah Palin, and the editorial board of *Forbes* magazine) have accused Francis of failing to appreciate the marvels of contemporary capitalism and even of leaning toward Marxism or some doctrinaire brand of crass socialism. Those who take exception to his questioning of the global financial system generally fail to see that Pope Francis defies all the standard political labels. He is not ideological in any conventional way, so the usual political spectrum of left to right displays no capacity to capture his priorities or categorize his perspective. A fitting way to close this chapter on human labor, then, is to offer an assessment of the pope's stance regarding human work. So, along with many commentators puzzled by the pope's recommendations regarding economic justice, we may ask, When it comes to the topic of labor in the globalizing economy, what does Pope Francis really stand for? How may we best describe his agenda?

Perhaps the most straightforward summary of the message of Francis on worker justice is that the well-being of ordinary working people must take priority over capital (that is, money invested and, by extension, the prerogatives of owners and managers of great wealth). The alliterative motto "putting people over profits" captures this priority quite accurately, though at the risk of oversimplification. As we have seen, the tradition of modern Catholic social teaching demonstrates a high regard for the institutions of private property, profitable business enterprises, and economic freedom. Indeed, a market system featuring these qualities has been affirmed as the best method of generating wealth, employment, and economic opportunities that can be distributed broadly to advance the common good of society. When gains experienced by both employers and employees are mutual, when the interests of owners and workers coincide, when all benefit from a fair social contract that distributes newly created wealth equitably, harmonious labor relations are easily achieved.

Things sometimes go wrong, both on the level of the individual business enterprise and on the larger stage of the macro economy, when priorities drift away from mutuality and shared benefits so that unbridled competition and greed take over. Under the pressures of a globalized economy, many managers look for every opportunity to squeeze workers of pay and benefits, and the trust that should characterize industrial relations breaks down in a war of words or worse. We are all familiar with the excesses and abuses of unfettered capitalism and absolutely autonomous markets. On one hand, carefully regulated markets, with legal protections for workers, consumers, and the environment, are capable of operating for the benefit of all. But on the other hand, a market economy lacking adequate regulation soon becomes our master, not the servant it is meant to be. Everything that Francis says and does regarding economic relations reflects his appreciation of the importance of recalling what he sees as the purpose of markets in the first place: serving the human needs of all, especially the most vulnerable.

A further point relating to culture and values is just as vital as the strictly economic analysis above. In a truly healthy economy, it is not just government agencies and courts that work as protective mechanisms to restrain greed and callous self-interest in economic transactions; it is also the internal moral codes that form part of the very character of virtuous individuals. Preventing economic abuses and steering the economy to optimal social outcomes is a combination of collective cultural understandings as well as personal virtues—forces more potent than any government agency or regulatory rule book. These internalized codes of ethical behavior are generally more influential in smooth social functioning than external written codes prescribing particular procedures. In a corrupt and callous economy, dysfunctions creep in at all levels—the personal, the corporate, the systemic, and the structural.

An imbalance of economic values quickly makes victims out of workers who are simply aspiring to contribute to the common good while providing a decent livelihood for themselves and their families. As children of God and heirs to the gifts of creation, the poor deserve to share the benefits of material and technological progress, which are increasingly hoarded by a few. Francis displayed his commitment to addressing these concerns when, in a June 2013 address to officials of the United

Nations Food and Agriculture Organization, he lamented the scandal of hoarding (both of food and of economic power). The pope affirmed that it is scandalous for any to go hungry, since in a world of relative abundance we can easily meet all dire needs but simply lack the political will to do so. In just his fourth month in office, Francis used the international platform provided by that occasion to declare, "A way has to be found to enable everyone to benefit from the fruits of the earth . . . to satisfy the demands of justice, fairness and respect for every human being. . . . There is a need to oppose the short-sighted economic interests and the mentality of power of a relative few who exclude the majority of the world's peoples, generating poverty and marginalization and causing a breakdown in society."[21]

With his structural perspective and eye for the excluded, Pope Francis is a tireless advocate for workers who find themselves exploited (in direct or indirect ways) by large multinational corporations operating in an increasingly globalized economy. In keeping with traditional Catholic social teachings on labor justice, Francis readily identifies the root cause of exploitation: greed that causes labor to be treated as a mere commodity, as merely an objective factor of production, with no recognition of the inherent human dignity of each worker. The result is indifference to the human tragedy of unemployment and a tolerance for unconscionably low wages that leave workers insecure and entire families hungry and desperate.

As noted in the previous chapter dealing with economic inequality, for Francis the status quo in labor relations is not tolerable. To put it mildly, it fosters exclusion; in the starker terms employed by Francis in "The Joy of the Gospel," such an economy kills. We have noted Francis's stern insistence that deep reforms are needed as workers in the globalized labor market struggle for survival at the mercy of economic forces they cannot control. Further, innovative production technologies (accelerating automation and robotization) are disrupting existing patterns of employment and trade. These trends threaten to leave millions of workers even further behind as the least-resourced workers and communities absorb the damaging effects of economic disruption and dislocation. We search in vain for easy institutional solutions. With declining membership in labor unions in most places, worker rights are being rolled back around the world, in developed as well as emerging economies. This is one of the reasons why faith-based advocacy for worker rights, such as that taken up by Pope Francis, is so important at this particular historical moment.

Simply put, the crux of the economic approach of Pope Francis is his keen desire to put the economy at the service of people. When he addresses economic topics such as inequality and labor justice, he deliberately shies away from growing overly specific about policy recommendations. "The Joy of the Gospel" and the 2015 address in Bolivia contain entire paragraphs explaining why no voice from Rome (or any location for that matter) should be heard insisting on specific measures that must be followed in detail in distant contexts. Church social teachings are intended to be value raisers, not answer providers, regarding the achievement of economic justice. In his Bolivia speech Francis even frankly admits, "So don't expect a recipe from this Pope. . . . I dare say that no recipe exists." In acknowledging the limits of Vatican social teaching, Francis is reprising the wise counsel of his predecessors, who aspired to offer not a blueprint for economic reforms but merely a set of criteria to judge an economy as just or unjust, as healthy or imbalanced, including in its spiritual dimensions. Indeed, his friend and confidant Cardinal Walter Kasper specifies, "Francis does not wish to propound a concrete economic program. He is concerned with the anthropological crisis, in which money has become mammon and an idol."[22]

We should, then, expect from Francis a paucity of details but an abundance of moral instruction and spiritual guidance along the way. While he steers us to recognize the need for deep structural changes, those expecting a detailed articulation of, say, a carefully prescribed mix of government policies and private charitable partnerships to boost employment opportunities will remain frustrated. By some standards, Francis is maddeningly unclear about the systematic remedies and alternatives he encourages his hearers to pursue. For ultimately, the most important thing any religious leader can do in commenting on the economy is to identify the overarching ethical goals that economic reforms should achieve. For Francis, there is no doubt that the key to these goals is the advancement of those currently poor and powerless, whose lives are so thoroughly controlled by the powerful. Drastic changes are needed if today's disenfranchised are to become what God intends: not mere objects of occasional charitable concern but fully empowered agents in their own lives and place in history.

Besides these questions regarding the content and level of detail of the economic teachings of Pope Francis, there is also the question of his tone. For some, he is too strident in his tenor, too adversarial in his challenge to those who hold power in the economy. For others, Pope Francis is too pessimistic about the workings of the current global economy; if relatively free markets are seen as part of the problem rather than as the solution to global poverty, then we appear to jettison practically all hope of better outcomes. In reply, defenders of Pope Francis are quick to point out that his economic teaching contains an abundant message of hope. But this is not some ungrounded hope that turns a blind eye to the serious problems yet to be overcome. Before we can entertain what Francis calls "creative alternatives," we first need to face up to even the most uncomfortable of global realities, such as "the cry of the excluded."[23] The entire thrust of his economic teachings is to challenge his audience to create conditions and new structures that will provide the excluded with more favorable conditions for their full flourishing. Even without specifying the details and mechanisms of such economic reforms, Francis is holding out the hopeful possibility of constructive change and real improvement.

If there is an uneasy mix of optimism and pessimism here, the tension may spring from the long experience of Francis in direct service of disadvantaged communities in his native South America. Jorge Bergoglio won renown for "walking the talk." Even as archbishop of Buenos Aires, he would wander the alleyways of the slums and shantytowns at the margins of the city to listen to the concerns of the families living in humble conditions there and to offer them some solace and hope. He took extraordinary steps, for example, to assist the efforts of trash pickers (*cartoneros*) to organize a profitable cooperative—contributing to constructive structural change at the grass roots.

His close contact with the misery of people struggling for material sustenance and self-respect has given Francis a profound sense of realism, which prompts him not to expect momentous overnight change. But at the same time, his rich personal experience over decades of pastoral work has shown him the resilience of even the most downtrodden people and their noble aspirations for a better life. He is able to recall vividly several occasions when successive governments of his native Argentina, working in concert with the business community and various institutions of civil society, actually responded in highly effective ways to demands for reform to assist those in need. The ministry of Francis on the global level as pope and Universal Pastor, then, is in essence a continuation of his remarkable service to the poor of his home city of Buenos Aires. Wherever he goes, we witness a church leader who is especially attentive to the voices of the humble and marginalized—those who are so often harmed by untamed economic forces.

But if long experience has given Francis a sense of patience, it has in no way robbed him of a sense of urgency. He is fearless in posing hard questions about economic justice; he knows that we cannot wait too long to address the misery of the suffering and the need for a thorough restructuring of our economy so that it may serve the needs of all. Francis certainly issues his challenges in stark terms, employing prophetic rhetorical flourishes used by no previous pope. But at the same time, his social and economic concerns are in close continuity with the best of the tradition of Catholic social teaching. The remaining four chapters each take up social issues and topics (the environment, family life, migrants and trafficked persons, and peacemaking) that exhibit numerous points of contact with economic justice. In each chapter, we will again observe deep ethical commitments held by Pope Francis that display both continuity with previous Catholic social thought and considerable innovation as well.

3

A BOLD CALL FOR INTEGRAL ECOLOGY

The middle two chapters of this book provide an opportunity to extend the analysis of Pope Francis into two additional areas of Catholic social teaching: ecology and family life. The previous two chapters focused squarely on economic issues, describing the ways that Pope Francis has renewed and expanded the Catholic tradition of advocacy for those left behind by economic progress. In addressing economic inequality and labor justice, Francis expresses a profound concern for the well-being of the poorest and most vulnerable members of society, who are so often excluded from opportunities and otherwise harmed by the interplay of harsh economic forces. In his eagerness to see their lives improved, Francis challenges all of us to support structural changes in a market system that, left to itself, will resist constructive change.

But the pope's concerns are by no means limited to the distribution of material resources. Anyone truly concerned about advancing the well-being of our marginalized neighbors will care about factors beyond the size of their bank accounts or other strictly economic measures. If we want to imagine a future in which those currently disadvantaged and excluded are truly thriving, we need to look at broader measures of well-being and security—taking up more holistic perspectives on their physical and social welfare.

Throughout his papacy, Francis has repeatedly called attention to more comprehensive indicators of personal and social well-being. In the interest of broadening the canvas and expanding our horizons, he has published two important documents that treat topics that are central to human flourishing. In June 2015 he published *Laudato Si'*, his first encyclical,[1] which bears the subtitle "On Care for Our Common Home." This long and highly authoritative document deals with the natural environment, the health of which is especially pivotal for the well-being of the poorest people on earth. The current chapter focuses on *Laudato Si'* and the topic of ecology in Catholic thought. In April 2016, Pope Francis published *Amoris Laetitia* (translated into English as "The Joy of Love" or "On Love in the Family"), an apostolic exhortation on the topic of healthy family life. Chapter 4 covers this important set of teachings.

While ecology and family relations may at first glance seem a bit peripheral to social justice and material progress, these two chapters demonstrate how Pope Francis, following the long trajectory of Catholic social thought, incorporates these themes into an integrated approach to promoting authentic human development and advancing the well-being of the most vulnerable. Reviewing the contents of these important papal documents on family and the environment will help us appreciate both the depth and the many faces of Francis's commitment to advancing the dignity of all humans (indeed, the integrity of all of creation).

Most of this chapter on ecology will consist of an explication of the message of *Laudato Si'* because of the great importance of its innovative contributions to Catholic thought on the environment. Before analyzing the 2015 document, we examine what preceded this groundbreaking encyclical. Besides noting the treatment of the environment early in the pontificate of Francis, we situate these new teachings within the context of previous Catholic social teaching on the environment.

PREPARING THE WAY FOR *LAUDATO SI'*

From the very start of his papacy, Francis has been very outspoken about the theme of respect for the environment. As he assumed office, he seemed especially eager to send the signal that ecological concerns would be front and center at the Vatican under his leadership. During his very first press conference, the new pope was asked to explain his choice of a papal name. Over the whir and click of camera shutters, he referred to his great admiration for Saint Francis of Assisi, whom he referred to as "the man of poverty, the man of peace, the man who loves and safeguards creation. . . . At this time, we do not have a very good relationship with creation, do we?" Many in attendance that day would have recalled that in 1979, Pope John Paul II declared Francis of Assisi the patron saint of ecology.[2] The first Jesuit pope in history was most evidently deeply inspired by the thirteenth-century founder of the Franciscans, and that Italian saint's reverence for the wonders of the natural world clearly sparked much of this admiration.

Days later, as Francis crafted and delivered his inaugural homily as pope, he demonstrated his environmental priority once again. Taking advantage of the fact that the Mass fell on the Solemnity of St. Joseph (the day the church sets aside for celebrating Jesus's earthly father, whose vocation was to be a protector of the Holy Family), Francis included an appeal to all to be protectors of creation, besides serving as protectors of our fellow human beings. His sermon on that important occasion contained these words of inclusion, challenge, and encouragement:

> Let us protect Christ in our lives so we can protect others; so that we can protect creation. The vocation of being a protector, however, is not just something involving us Christians alone; it also has a prior dimension which is simply human, involving everyone. It means protecting all creation, the beauty of the created world, as the Book of Genesis and as Saint Francis of Assisi showed us. It means respecting each of God's creatures and respecting the environment in which we live. . . . In the end, everything has been entrusted to our protection. . . . I would like to ask all those who have positions of responsibility in economic, political and social life, and all men and women of goodwill: let us be 'protectors' of creation, protectors of God's plan inscribed in nature, protectors of one another and of the environment. Let us not allow omens of destruction and death to accompany the advance of this world!"[3]

Although we can only speculate about when the pope decided to write the first-ever encyclical on environmental concerns, it is easy to follow the trail of hints he dropped on many occasions that ecology was close to his heart. Especially in his first year in office, he went out of his way to include in public addresses prominent mention of the importance of respecting the earth and all its creatures. His daily homilies, speeches to general audiences, and addresses to groups of visiting dignitaries frequently struck the same notes. Even his Twitter feed often urged readers to preserve the earth and reduce waste.[4]

Francis also utilized a variety of more formal opportunities to highlight his ecological message. For example, his first message for the annual World Day of Peace (January 1, 2014) included several paragraphs identifying the imperative of preserving the earth ("a common gift from the Creator") and fulfilling our "truly pressing duty to use the earth's resources in such a way that all may be free from hunger."[5] Each of his addresses to the World Meetings of Popular Movements (explored in detail in chapter 2), especially his October 28, 2014, address to that first gathering in Rome, touched upon environmental concerns, including the devastating effects of global climate change upon the poorest people of the Global South. Finally, recall that his November 2013 apostolic exhortation "The Joy of the Gospel" serves as a programmatic agenda for his entire papacy. Francis touches on the environment just a few times (paragraphs 56, 215, and 216) in that long document. However, it is easy to imagine that the pope was deliberately reserving a fuller treatment of this important topic for the full-scale environmental encyclical that he was presumably already considering writing by late 2013.

Francis's encyclical *Laudato Si'*, eagerly awaited for many months by Vatican watchers who had been alerted that it was in the works, finally appeared on June 18, 2015. In slightly over 40,000 words contained in 246 paragraphs spread out over 184 pages (as the official English version is laid out on the Vatican website), the depth and complexity of its message surpasses anything Pope Francis had said or written before on the environment. To fully appreciate the groundbreaking contribution of this encyclical letter, of course, we must look further back than just the papacy of Francis. It is especially illuminating to situate this new document against the background of Catholic social teaching on the environment over the past half century.

It is not surprising that social encyclicals published before the Second Vatican Council (1962–1965) barely mention ecology; the environmental movement only began in earnest in the 1960s. Of the sixteen major documents of Vatican II, *Gaudium et Spes* ("The Pastoral Constitution of the Church in the Modern World") includes most of the council's social teachings—those topics that reach out beyond internal church matters. This document's stirring call to greater social concern and action on the part of Catholics to improve the world contains three paragraphs (12, 33, and 34) that treat the natural environment. A close examination of these three paragraphs reveals that the council fathers were relying on a pattern of thought that a contemporary observer might find to be quaint at best and ultimately troubling upon deeper reflection. The simplest label for the approach to the natural environment invoked here is the "dominion approach" to the natural world. It portrays the natural world as a resource created by God and intended solely for the benefit of humans, who are its sole beneficiary. A particular reading of the creation accounts in Genesis (the first book of the Bible) supports this approach, as it understands the divine mandate to "subdue the earth" in a way that is rather harsh and lacking in nuance. Paragraph 33 of *Gaudium et Spes* looks approvingly on the supposed divine mission "to extend [human] mastery over nearly the whole of nature."

The environment made only cameo appearances in the several major social teaching documents published by the Vatican in the quarter century after Vatican II. For the most part, these documents from popes and worldwide synods of bishops perpetuated this dominion approach, though sometimes with a constructive twist. Documents from Pope Paul VI[6] and the 1971 Synod of Bishops[7] took notice of growing pollution and environmental degradation and expressed concern that by damaging the natural environment humankind would in the long run be hurting itself. These documents were especially eager to offer ethical guidance to world leaders as they pursued economic development, extending industrialization to newly independent nations in the immediate wake of decolonization.

Further, Vatican officials were often present at international proceedings dealing with sensitive development issues that involved potential threats to the environment. For example, if fragile ecosystems such as rain forests and wetlands are developed too rapidly or imprudently, such as through the construction of major dams and levee projects that will disrupt natural watercourses, millions of people might suffer dire consequences. The appropriate response, then, is to exercise greater caution in our use of the earth's resources, including its land, water, and air. Hasty development initiatives could backfire and harm millions of people in the long run as well as the short term. The church felt an ethical duty to utter a word of restraint and encourage greater fore-thought. Catholic teaching documents of this era began to reflect this awareness, though the focus of concern remained exclusively on pro-tecting humans, not ecosystems and the nonhuman species within them, from harm.

To capture this duty, common church parlance often invokes the scriptural concept of stewardship, a theological term that denotes an obligation to act prudently to develop our God-given talents and re-sources, mindful of the effects of our actions on others. At this point in the church's environmental teachings, those others appeared to be con-fined to other humans (as opposed to members of other species or their natural habitats). The reasons cited for halting pollution or avoiding undue exploitation of natural resources were limited to the potential boomerang effects on people. If their words are taken at face value, the church documents in question recognize no intrinsic value in the non-human material world. The value of all these creatures remains merely instrumental, limited to how they may serve human purposes. There-fore, Catholic teachings of that era contain no critique of human selfish-ness or myopia in the wanton abuse of nature. The operative reading of biblical texts (such as God's command to the first humans to "fill the earth and subdue it" in Genesis 1:28) prevented church voices from acknowledging the possibility that we might be exceeding proper and prudent limits in our interactions with creation. The status quo was sacralized by the received view that the earth, including other species and the entire ecosystem, exists for the benefit of humans alone.

The early 1990s witnessed a breakthrough to a far more robust Cath-olic theology of the natural environment. Pope John Paul II titled his 1990 World Day of Peace message "The Ecological Crisis: A Common Responsibility." It staked out new ground (including the stunning claim "The cosmos is endowed with its own integrity, its own internal, dynam-ic balance. This order must be respected"[8]) that signaled a major shift in perspective from the previous models of dominion and stewardship. John Paul's 1991 social encyclical *Centesimus Annus* followed up these challenging words with a summons to respect the cosmos by curtailing "the senseless destruction of the natural environment" and "arbitrary use of the earth."[9] Bishops' conferences around the world, taking their cue as they often do from papal initiatives, began to produce pastoral letters that echoed the words of the Polish pope. A prime example is

"Renewing the Earth: An Invitation to Reflection and Action on the Environment" published by the United States Conference of Catholic Bishops in November 1991. That influential document helped fill in a major lacuna in previous Catholic thought regarding the environment by supplying a richer understanding of humanity's place in the universe. In a compact twenty pages, this bishops' document provides a framework of several rich theological themes that rightly feed Catholic concern about the state of the earth. Among the noteworthy resources that the bishops' document sought to revive were venerable Christian spiritual traditions (such as Franciscan spirituality) that interject a much-needed note of humility regarding our role with respect to the natural world—a relationship that should be characterized by service and care rather than domination and ruthless exploitation.[10]

In the introductory paragraphs of *Laudato Si'*, Pope Francis extends a word of genuine appreciation to John Paul II for enabling this pivotal advance in Catholic theology. He devotes the entirety of paragraph 5 to Saint John Paul (over whose canonization ceremony Francis presided in April 2014), praising him for his summons to "be concerned for the world around us" and for pointing out that our respect for the earth "must proceed in line with God's original gift of all that is."[11] In the very next paragraph of *Laudato Si'*, Francis notes the great contribution to Catholic ecological thought of his immediate predecessor, Pope Benedict XVI, who was often called "The Green Pope" during the years of his own papacy (2005–2013). There were good reasons for Benedict's stellar reputation regarding environmental progress. The scholarly German pope used both words and actions to advance his ecological agenda. To a variety of audiences, he repeatedly emphasized the urgency of undertaking structural changes to prevent further ecological degradation, such as by implementing international standards for reducing carbon emissions. He arranged for the Vatican to install a large number of photovoltaic solar panels on the roofs of church buildings in Rome and actively encouraged Catholic institutions to participate in carbon emission offset initiatives. Pope Francis was grateful to inherit the positive ecological legacy of Benedict, who made substantial progress toward the goal of making Vatican City the world's first carbon-neutral nation-state.[12]

In his words of praise for his predecessor's environmental leadership, Pope Francis cites several sentences that Benedict delivered within longer addresses to gatherings of three different groups (of German legislators, of diplomats, and of clergy). There is also one citation from Benedict's landmark 2009 social encyclical *Caritas in Veritate* ("Charity in Truth"), a document that richly deserves the attention of anyone tracking the progress of Catholic teaching on the environment. This was the first encyclical of any pope to include an entire section on the environment—at last, ecology made more than a cameo appearance. Benedict devotes four long paragraphs (48–51) to detailing the urgency of ecological progress, especially involving the need for cooperative global management of energy resources. In many ways, Benedict prepared the ground for Francis to undertake the writing of *Laudato Si'*. Without the bold leadership of the German pope, the Argentinian pope would not have been so well positioned to take an additional step in the long overdue development of Catholic teaching on the environment.

THE MANY CONTRIBUTIONS OF *LAUDATO SI'*

If Catholic theology regarding the environment had come a long way since Vatican II, Pope Francis was aware that it still had some distance to cover before it reflected the full range of ethical values at stake. Perhaps he was inspired to prioritize the promotion of environmental responsibility by other Christian communities. The World Council of Churches (a Geneva-based organization of many affiliated Christian denominations that does not include Roman Catholicism) had decades earlier adopted "the integrity of creation" as one of its ecumenical ethical goals (alongside the promotion of justice and peace). Perhaps Francis was further inspired by the deep respect for the earth displayed by a variety of indigenous peoples in his native South America (and indeed, around the world), who deeply lament the degradation of the earth and the wanton disruption of its delicate patterns of activity, to which these communities are so close and so attentive. In any case, he came into papal office with a firm commitment to advancing Catholic teaching on the environment even beyond the considerable achievements of his two immediate predecessors in the Chair of Peter. While Francis is in many ways a traditionalist, intent upon preserving received church teachings, ecology is one area where he eagerly took advantage of the opportunity to contribute to a substantial development of Catholic doctrine.

The primary vehicle for advancing Catholic teaching on the environment was an ambitious social encyclical which Francis divided into six chapters. *Laudato Si'* starts by offering a litany of concerns, including a stunning survey of ecological degradation, pollution, and wanton destruction of our planet. The first chapter, called "What Is Happening to Our Common Home," reaches a high point in paragraph 21 with the sweeping observation that "the earth, our home, is looking more and more like an immense pile of filth." The dire need for an abrupt about-face is obvious. Of course, the most vexing and dangerous problem of all is global climate change, which Francis is not afraid to attribute to human activity such as the burning of fossil fuels. In affirming the consensus of the vast majority of responsible scientists, Francis does find himself wading into the fierce political arena often dominated by the vitriol of climate change deniers. Undeterred by the whiff of controversy, the pope contends that he is by no means seeking to usurp the role of scientists (or politicians for that matter). He is forthright in stating that he is simply "drawing upon the results of the best scientific research available today" (paragraph 15). His confidence in his reading of overwhelming evidence to support the hypothesis of human-caused climate change allows him matter-of-factly to proceed with his project in this encyclical. He displays firm determination to do what is necessary to provide pastoral leadership to people of faith (and, he repeatedly affirms, all people of goodwill who care to listen) who seek to improve the state of the earth.

After recounting all this bad news, the encyclical turns to sources of hope and potential action. Like so many church documents, it looks first to scriptural materials (chapter 2 is titled "The Gospel of Creation") that direct Christians to care for the earth, even when this project comes at a substantial cost. It is not enough simply to identify and read the parts of the Bible that portray the appropriate human role in the created world; we must also interpret the scriptural narrative properly and avoid errant understandings of the revealed Word of God that would rationalize wanton exploitation of nature. The next three chapters ("The Human Roots of the Ecological Crisis," "Integral Ecology," and "Lines of Approach and Action") provide a diagnosis and prescription for the ecological crisis we are facing. Employing a structuralist lens once again to probe the causes of society-wide dysfunction, Francis does not hesitate to identify deep cultural imbalances and social sins that have caused humans to destroy so much of the natural world. Nor does he shy away from demanding that people everywhere transform their mentality and reform their institutions in far-reaching ways. We can no longer afford to operate according to a logic of selfish acquisitiveness; rather, for the benefit of ourselves and the entirety of creation, we must adopt the ways of universal solidarity. Only by first making internal changes within our hearts and souls will the urgent changes in external behavior be possible.

In a final chapter charting the path ahead (chapter 6 is titled "Ecological Education and Spirituality"), Francis urges the formation and practice of new habits and ways of behavior that will respect the earth more fully. Besides offering some rather profound pastoral and spiritual insights, the pope ventures some homespun practical advice (he recommends, for example, donning an extra sweater instead of turning up the thermostat at home and repurposing paper wrapping and plastic bags). Demonstrating his sensitivity to people of all faiths, Francis concludes his encyclical with two prayers for the earth. One is "a Christian prayer in union with creation" (employing a variety of explicitly Christian religious symbols and imagery), and the other is "for all who believe in a God who is the all-powerful Creator." Addressed to the "all-powerful God," this prayer includes a request that is fitting for a compassionate mystic who chose the papal name Francis: "Teach us to discover the worth of each thing, to be filled with awe and contemplation, to recognize that we are profoundly united with every creature as we journey toward your infinite light." These are apt words indeed to conclude an encyclical of such profound ecological sensitivity.

In a sense, the encyclical also begins with a prayer, or at least a brief citation from a stanza of the famous prayer "Canticle of the Creatures," attributed to Saint Francis of Assisi. This prayer praises God for the gift of fellow creatures, celebrates our closeness to particular creatures (including Brother Sun and Sister Moon), and reverences creation in general. It is highly significant that this prayer provides this encyclical with its name. (Encyclicals are customarily referred to by their initial two or three words in Latin, so it is by way of great exception that Francis begins his encyclical with a non-Latin phrase). The Italian *Laudato si', mi' Signore* is usually translated "Praise be to you, my Lord," so English speakers may refer to the encyclical as "Praise Be," "Be Praised," or even "May You Be Praised." As we shall see, Pope Francis proceeds to develop a large number of theological themes, all of which bear eloquent witness to the value of establishing harmony with God, other people, and all creatures. Citing the "Canticle of the Creatures" allows the pope to strike just the right note at the very beginning of his effort.

If there is a single phrase that summarizes the message of Francis throughout the encyclical, it is "integral ecology." Francis employs this term eight times in the course of the encyclical (in paragraphs 10, 11, 62, 124, 137, 159, 225, 230), and it provides the topic and title of the pivotal fourth chapter. It is not a completely new term in church circles; the International Theological Commission had referred to the notion of integral ecology in an important 2009 document on natural law, and Catholic theologians had for decades followed secular writers in appealing to this concept. Integral ecology combines our concern for natural ecology and human ecology, leaving out nothing in the visible universe. The phrase has positive resonance with concepts such as integral development and integral liberation, buzzwords in recent Christian theology as well. Integral ecology may be considered a new name for an old insight, one understood almost instinctively by parties (for instance, members of the venerable Franciscan communities) who dedicate themselves to caring holistically for the earth and its inhabitants, such as by practicing the virtues of hospitality and environmental husbandry. Any act of generous attention and practical compassion for poor and needy humans or for preserving fragile ecosystems and the species within them constitutes an act of integral ecology.

To claim that ecology must be integral is to call attention to the close link between the well-being of humans and the natural environment, refusing to view either one in isolation. In any adequate vision of ecological flourishing, the key is to "get the relationships right," and these must always include the relationships within and beyond the human community. This explains why Francis repeatedly expresses (at least a dozen times in *Laudato Si'*, phrasing the point in various ways) an insight that appears early in his chapter on integral ecology: "It cannot be emphasized enough how everything is interconnected. . . . [Nothing] can be considered in isolation" (paragraph 138). Above all, the pope is calling for a deeper appreciation of the ways that human society and the natural world are interrelated. He wants to impress upon his readers the importance of paying adequate attention to the networks of relationships in which we find ourselves—networks which are never simply natural or social but always both at once.

While this might sound like an obvious insight, Francis is eager to drive this point home, perhaps because of a certain recent contentiousness in Catholic circles regarding proper terminology. For all their contributions to Catholic ecological awareness, Popes John Paul II and Benedict XVI continued to draw a sharp distinction between human (or social) ecology and environmental (or natural) ecology. In their writings and addresses, these two predecessors of Francis took pains to preserve a separation between nature and society, perhaps in the interest of underlining the uniqueness of humankind among all other creatures of God. While Francis clearly affirms the special place of humans in the universe, he proposes the framework of integral ecology as a corrective to an overly rugged distinction that prevents constructive engagement with environmental problems.[13] His clearest statement of this concern comes in paragraph 139: "We are faced not with two separate crises, one environmental and the other social, but with one complex crisis which is both social and environmental. Strategies for a solution demand an integrated approach to combating poverty, restoring dignity to the excluded, and at the same time protecting nature."

Two weighty factors motivate Pope Francis to adopt this stance. One is the utter urgency of addressing ecological degradation, such as the realities of pollution and climate change he had already described. The time for enacting solutions is running out; because we simply cannot delay any further, all excuses for inaction must be challenged. The second factor at play is the pope's awareness that the ecological crisis is at root a moral problem, one tied to the ethical blindness and selfishness of humans around the world who have been cavalierly exploiting natural resources for centuries. The grave threats to the health of the planet are not inevitable but the result of poor human choices and patterns of behavior. Human society is not likely to rein in wanton abuse of the earth until we reconceive ourselves as very much a part of nature, not as overlords operating somehow with impunity above the rest of God's creation. Only by addressing the environmental damage in which we are complicit can we assume our proper social responsibility and prevent digging our own graves. Unless we break down the previously recognized distinction between human ecology and natural ecology, we are unlikely to enact effective change or make sacrifices to support the needed improvements. Preserving the customary distinction we have inherited is a dangerous impediment to true progress and an obstacle to the deep reforms required today.

As we have seen, Catholic social teaching has for decades witnessed a gradual growth in sensitivity to threats to nonhuman creatures, for example, expressing increasing concern for their vanishing habitats. Pope Francis is of course eager to continue this trajectory, as he does when he devotes an entire section of *Laudato Si'* (paragraphs 32 to 42) to the necessity of addressing one particular face of the ecological crisis: the loss of biodiversity. Here we find a sincere lament for the extinction of "thousands of species, which will no longer give glory to God by their very existence" because of imprudent human activity (paragraph 33). But he is also adding a revolutionary new angle, completing some of the intellectual work that was left to be done even after the great contributions of previous popes.

The most urgent appeal now is not simply to alter our external behavior in a few marginal ways by making more prudent choices about allocating resources, such as setting aside more land for wildlife sanctuaries and less for agriculture and commercial development. The choice before humankind can no longer be portrayed as a matter of such simple and practical calculations regarding how to balance our needs with those of other species. Such necessary reallocations will surely impose costs and inconveniences upon human society, but they remain merely external matters. The imbalances that require the most urgent correction nowadays lie within us, involving the internal dynamics of human self-understanding, the wellsprings of human culture and human identity itself. This is why Francis makes this stunning and challenging statement linking humanity and its natural environment in paragraph 118: "There can be no renewal of our relationship with nature without a renewal of humanity itself. There can be no ecology without an adequate anthropology."

Francis is using the term "anthropology" here in a way customary for theologians, to describe an all-encompassing understanding of who human persons are in relation to God and all of creation. He is calling for a comprehensive reconsideration of humanity's place in the universe. We have gotten off on the wrong track, he laments, relying on a model that has inordinately emphasized human mastery over creation. He even provides an imposing name for the root error that leads us astray as individuals and as a culture: tyrannical anthropocentrism. By placing the human race at the center of all concern, we find ourselves justifying all manner of unnecessary exploitation, treating created things as mere resources for our own purposes. Francis presents his fullest diagnosis of this fundamental human mistake in paragraphs 67 and 68 of *Laudato Si'*. He returns to the topic in paragraph 118, where he laments the many costs of what he calls "a misguided anthropocentrism."

Pope Francis claims that the error of exaggerated anthropocentrism is based on a misreading of the creation story in the book of Genesis, one that exaggerates the mandate to exercise dominion over the earth. Of course, mainstream Christian theology has traditionally been unabashedly anthropocentric, concerned primarily with God's offer of salvation to human beings and relegating other parts of the created order to afterthoughts in the narrative of human redemption from sin. Even with the revision Francis is urging, it is of course still possible to preserve the traditional Christian orthodox views that humanity has a unique role in the universe and that human dignity somehow surpasses the innate dignity of our fellow creatures. However, Francis explains, the balance that needs to be struck will involve "putting an end to [humans'] claim to absolute dominion over the earth," to "usurping the place of God," and to "claiming an unlimited right to trample his creation underfoot" (paragraph 75). We will never develop adequate respect for the earth and for other species until we accept the central lesson of integral ecology: that humans are part of a larger web of life, an integral part of a larger whole that we are called to serve rather than to dominate exclusively for our own benefit. Francis is ushering Catholic theology away from a crass anthropocentrism and toward a creation-centered theology that is more open to the widest intentions of a loving Creator God for the entire universe.

Another memorable phrase used by Francis to describe this problem is the dominance of the "technocratic paradigm," a term invoked throughout the encyclical's third chapter, which treats "the human roots of the ecological crisis." Francis calls an exaggerated reliance on a scientific model "a reductionism which affects every aspect of human and social life" (paragraph 107). Like tyrannical anthropocentrism, technocratic ways of thinking can stunt our moral imagination and prevent us from viewing ourselves as an integral part of creation. Now, by no means is Pope Francis or the church leadership in general opposed to

the appropriate use of technology; it is only when an instrumental mentality becomes omnipresent and dominates all our relationships that we
need to reevaluate our reliance on the methods and aims of science. An
unduly high regard for our own ability to manage the challenges of life
on earth reveals the tragic vice of hubris and leads us to overlook our
connections to other beings. The result is an exaggerated self-reliance
unchecked by a realistic sense of our own limits and vulnerabilities.

While he does us a great service in issuing this ethical guidance,
Francis is hardly breaking new ground here. Ever since the presentation of the cautionary tale involving the Tower of Babel (see Genesis
11:1–9), Western religious traditions have featured an acute awareness
of the dangerous tendency for technological advances to lead us astray.
Catholic moral teaching documents are full of admonitions to subject
both the ends and means of scientific advances to close ethical scrutiny,
and Pope Benedict frequently noted the need to counter the "technical
mind-set" when it leaves behind important moral considerations. In
several places in *Laudato Si'*, Pope Francis cites the mid-twentieth-
century work of Romano Guardini, one of his favorite theologians, who
is famous for advocating vigilance in applying ethical checks upon technological development.

As ever, Francis is eager to accentuate the positive. He is clearly
more interested in proposing innovative and constructive approaches to
these profound issues of our age than he is in condemning the inadequate approaches that brought us to the ecological precipice. If social
change is to come, the kind of change that will empower people around
the world to address the threat of environmental degradation, a set of
renewed cultural values will lead the way. Again and again, Pope Francis demonstrates his unique talent for appealing for cultural change in
ways that are capable of sparking enthusiasm and effective response.
Elsewhere in this study, we see him describing the heartwarming effects of embracing a culture of encounter, a culture of accompaniment,
and a culture of inclusion. In the closing paragraphs of *Laudato Si'*, he
proposes the phrase "a culture of care" as a summary of the changes
that will be required to transform the currently bleak prospects for the
natural environment into something more promising.

A society-wide embrace of a culture of care provides a particularly
sharp contrast to the notion of "the throwaway culture," which Francis
laments so often at the beginning of the encyclical (most prominently in

paragraphs 16 and 22) in presenting his litany of environmental woes. Indeed, the entire encyclical can be summarized as an appeal to grow in ecological awareness by replacing the throwaway culture with a culture of care. This naturally leads us to inquire about the conditions that would favor such a momentously important turnaround. What cultural variable accounts for the crucial difference between disastrous and constructive outcomes? Once again, Pope Francis provides an answer that requires all humans to dig deep and change their selfish ways. The pivotal change arises when indifference (a key problem Francis cites in paragraph 14) is replaced by solidarity—the virtue of fellow feeling that is absolutely central to Francis's vision of economic justice and concern for the most disadvantaged.

When Francis inserts that novel and appealing phrase "a culture of care" into paragraph 231 near the end of *Laudato Si'*, he equates it with "social love" (a more familiar term within Catholic social teaching), which is understood as a force that motivates generous service for the common good. He concludes paragraph 231 with this invitation: "When we feel that God is calling us to intervene with others in these social dynamics, we should realize that this too is part of our spirituality, which is an exercise of charity and, as such, matures and sanctifies us." While nobody would be surprised that this great religious leader concludes such a wide-ranging analysis of historic challenges to the very existence of humanity with an appeal to spirituality, this is nevertheless a highly noteworthy move.

Halfway into the encyclical (in paragraph 114), Francis identifies "the urgent need for us to move forward in a bold cultural revolution." Attentive readers will naturally be wondering how the pope proposes to launch this revolution. In the closing pages of *Laudato Si'*, Francis reveals his plan and proclaims his desire to share with the reader the riches of Christian spiritual traditions, many of which have long been revered for their love of the environment. As noted above, the entire final chapter of *Laudato Si'* is titled "Ecological Education and Spirituality." If deeper values are to replace superficial ones, if humanity is to transcend its most destructive blind spots and limitations, if new cultural priorities can provide an antidote to the worst excesses of anthropocentrism and technocratic mind-sets, spirituality will provide essential resources in this endeavor.

Spirituality is most broadly defined as our entire way of being in the world, the path of life we follow, a way that includes spiritual dimensions that transcend (but in no way denigrate) the material level of existence. Spiritualties naturally gravitate toward holistic visions, inviting their practitioners (those who participate in particular rituals, prayer, and other disciplines) to broaden their horizons and even to forget themselves entirely. Getting in touch with common spiritual hungers to experience wholeness and to overcome artificial separations among God's creatures are frequent motifs in spiritual traditions that readily overlap with ecological concern. In many schools of spirituality, both within and beyond Christianity, the summit of spiritual life is a rich experience of mystical union with God—an intimate knowledge of the Creator. While some traditions even aspire to an unmediated (or direct) experience of God, for most the Creator is known precisely through created things and is approached through loving relationships with all manner of creatures. All these themes common to many spiritual traditions support the development (indeed, the urgent priority) of respect for the nonhuman natural world.

Spirituality goes hand in hand with morality, so it is easy to see the linkages between a holistic spirituality of creation and ethical principles relating to the environment as Pope Francis frames the topic in *Laudato Si'*. The sincere desire to enter into a spiritual relationship with the Creator and a deeper kinship with the created order requires a range of moral virtues, including humility, care, and simplicity of life (paragraph 222 of *Laudato Si'* urges us "to be spiritually detached from what we possess"). Those aspiring to practice a creation-centered spirituality seek to transcend self-centeredness, to embark on a path that is more deliberate in valuing all things within the universe, which is experienced as a vessel of God's presence. For proponents of this type of ecological mindfulness, there is no place for plundering creation or exploiting its riches.

With its own distinctive grammar, *Laudato Si'* speaks of all these spiritual realities and more. Pope Francis calls for an "ecological spirituality" (paragraph 216) and, as supports for the conversion process that will enhance it, recommends human emotions and attitudes rarely mentioned in papal encyclicals; he lauds the gifts of awe, wonder, tenderness, and beauty on many occasions throughout the encyclical.[14] Sometimes the tone of his appeal is quite affirming, as when paragraph 207 calls us to "a new reverence for life . . . and the joyful celebration of life," or when, in paragraph 12, Francis declares, "Rather than a problem to be solved, the world is a joyful mystery to be contemplated with gladness and praise." Elsewhere, he offers stern words of caution or even disapproval, as when he challenges his readers to grow beyond "obsession with a consumerist lifestyle" (paragraph 204).

Because the stakes are so high, it is certainly appropriate that this encyclical challenges us to a thoroughgoing change of perspective, an "ecological conversion" (this phrase serves as the section title for paragraphs 217 to 221). Once again, Francis invites us to see the connections between our external actions and our internal states of mind, driven as they are by our culture and spiritual motivations. Nowhere is this linkage put more lyrically than in an observation (in paragraph 217) that Francis borrows from his predecessor. Precisely ten years before *Laudato Si'*, in the inaugural sermon of his own papacy, Pope Benedict had lamented, "The external deserts in the world are growing, because the internal deserts have become so vast." Since everything is so intimately connected, we need to recognize the linkage between the work of our hands and the state of our hearts and our heads; only interior intellectual and spiritual conversion will enable constructive external efforts to renew the earth.

ADVANCES IN CATHOLIC THOUGHT ON THE ENVIRONMENT

Just as Francis builds on the foundation laid by his predecessors in ecological awareness and spirituality, *Laudato Si'* also contributes to the development of existing Catholic teaching on a number of discrete topics related to ecology. A good example is the notion of a right to clean water, which had been mentioned in previous Vatican documents as a sincere concern but had never been highlighted as prominently as in the five paragraphs (27–31) of *Laudato Si'* dedicated to this pressing issue of social justice. Here Francis is unequivocal in his stance that adequate access to safe drinking water is essential for life and must never be denied or withheld. It is, of course, the poorest communities whose water supplies are most often threatened by pollution and the increasing privatization of waterworks. He laments that water, a gift of

God intended for all to share in common, is turning into "a commodity subject to the laws of the market," while in reality "access to safe drinking water is a basic and universal human right, since it is essential for human survival" (paragraph 30).

When the poorest and most vulnerable have to make do with unclean water, we witness a further increase in the whole range of human suffering: from the minor indignities associated with the daily struggle for better sanitation and hygiene to life-threatening dangers from waterborne diseases. To generalize this deplorable case and to take up a related topic that is evidently close to the heart of Pope Francis, it is well documented that the poor are the ones who most often fall victim to environmental degradation of all sorts. The most dramatic manifestation today is, of course, the threat of massive climate change. The "climate vulnerable" disproportionately come from communities of modest means attempting to eke out an existence on marginal lands increasingly threatened by desertification or coastal flooding caused by global warming and climate disruption. Poorer nations and the highly precarious communities within them suffer disproportionately from toxic chemicals, resource depletion, and threats to wildlife easily traced back to exploitative practices that have for centuries served the affluent and harmed the already disadvantaged. Rich nations and classes reap the benefits, and the poor pay the ecological cost.

Laudato Si' amply displays Pope Francis's keen awareness of these regrettable facts of contemporary life. Francis highlights this particularly galling face of environmental injustice in a number of places in the document, most notably in a section of chapter 1 titled "Global Inequality." Paragraph 49 (in the middle of that section) includes the pope's challenge to all people to begin addressing the issue by listening more closely to the voices of the excluded, so as "to hear both the cry of the earth and the cry of the poor."[15] Prioritizing this agenda would advance the Catholic social principles of the common good and the preferential option for the poor. As hard as it might be to turn our ears to these cries, we have a moral obligation to heed the key insight Pope Francis shares in this encyclical: that social disorder and environmental abuse accompany one another.

Recognizing the inseparability of the social and ecological crises may sound like a reason to despair but can in actuality supply reason for hope. It is helpful to point out the positive synergies that are possible, including the insight that making "an option for the earth" goes hand in hand with making "an option for the poor." So any efforts we make to end the mistreatment of the planet will likely most benefit the poorest. On the largest of scales, a new global economic order committed to sustainable development (consider the 2030 Sustainable Development Goals adopted in 2015 by the United Nations) will be simultaneously pro-environment and pro-poor. The encouraging foci of this international instrument for promoting the welfare of both humanity and the natural world are further examples of the convergence among Catholic social teaching, the social ethics of other religious communities, and the growing consensus of secular thought on overlapping goals garnering mutual support.

Another topic on which *Laudato Si'* greatly advances Catholic social thought involves intergenerational solidarity. Although this phrase was only rarely used previously in Catholic theological circles, Pope Francis's 2015 encyclical launched it into new prominence. Chapter 4 of *Laudato Si'* concludes with a section titled "Justice between the Generations," consisting of four long paragraphs (159–162). Here Francis calls us to extend the familiar notion of the common good (the basis of our duties to others, which often call for attendant sacrifices on the part of the affluent) to the well-being of those who will come after us. In paragraph 160, Francis poignantly asks, "What kind of world do we want to leave to those who come after us, to children who are now growing up?" The answer is obvious; any morally serious person will embrace the "broader vision" to which Francis appeals, a vision that includes universal solidarity not only with those currently alive but with those whose very lives will depend upon our current treatment of the earth.

Providing for the well-being of future generations is a matter of expanding the circle of concern. It takes the classical understanding of the virtue of justice—as the willingness to enter into a fair sharing of burdens and benefits within society—and expands upon it in the spirit of objectivity and equity. Practicing principles of sustainability allows us to say with honesty that we are fulfilling our duties to those who will come after us on this fragile planet. Here Francis is calling on us to recognize a thicker notion of solidarity and to imagine that our obligations to lead a socially responsible lifestyle extend across time as well as space, encompassing the entirety of creation. Intergenerational solidarity is yet another face of Francis's insight that "everything is connected," even those things and persons we cannot yet see or imagine.

A final area where *Laudato Si'* advances Catholic teaching on the environment is perhaps the most keenly anticipated of all: the threat of global climate change. Although this topic has been mentioned briefly in earlier sections of this chapter, deliberately delaying the treatment of this crisis coheres surprisingly well with a message that Pope Francis has reiterated on many occasions. He clearly does not wish *Laudato Si'* to be remembered exclusively as "the climate change encyclical." In the face of press coverage that all too often focused narrowly on that one issue, Francis and his spokesmen (including Cardinal Peter Turkson of Ghana, who coordinated the encyclical drafting process) repeatedly encouraged a broader reading of the document and its significance. Even the text of the encyclical (see paragraph 15) warns against a narrow understanding of its concerns, making the point that this is fully a "social encyclical" featuring the broadness of scope (treating economics, politics, and culture) that is characteristic of documents in this genre. As this chapter has shown, *Laudato Si'* touches upon every aspect of humanity's relationship with the environment; indeed it addresses the deepest wellsprings of human identity and destiny, including our need for spiritual renewal that transcends any physical challenges we may face.

But, of course, the encyclical does treat global warming, its causes, and its potential solution. Paragraphs 23 to 26 present the pope's analysis of the problem of climate change and contain an invitation to discernment and dialogue about the path forward. Although these paragraphs engage the central issues at stake (including, most controversially, the mounting evidence that excessive carbon emissions are causing a rise in global temperatures), Francis is not writing primarily to pronounce a verdict on the findings of climate scientists. Rather than posing as an all-purpose "answer man," the pope assumes his characteristic role as a teacher and pastor of souls, calling his readers to shake off apathy and embrace a responsible ethical path. The proper Christian response to this global crisis is to take action to assist our neighbors already suffering the worst effects of these documented alternations in the climate and to stave off further harm that will eventually affect all humans as well as every creature and ecosystem on earth.

Francis returns to climate change issues much later in the document, where he devotes a dozen paragraphs (164–175) to the topic of "dialogue on the environment in the international community." Here Francis announces his strong support for the many existing conventions and protocols to protect the environment. He approves of existing efforts to meet the voluntary guidelines proposed and goes so far as to call for "enforceable international agreements" on carbon emissions and the reduction of greenhouse gases. With this call to keep the dialogue going, he is signaling his particular support for the ongoing international deliberations that culminated in the successful Paris Conference on Climate Change in December 2015—held less than six months after the release of *Laudato Si'*. The Vatican made no secret of its desire to contribute to the momentum that produced the Paris climate accords and continues to work for adoption of measures to reduce reliance on fossil fuels worldwide.

There is, however, one carbon-reduction mechanism about which *Laudato Si'* expresses certain reservations: the use of carbon offset credits and cap-and-trade policies. These approaches, pioneered with some success in parts of Europe and even in the state of California, provide industries with market incentives to control carbon dioxide emissions, in effect making it profitable to reduce the pollution that contributes to greenhouse gases. The pope's expression of skepticism about the wisdom of relying on this mechanism sparked much criticism in the media immediately upon the release of *Laudato Si'*, with some detractors accusing Francis of prematurely dismissing this approach and far exceeding his scientific competence.

However, a close look at the paragraph in question (171) reveals that these charges do not really hit the mark. The final two sentences of this three-sentence paragraph on "this strategy of buying and selling carbon credits" read thus: "This system seems to provide a quick and easy solution under the guise of a certain commitment to the environment, but in no way does it allow for the radical change which present circumstances require. Rather, it may simply become a ploy which permits maintaining the excessive consumption of some countries and sectors." The careful reader will note the provisional language ("seems to" and "may simply become") employed here, indicating that this assessment does not represent a definitive rejection of such policies. In light of all that Francis attempts to achieve in the other 245 paragraphs of this encyclical (namely, to extend an invitation to a thoroughgoing ecological conversion), this demurral from a proposed market-oriented strategy to curb carbon effluents should hardly have been judged as a major stumbling block to an enthusiastic reception of the document by environmentalists. Perhaps the deeper root of this overblown momentary controversy was the long-standing clash between a market-based policy approach versus a culture-based approach to motivating people to achieve social aims such as pollution control. Taking the long view, the most damaging fallout of that brouhaha in summer 2015 is the missed opportunity for early press coverage of the release of *Laudato Si'* to focus on more central components of the pope's ecological agenda.[16]

BEYOND *LAUDATO SI'*

We have seen several ways that *Laudato Si'* advances Catholic social thought, often by consolidating insights that had been mentioned but underdeveloped in previous church documents and teachings. But, of course, simply writing and publishing a document does not in itself constitute a great accomplishment; an encyclical remains just aspirational words on paper unless it is somehow implemented and translated into action in the practical realm. We might well ask, Has *Laudato Si'* gained a significant audience for itself? How may the church implement its valuable teachings? What signs might we look for to judge its effectiveness in the real world?

In the months after the publication of *Laudato Si'*, there were indeed several efforts in the United States alone to measure the encyclical's effects upon public opinion regarding faith-based environmental concern. For example, a reader poll conducted by the publication *U.S. Catholic* in spring 2016 revealed some highly encouraging numbers. The results of this magazine's web survey suggest that a solid majority of American Catholics (as much as 95 percent of this self-selected group) were familiar with the content of the encyclical and supported its message. Very high percentages of respondents registered greater eagerness than ever before to participate in parish-based opportunities for enhanced ecological activism, such as mobilizing for a reduction of carbon footprints.[17] Just a few months earlier, a more scientific opinion survey conducted by researchers from George Mason and Yale universities turned up similarly encouraging data. Their cosponsored ninety-two-page study ("The Francis Effect: How Pope Francis Changed the Conversation about Global Warming") demonstrates that 35 percent of Catholics (and up to half that percentage of non-Catholics as well) report that the pope's position on global warming had exerted an impact on their views about the issue.[18] These numbers far exceed the effects associated with the release of previous Catholic social teaching documents, such as pastoral letters on peace, justice, or climate change promulgated by the U.S. Catholic bishops (for example, their 2001 pastoral letter "Global Climate Change: A Plea for Dialogue").

These results were confirmed by an equally impressive study conducted six months later (during May 2016) by researchers at the Center for Applied Research in the Apostolate, a nonprofit affiliated with Georgetown University. The findings give *Laudato Si'* high marks on a number of crucial indices: how widely its message has been disseminated and its effectiveness in persuading a high percentage of those familiar with it that the facts of climate change demand a strong ethical response and significant changes in human behavior and lifestyle.[19] In the language of these researchers, the pope's message of ecological concern is exerting a measurable effect on large numbers of those exposed to it. While most of the data collected in these studies pertain to the single issue of global warming (rather than the broader ethical and even spiritual topics covered in the encyclical), Pope Francis has clearly won a wide and appreciative audience with his environmental teachings.

Of course, only a minority of Catholics (not to mention those with other religious affiliations and nonbelievers as well) will likely read any church document, much less a very long and closely argued encyclical letter. If greater engagement of Catholics and others in these areas of ecological concern is to come, it will need to be inspired by some additional measures that more directly touch the lives of people, both within and beyond religious communities. Once again, the aptitude of Pope Francis for meaningful gestures is a great asset; even his small symbolic actions on the level of popular piety are capable of motivating people to act. One example is his initiative (in August 2016) to promote "care for our common home" (the subtitle of *Laudato Si'*) by adding this item to the traditional lists of spiritual and corporal works of mercy recommended to Roman Catholics. It now appears as the eighth item on those lists of acts of compassion and service expected of all members of the church.

Similarly, Francis acted to establish a World Day of Prayer for the Care of Creation.[20] This annual observance was celebrated by Roman Catholics for the first time on September 1, 2015, having long been observed within Orthodox Christianity. Further, as previously mentioned, the efforts of Francis to reorganize the Vatican's administrative departments include the creation of a "super dicastery" for promoting integral human development (with a portfolio that subsumes that of the former Pontifical Commission for Justice and Peace). This reorganization raises the profile of ecological concern in numerous ways and dedicates additional resources to these important church efforts. Francis has also signaled his ongoing commitment to ensuring maximal Vatican representation at all international deliberations regarding environmental sustainability—including those under the auspices of the United Nations and beyond.

Each of these initiatives represents significant papal support for the project of insuring that ecological concerns remain prominent within Catholic circles. But obviously, there is a limit to what any one person, even a pope, can accomplish to keep the natural environment on the radar screens of Catholics. Much of the work of publicizing the church's ecological message and expanding the commitment to environmental justice must unfold at the national, regional, and local levels. In the organizational structure of Catholicism, the role of national and regional bishops' conferences is key in promoting activism in support of care for creation. Pope Francis gives a strong nod to the importance of episcopal conferences by citing pastoral letters from eighteen of these groupings of bishops in the footnotes of *Laudato Si'*—according an unprecedented prominence to documents of this sort.[21]

The United States Conference of Catholic Bishops has already undertaken considerable efforts to spread and implement the ecological message of Pope Francis. One promising initiative is a training program for priests and deacons to prepare and encourage them to preach homilies on environmental justice. Cosponsored with the faith-based nonprofit advocacy organization Catholic Climate Covenant, this series of workshops in dioceses across the country is called "*Laudato Si'* in the Parish: Preaching, Practice, and Pastoral Strategies on Caring for Creation."[22] The success of this program contributes to numerous efforts to

expose millions of Catholics to the call of Pope Francis for action to
protect the earth and to safeguard its fragile ecosystems.

Even in light of all these encouraging developments, we should never be surprised by the persistence of apathy and the strength of resistance to calls for environmental responsibility and sustainability. It is
rarely popular to testify to the need for sacrifices and the urgency of
enacting lifestyle changes. Pope Francis himself has been criticized for
many alleged errors—from embracing doomsday predictions to engaging in sentimental romanticism to displaying unduly alarmist tenden-
cies—in arguing for new ecological protections. Some observers find his
tone and style of presentation too harsh and demanding, while others
chide him for providing insufficient specificity about action steps and
the practical changes we need to make. Still others are well satisfied
with the moral leadership he has demonstrated on the environment,
complimenting him for "putting ecology at the very heart of Catholic
social teaching and doing this in a way that emphasizes the inseparable
link between justice and ecology."[23]

It is helpful to conclude our consideration of *Laudato Si'* by recalling
the fundamental purpose of this encyclical. As a moral teacher and
pastor, Pope Francis has over the years discerned the need to address
an urgent threat that endangers the entire planet. He ardently under-
took the task of calling us to both personal conversion and structural
reform, since thoroughgoing changes in both awareness and collective
activity will be required to address the historic challenges we face. In a
document that took great effort and many months to write, he shares
his insight that addressing the ecological crisis in an effective way will
require two types of changes: first in our culture, consciousness, and
spirituality, and second in the routine operations of large-scale organizations such as corporations and governments.

If Pope Francis assumes a scolding and prophetic stance at times,
even at the risk of alienating his guilt-ridden audience, the finger-
wagging indictment we may detect is in fearless service of this urgent
message. Indeed, the pope adopts certain passionate rhetorical strategies precisely to overcome our natural apathy and the temptation to
indifference. For the most part, however, the message of *Laudato Si'*
proceeds by the method of gentle invitation to ongoing dialogue—proposing rather than imposing constructive courses of action to forge a
better future. Above all, the messenger delivering these challenging

words shows no sign of giving in to discouragement or despair. Pope Francis consistently exhibits fervent hope in the possibility that a world created in love will be healed and renewed with our generous cooperation.

4

PROMOTING HEALTHY FAMILY LIFE IN CHALLENGING TIMES

This chapter on the topic of marriage and family life resembles the previous chapter on care for the natural environment in at least two important ways. First, these two topics are the subjects of very comprehensive documents by Pope Francis released within the span of a calendar year. While many were still reading and absorbing the insights of *Laudato Si'*, Pope Francis published *Amoris Laetitia* (in English, usually rendered as "The Joy of Love" or "On Love in the Family"). The Vatican released it with great fanfare on April 8, 2016, although the text is dated March 19 (appropriately, the Solemnity of Saint Joseph, a member of the Holy Family).

The remarkable document *Amoris Laetitia* is not an encyclical letter but rather an apostolic exhortation, in the same genre as the teaching document *Evangelii Gaudium*, treated extensively in chapter 1. Both *Amoris Laetitia* and *Evangelii Gaudium* are considered postsynodal exhortations because they represent the pope's response to regularly scheduled worldwide synods of bishops called to confer on specific themes (more details of the synod process will follow). Vatican watchers noted that no papal encyclical or exhortation had ever approached 60,000 words in length—the English word count of this document on the family. Just as *Laudato Si'* represents a breakthrough in its thorough coverage of ecological issues from a Catholic Church perspective, *Amoris Laetitia* provides unprecedented treatment of the many challenges facing family life today.

A second point of similarity is that both *Laudato Si'* and *Amoris Laetitia* treat topics that, while clearly close to the heart of Pope Francis, are often neglected when commentators consider themes of social justice within Catholic social thought. While we readily associate the struggle for social justice with addressing inequality, alleviating global poverty, and advocating for worker rights (the subjects of chapters 1 and 2), it is often necessary to make the case for considering environmental justice and the promotion of healthy family life as central parts of the social justice message of the church. We have already seen how Pope Francis achieves this objective with respect to the environment, linking the need for care for our common home with the injustice of poverty, the shortcomings of an exclusively technocratic mind-set, and the full array of social concerns. He went out of his way to call attention to the status of *Laudato Si'* as fully a social encyclical (see paragraph 15), not merely a narrow consideration of the topic of ecology in isolation. Beyond acknowledging what Francis says explicitly in *Amoris Laetitia* about the linkage of family life with many social justice issues, we will consider briefly how the Catholic tradition of reflection on the family connects to the broader social context.

CATHOLIC TEACHINGS ON HEALTHY FAMILIES IN ALL SOCIETIES AND CULTURES

An important anchor of Roman Catholic approaches to the family is an affirmation of the inherently social nature of humankind. Mainstream Christian anthropology portrays members of humanity as more than atomistic individuals whose social interactions are casual, incidental, and completely voluntary. Rather, humans are fundamentally social in nature, belonging to groupings as small as the family and as large as nations and all humankind. Like the Triune God in whose image we are created, all humans are persons-in-community. Our membership in a community of mutual regard and respect makes us who we are. Participation in social life bestows upon us our very identity and allows us to fulfill all aspects of our God-given purposes—both earthly flourishing and even our supernatural destiny. Drawing upon divine revelation in scripture (e.g., the creation story, the experience of God's chosen people of Israel, the public ministry of Jesus Christ, and the life of the early

Christian community) and even upon the insights of non-Christian philosophers such as Aristotle and Cicero, mainstream Christian social theory emphasizes family life as a key component of discipleship and vocation. It is in the context of family life that we encounter God, experience the loving offer of salvation, and respond to human and divine love in a life of committed discipleship.

Rejecting any approach that would denigrate life in the family, church teachings and practice have proposed specific expectations of members of families, such as sexual fidelity and solemn parental responsibility for the education and growth of their children in faith. Reflecting the Christian consensus on the vital significance of strong families, ecclesial communities have consistently emphasized the many virtues associated with committed relationships within healthy families, even as various eras and many cultures naturally display their own distinctive approaches to supporting marriage and family life. This latter point calls attention to the importance of the church's engaging in a program of sensitive inculturation, or cultural adaptation. Churches and other organizations should of course be careful not to assume uniformity in institutions (such as family life) across cultural boundaries, since even people who use the same word "family" may mean vastly different things by this term.

An illuminating example of this need for sensitivity to cultural variety involves the portrayal of normative forms of family life. The currently dominant Western model of family formation and households, consisting almost exclusively of the nuclear family in isolation, has hardly been the norm throughout the centuries and across cultures. In many times and places the term "family" has embraced more extended kinship relations (and not infrequently the institution of polygamy), and "household" in these settings denotes more thoroughly communal living arrangements than a twenty-first-century American or European would customarily imagine. Pope Francis went out of his way to underscore this point about cultural variety in a pivotal moment in his leadership on family life.[1] His efforts as pope to address family life in a constructive and culturally sensitive way represent the continuation of centuries of church leaders' sincere efforts to discern and fulfill the will of God for humanity in all its cultural variety. Even while maintaining a stance of modesty about our claims about normative family arrangements, recognizing the profound social significance of healthy family life is rightly a recurring theme of this ongoing task.

The advent of modern Catholic social teaching in the context of industrialization in the nineteenth century gave the church an opportunity to renew and deepen these central affirmations about the meaning, value, and shape of healthy family life. Marriage and family life make cameo appearances in most of the major Vatican social teaching documents, often with the agenda of bolstering domestic life in the face of hostile external forces such as markets and totalitarian governments. With the enhanced dominance of a public sphere characterized by economic competition and political contentiousness, there has been a tendency in recent decades to portray the family as a private realm of intimacy and self-giving that serves as a counterbalance and corrective to the selfish individualism that prevails beyond the walls of the family home. Indeed, many observers have taken the church to task for unduly exaggerating the split between the private and public realms and thus reducing the family to a mere self-enclosed haven in a heartless world, without much significance for public life.[2]

A number of insightful scholars have responded constructively to the task of identifying and reviving elements of Catholic social thought that enable a bridging of the two spheres. On closer inspection, the church's social teaching does offer valuable resources that support a model of the family as an engaged unit that turns its face outward to effect social change rather than only looking inward after its own members in a supposedly sealed-off private sphere.[3] As we shall see, the text of *Amoris Laetitia* reflects Pope Francis's awareness of these insights about the potential of the family to play a constructive social role, embodying virtues such as generosity and hospitality to the needy and solidarity with the poor.

In the course of the twentieth century in particular, Catholic leaders developed especially high expectations for the conduct of family life and the nurturing of the relationships in the domestic sphere. Church documents of that era such as *Casti Connubii* ("On Chaste Wedlock"), a 1930 encyclical letter on the family by Pope Pius XI, make the claim that the well-being of the entire society depends upon healthy families, committed marriages, and responsible parenthood. The 1965 Vatican II document *Gaudium et Spes* devoted an entire chapter to this vital topic (paragraphs 47–52 are titled "Fostering the Dignity of Marriage and

Family Life"). Recent popes have frequently extolled the family as the locus for the transmission of crucial values, most notably when John Paul II published the 1981 document *Familiaris Consortio* ("The Role of the Christian Family in the Modern World") as his postsynodal exhortation responding to a 1980 worldwide meeting of bishops to discuss the importance of families. In 1983, as a follow-up to that same synod, the Vatican published its "Charter of the Rights of the Family," spelling out the pivotal rights of families that require protection in the public, legal, and policy spheres.[4] The next sections of this chapter examine more of the content of the rights, values, and virtues associated with marriage and the family, as expressed by Pope Francis as well as his predecessor popes and other church leaders.

TWO SYNODS ON THE FAMILY

The most helpful of the church documents on family life are not satisfied merely to laud the family in flowery language and with pious images but rather attempt to engage difficult issues and "roll up their sleeves" to enumerate and express real-life challenges to the health of marriages and families of all sorts. For church guidance to be credible to the people in the pews and beyond, excessive idealism needs to give way to reality checks—to consulting "facts on the ground." As a long-time pastor of churches in struggling communities in Argentina, with ample exposure to every personal and social hardship imaginable, Pope Francis appreciates this insight well.

The need for deeper engagement with concrete challenges to family life today is a recurring theme in the brief treatments of family offered by Francis in the early months of his papacy. He took advantage of many opportunities to offer written and spoken words of pastoral guidance on family themes, including the vital importance of specific roles and relationships within the family, Christian education, and the nurturing of children. In daily homilies and especially in a series of brief addresses on the topic during general audiences from December 2014 to September 2015, Francis offered a wide array of observations and teachings about the conditions that both foster and challenge healthy family life. Several edited collections of these brief addresses (typically five or fewer pages in length) from the first two years or so of his papacy are readily available in print.[5] In addition, the Vatican website posts practically every word the pope speaks or publishes.

Francis's evident interest in addressing challenges to family life led him to take the unprecedented step of calling not one but two world-wide synods of bishops on this topic. By the time he became pope in March 2013, the next of these triennial meetings had already been scheduled to take place in Rome in October 2015. Francis quickly up-ended convention by announcing his intention to call an extra synod meeting a year in advance, explaining that the importance of the topic of family life justified an expansion of the deliberation process and that the prolonged attention to this vital topic would widen participation. So for only the third time since regular synods were established by the Second Vatican Council, there was an extraordinary general assembly of the Synod of Bishops. The meeting was held from October 5 to 19, 2014, and its official topic was "The Pastoral Challenges of the Family in the Context of Evangelization." It was followed a year later by the regularly scheduled Fourteenth General Assembly of the Synod of Bishops, which met from October 4 to 25 and was titled "The Vocation and Mission of the Family in the Church and the Contemporary World." There were 260 delegates at the first meeting and 318 at the second, most of whom were bishops selected by national or regional bishops' conferences. A few dozen lay people (mostly married couples) participated in each meeting as nonvoting attendees. Such limited par-ticipation of women and laity in general (those with the most direct experience of marriage, parenting, and family life, after all) did not escape the eye of critics.

The twelve months between these two meetings allowed people at all levels of the church to digest and discuss the content of the interim report (or *relatio*) of the first synod, which summarized the wide-ranging proceedings of the 2014 synod. Besides various internal church consultations on the topic that took place behind closed doors during that year, there were some noteworthy public events focusing on the theme of family life. None enjoyed a higher profile than the Eighth World Meeting of Families held from September 22 to 27, 2015, and sponsored by the Pontifical Council for the Family. Pope Francis at-tended this meeting (hosted, most appropriately, by Philadelphia, known as the City of Brotherly Love) to continue the tradition (started by John Paul II in 1994) of promoting these triennial meetings dedicated to dialogue on ways to encourage healthy family life. The conference theme that year was "Love Is Our Mission: The Family Fully Alive." Pope Francis included this Philadelphia appearance in his U.S. itinerary, which included visits to Washington and New York to address the U.S. Congress and the United Nations General Assembly. At each venue in his first-ever visit to the United States, the pope displayed his eagerness to call attention to the vital importance of healthy families in contemporary society.

Those unfamiliar with the synod process may wonder how those meetings relate to papal leadership and other church initiatives. The work of such synods, which includes plenary speeches and small-group work by the participants, is of course primarily advisory to the pope, who takes all the discussions and recommendations into account in writing his postsynodal exhortation. And indeed *Amoris Laetitia*, which appeared six months after the close of the second synod, takes most seriously what Francis heard and saw in attending all the sessions of the two synods he had convened. Of the 391 footnotes contained in *Amoris Laetitia*, 75 reference the final report of the synod, which consists of 93 propositions that garnered the support of at least two-thirds of the voting delegates. As described below, the text that Francis produced bears the personal stamp of his own distinctive perspective, but it also draws richly on the hard work of the hundreds of delegates to the synods on the family.

Throughout the multiyear synod process, Francis displayed a further commendable commitment to wider-than-usual participation and openness. For example, he took the unprecedented step of preparing for the synods by encouraging the distribution of a survey instrument intended to reach clergy and laity in dioceses around the world, starting in December 2013. Although the questionnaire containing thirty-nine items was unevenly promulgated by bishops, the goal of gathering reliable information about how the church's teachings on family were understood and practiced by Catholics was widely appreciated and eminently useful. Once the synod itself started, experienced delegates remarked that the processes of tallying the votes and releasing the interim and final reports was speedier and more transparent than ever before—a welcome change from the secretiveness and delays that marred some previous synods.

Even more impressive than these improvements in the nuts-and-bolts mechanics of the meetings were Francis's opening addresses, which inspired the synod delegates and struck a much-needed note regarding the style of the consultation that he was anticipating. In one, Francis used the Greek word *parrhēsia*—meaning openness, frankness, even boldness—which captured his hopes for how the delegates would approach the proceedings. He encouraged the deliberations on the most sensitive issues regarding family life to proceed as a true dialogue, not as the tightly scripted monologues and ceremonial set pieces into which too many previous synods had devolved. No topic should be considered off the table; no one should be afraid to disagree with others, Francis advised. His sincere appeal to the delegates to speak their minds—sharing what was in their hearts rather than merely mouthing words they might suppose their peers or superiors would prefer to hear—changed the dynamics of the meeting in remarkable ways and by most accounts produced highly constructive results.

Some naysayers clucked that Francis got more than he bargained for with this appeal to openness, pointing to a palpable contentiousness that at times affected the proceedings (and which came to be exaggerated by coverage in certain media outlets that appeared to be hungry for rumors of conflict). Overall, the oft-repeated hope of Francis—to gather wisdom from all parts of the world on understanding and meeting the challenges to healthy family life today—was fully realized. Although complete consensus on the full range of relevant issues eluded the hundreds of assembled delegates (as might well be expected), the deliberations certainly positioned the pope very well to accomplish one of the signature achievements of his papacy. In less than six months, he was able to produce a momentous postsynodal exhortation containing a credible and comprehensive theology of marriage and the family.

FRANCIS ADDRESSES THE MANY CHALLENGES FACING FAMILIES TODAY

Time and time again, the text of *Amoris Laetitia* demonstrates that Pope Francis was listening intently to the proceedings of the two synods he had called. Many of his paragraphs begin with phrases like "As the Synod Fathers stated" or "The Synod Fathers noted" (see paragraphs

62 and 82 as examples). But rather than simply mirroring the conclusions of the synods, his overall treatment of family life amply displays his own preferred approach to social problems, replete with the structuralist perspective described in earlier chapters of this book. Francis exhibits a particular concern for addressing the severe hardships plaguing families around the world that are caused by an array of social and economic forces. He analyzes disturbing trends such as skyrocketing divorce rates and out-of-wedlock births, an increase in the incidence of absentee parents, and even the "time crunch" that so often burdens dual-breadwinner families. He laments domestic violence, sex trafficking, and deepening poverty that forces families to raise children in unsafe neighborhoods and precarious situations. In the course of the long document, Francis once again applies his structuralist lens to spotlight those challenges that can be traced back to cultural imbalances, policies of large-scale organizations, and social forces beyond the control of family members themselves.

While he is eager to call attention to the deplorable suffering generated by massive social forces, the pope is also fully aware that there is plenty of blame to go around for this adversity, some of which is justifiably laid at the feet of individuals. Personal shortcomings and culpable human weaknesses such as greed, impatience, and other selfish behaviors account for much hardship and contribute mightily to family breakdown as well. The struggle to create a more hospitable environment where families may truly thrive must account for both individual sins and social sin, and no two cultures or locales feature identical problems or solutions that can be proposed in a papal document.

Amoris Laetitia is divided into nine chapters of roughly equal length. Like many church documents, this one resists easy summary since it contains such a wide variety of materials—from scriptural exegesis to social theory to folksy pastoral advice for couples and fellow pastoral ministers from an experienced priest. While there is no substitute for a thorough reading of its 325 paragraphs spread out over about 250 pages of text, the brief treatment that follows highlights the essential points that are most relevant to the central concerns of Catholic social teaching. If one were looking for a single insight that captures the core message of the document, he or she would be wise to look to the title Francis very deliberately chose for his definitive statement on family life: "The Joy of Love." The relationships among members of any family are intended to be characterized by the abiding emotion of joy that Christians proclaim by virtue of their belief in the resurrection of Jesus Christ and the hope of their own salvation, to which family nurturance contributes.

As the positive tone of *Amoris Laetitia* attests, this spiritual quality of joy is in no way threatened by any temporary state of affairs, such as material deprivation or emotional distress of any kind. Christian joy contains resources that energize us to persevere despite the endemic worldly suffering it readily acknowledges because genuine joy is in touch with deeper memories and hopes—including the very purpose and destiny of our families of love. Thus, to construe this document merely as a list of dire challenges along with certain problem-solving proposals, as much media coverage has tended to do, misses the main point entirely. Consider this emblematic affirmation about one of the church's joy-filled resources (namely, holy scripture) from paragraph 22: "The word of God is not a series of abstract ideas but rather a source of comfort and companionship for every family that experiences difficulty or suffering." In these lines about the guidance offered by the Bible, and truly in the entirety of his exhortation, Francis is offering a manifesto for living out joyful family relationships despite the weighty challenges presented by social realities today. And he does so with highly evident confidence. The pope would not have gone to all the trouble to steer a complex multiyear synod process to this conclusion and to write such an imposing document if he did not consider it possible to sustain a full complement of joy even under trying circumstances.

As Francis instructs the reader in paragraph 6, the first three chapters of *Amoris Laetitia* form a unit that lays out a framework for a contemporary consideration of family life—both its great strengths and the considerable challenges it faces. Here we find one chapter offering scriptural perspectives on the family, another surveying contemporary social and economic challenges to family life, and yet another on the vocation of the family viewed through the inheritance of Christian theology and church doctrine. In these chapters Francis appears eager to establish a strong sense of continuity with previous church teachings on the family, providing ample reference to documents of his papal predecessors (especially John Paul II, whose writings are cited about fifty times overall) and church councils (Vatican II's *Gaudium et Spes* garners sixteen footnote references). The pope shares his confident judgment that, even as we survey anew contemporary developments that challenge family life in unprecedented ways, the traditional teachings of the church are worthy of reaffirmation.

In these three opening chapters Francis confirms the church's long-standing appreciation of marriage as a natural institution established by God for the good of humankind—a covenant of love and fidelity, wonderfully and beautifully open to the transmission of life. The traditional understanding of the ends of marriage (articulated in various ways since Saint Augustine of Hippo addressed the topic in the fifth century) is still relevant. The union of spouses is intended for procreation and the raising of children ("the supreme gift of marriage," as catechism formulas have long taught) as well as the unity and sanctification of the spouses. The qualities of permanence, intimacy, and exclusivity that characterize a sacramental marriage carry rich benefits to all members of the family.[6]

Francis also readily affirms the bright moral lines that the church has traditionally recognized as pertaining to conjugal love and reproduction. These include the indissolubility of marriage, the impermissibility of artificial contraception,[7] and the normativity of the two-parent family based on a heterosexual married partnership. If we are successfully to meet the challenges of contemporary problems such as alienation, narcissism, and sexual libertinism (chapter 2 of the exhortation treats these and other concerns that inhibit or at least delay family formation in many cases), then the traditional church teachings on marriage and the family are the proper place to start. Pope Francis also upholds the church's opposition to procured abortion, emphasizing a consistent pro-life stance that includes opposition to capital punishment, euthanasia, and any situation "where life is rejected and destroyed" (paragraph 83).

In endorsing the continued applicability of these positions of the Catholic Church relating to family, Francis employs some distinctive terminology that will be familiar to readers of twentieth-century church documents on this topic. One is his portrayal of the family as "a domestic church"—an image from Vatican II that calls attention to the proper orientation of Christian families to God and especially to the promotion of divine worship and religious education.[8] A second metaphor Francis evokes in several places acknowledges the family as "the first cell of society" or "the original vital cell of social life." This is a nearly ubiqui-

tous notion in recent Catholic discourse about family, which coheres
with the communitarian social theory that the mainstream of Christian
thought has long affirmed.[9] It grounds its affirmation of the social rights
and obligations that exist at the highest levels of society upon the foundation of family life, where we first and most intimately experience our
reliance on others in social interactions. A third recurring motif of *Amoris Laetitia* is the phrase "family is the way of the church," an insight
offered by John Paul II in his writings on the topic that fits well into the
program of social and church renewal that Francis outlines in this document.[10]

The content of the fifth chapter (titled "Love Made Fruitful"), which
treats responsible parenthood, is solidly rooted in all three of these
inherited church insights, as well as further key Christian ethical materials, such as the Fourth Commandment ("Honor your father and
mother"). Well-socialized children readily recognize their social obligations and practice the virtues of hospitality and generosity to the less
fortunate. There is no place in a Christian household for rank individualism or social isolation. Paragraph 187 introduces this insight, but it is
driven home poignantly much later in the document by the lament in
paragraph 278 about this all-too-familiar occurrence: "when at dinner-
time everyone is surfing on a mobile phone." Indeed, part of the mission of every family is to break down the barriers of self-enclosure and
to foster solidarity with the poor (paragraphs 182–86).

The project of reaching out to the excluded can even begin at home:
with our care for the elderly within our own families, who amply deserve our respect. As Francis had been emphasizing in homilies and
addresses since his first week as pope, elder care often makes sizable
demands on the young, who should never resent the sacrifices required
to accommodate the needs of aging parents, older relatives, and all
members of the extended family (paragraphs 187–98). Chapter 5
touches on many weighty topics regarding the proper raising of children, but covering that ground would take us too far afield for present
purposes. Similarly, there is only modest further development of social
teaching themes in chapter 6 (proposing better pastoral care for families, including stronger marriage-preparation programs), in chapter 7
(on the educational roles families must play), and in chapter 9 (titled
"The Spirituality of Marriage and the Family"). We may now return to
the content of *Amoris Laetitia*'s pivotal chapters 4 and 8, which open up

a consideration of Francis's signature themes of mercy and tenderness, which have social implications that extend beyond his treatment of marriage and family.

Chapter 4 contains a lengthy word-by-word exposition of the famous New Testament passage (from chapter 13 of Saint Paul's First Letter to the Corinthians) describing love as patient, kind, and so forth. Francis unpacks this "hymn to love" (a staple of wedding liturgies worldwide, appropriately enough) with an eye toward identifying the virtues and practices that sustain successful spousal unions and families. Commentators have recommended this forty-page chapter as a stand-alone instructional primer worthy of distribution to all engaged and married couples. The reader emerges not only with a fuller understanding of the Christian view of marital love and the way it supports family life but also with a trove of pastoral advice pertaining to what works (for example, prioritizing spending quality time alone with a spouse) and does not work (allowing resentments to fester overnight) in marriage. As every husband and wife can attest, marital love requires diligent effort and cultivation, and it is surely worth every bit of effort expended.

But even amid the lyrical meditation he offers on love within marriage, the pope does not shy away from considering tragic outcomes (the threat of domestic violence is alluded to in paragraph 119) as well as the possibility of garden-variety dysfunction and fragility within a marriage (paragraph 123). Perhaps most poignantly, paragraphs 128 and 137 report a number of heartbreaking complaints that the pastor Francis might well have heard from his parishioners whose spouses have simply lost interest in them over time ("My wife no longer looks at me . . . it is as if I did not exist" and "He [my husband] does not listen to me"). Francis well knows that for each case where the spouses persevere and muster the effort required to improve the situation, there are others where the strain on the marriage results in permanent separation, abandonment of a spouse (and often children as well), and the utter dissolution of the relationship.

For all its disheartening qualities, this note of realism will likely be remembered as one of the great contributions of Francis to a credible Catholic theology of marriage—a breath of fresh air in a genre of papal documents that rarely venture into such specificity and such honesty about human frailty. Despite his continuing affirmation of marriage as a lifetime covenant of love and fidelity, captured in the Catholic Church's professed norm of the indissolubility of marriage, this pope is eager to acknowledge that some spouses witness their marriages falling apart through no particular fault of their own. No doubt drawing upon his experience of the broken families who populate the vice-ridden and economically desperate barrios of Buenos Aires, Francis is clearly less interested in assigning blame than in helping abandoned spouses pick up the pieces of their lives. What good is accomplished by church policies that emphasize holding a grieving ex-spouse culpable for this failure to live out the norm of permanent commitment? Paragraph 119 alludes to the most extreme cases ("men or women who have had to separate from their spouse for their own protection"), but of course marital failure occurs for a wide variety of reasons many millions of times each year. Sensitive pastoral practice will recognize that not every marital union ends up exemplifying the ideals of love described in chapter 4 of *Amoris Laetitia* or fulfilling the spouses' longing for total self-giving and permanent commitment.

The pope's acknowledgment of human frailty in chapter 4 provides a point of entry to the document's eighth chapter, which bears the title "Accompanying, Discerning and Integrating Weakness." Here we find a carefully nuanced consideration of difficult cases that challenge current pastoral practice and some provisional suggestions for future directions. Clearly, Francis is not satisfied with how the Roman Catholic Church has been engaging people who have experienced the breakdown of a first marriage (a sacramental marriage in the church) and have subsequently remarried civilly (or "outside the church"). By way of explanation for readers less familiar with church policies, a second marriage recognized by the Catholic Church would be possible if a spouse had secured an annulment (a declaration by church authorities that the first marriage was somehow defective from the start and thus void). However, for a variety of reasons, the long and often expensive juridical process of annulment is often not within the realistic reach of many spouses facing this painful situation. If they remarry civilly without benefit of an annulment, such Catholics are considered to be in violation of church law (living in what canon law labels "an irregular situation") and ineligible to receive the sacraments of the church until their marital circumstances change.

Francis had already in 2015 used his papal power to set in motion a streamlining of the annulment process and to encourage a more generous treatment of applicants at all levels of church administration.[11] In the eighth chapter of this document, he explores the need for additional concessions to human frailty and the possibility of new directions in the church's pastoral care of the divorced and civilly remarried. From the chapter's opening paragraph (291) on, he frankly acknowledges the difficult balancing act he is attempting. Joining the Synod Fathers whose consensus he cites frequently, he wishes to uphold the Christian call to perfection and specifically the traditional principles of the sacredness and permanence of marriage, which have long led church leaders to discourage any practice that might appear to condone a breach of the holy bond of matrimony. It goes without saying that none of these respected church leaders is considering simply scrapping the inherited high standards regarding marital fidelity among the faithful or tolerating a lax stance that cavalierly "looks the other way" when parishioners casually move from partner to partner.

At the same time, Francis detects that the synod's final document left the door open to prudential changes in how church laws are applied in difficult circumstances, and he proceeds to identify sound reasons for openness to potential alternative practices. One is the already accepted Catholic moral principle of gradualness in pastoral care (treated in paragraphs 293–95), which involves prudential ways of applying an ethical law to specific cases. Catholic moral theologians since the Middle Ages (Francis cites the highly respected work of Saint Thomas Aquinas several times in chapter 8) had considered many subtle arguments regarding the best way to adjust our mode of following laws to specific circumstances, a practice known as casuistry.

Francis is thus building on a long tradition whereby moralists pay close attention to the particular details of a situation before rendering a judgment about ethical culpability. The "law of gradualness" encourages pastors working with people in difficult circumstances to situate the laws and disciplinary practices of the church in the broader context of personal development and to consider extenuating factors. At its best, this ethical approach accounts for human imperfection without compromising core ideals and favors fitting punishments and remedies for sinful behavior to actual life circumstances rather than operating out of a framework where harsh judgments are rendered summarily.[12] Human morality emerges as the art it truly is rather than the science some might imagine.

Another resource for more flexible alternative practices is the key notion of conscience—a staple of moral theology since the dawn of Christianity. To invoke the human faculty of conscience is to invite deep reflection on the application of laws to individual cases, which always includes an appreciation for the particulars of a situation. Early in *Amoris Laetitia*, signaling his desire to revive serious consideration of the role of conscience, Francis laments, "We also find it hard to make room for the consciences of the faithful, who very often respond as best they can to the Gospel amid their limitations, and are capable of carrying out their own discernment in complex situations. We have been called to form consciences, not to replace them" (paragraph 37). In the long and carefully worded paragraph 300, Francis invites pastors to facilitate the traditional practice of "the examination of conscience through moments of reflection and repentance" so that those involved may fully appreciate the subjective as well as objective dimensions of these failed marriages. He raises the prospect that close attention to the details of a ruptured union will in some cases reveal potentially "mitigating factors and situations" (paragraph 301) that might have the effect of depriving some partners of full agency, freedom, and responsibility in the breakup of their first marriage, thus reducing their culpability for forming a second relationship.

It is worth noting that a close reading of chapter 8 reveals that Francis is eager to tread lightly on these points, with an evident desire to suggest the possibility of licitly selected particular courses of pastoral practice rather than to mandate new ecclesial procedures and policies. He couches his treatment of these sensitive points in carefully qualified clauses in order to avoid the mistake of proposing a new rigidity that might be perceived as coming down unilaterally from the papal throne. Consequently, paragraph 300 states, "Neither the Synod nor this exhortation could be expected to provide a new set of general rules, canonical in nature and applicable to all cases." In this subtle chapter on discernment and accompaniment of people in distress, Francis is primarily playing the role of the senior pastor rather than the legislator or canon lawyer. He appears to be consciously donning the vestments of the "pastoral magisterium"—a new model of teaching authority that includes greater flexibility and enhanced attention to specific personal needs—that Vatican II proposed but which had languished for a half century. While church leaders will continue to function as authoritative teachers and even arbiters of ethical questions, Francis de-emphasizes the expectation that they will be proposing one-size-fits-all solutions to profound pastoral quandaries.

Indeed, the pope's careful way of proceeding fits what we know about his intentions in addressing family life. From the start of the synod process, Francis had resisted the charge that the entire process was motivated by his own ardent desire to readmit divorced and remarried Catholics to the Eucharist, even without benefit of an annulment.[13] Perhaps to discourage this narrow construal of such a broad agenda regarding the joy associated with family life, he engaged in a technique sometimes employed by scholars facing potential opposition: burying explanatory points in the footnotes. Francis chose to place subtle arguments supporting the most venturesome of his proposals for new pastoral practice (the ones involving the possibility of offering the sacraments to the civilly remarried) only in the footnotes that accompany chapter 8. Here he does not explicitly alter Catholic doctrine but opens the possibility of a legitimate pathway to communion for those currently excluded. His desire to maintain this distinction may explain the oddity whereby the six longest and most substantial footnotes in the entire document (numbers 329, 336, 344, 348, 351, and 364) are those treating this one delicate matter. Shortly after the document's publication, one perceptive moral theologian noted that the "oblique accompanying footnotes have been the subject of much debate."[14]

Indeed, voices from both the progressive and the traditionalist camps have chided Francis for leaving his positions so ambiguous and open to misinterpretation. One small group of elderly cardinals even submitted *dubia* (questions seeking clarification on points of doctrinal interpretation) in an attempt to pin Francis down on precisely what courses of pastoral action are now allowable after the publication of *Amoris Laetitia*. Traditionalists have certainly not hidden their concern that the pope is sowing seeds of confusion among the faithful.[15] In resisting requests to provide further clarity on his message in this text, Francis has communicated that he is satisfied to share his overall vision of the key values at stake and leave to the level of local pastoral application the precise determination of access to the sacraments for the affected parishioners.[16]

For Pope Francis, a pastoral approach that consists of "taking people where they are" and helping them take the next constructive step in good faith to improve their family situation is more than just a common-sense guideline. It is also a cornerstone of his vision of the mission of the church. He signals this early in chapter 8 when he cites his oft-repeated analogy of the church operating like a "field hospital after battle" (paragraph 291). This compelling analogy suggests that the crucial task facing the church is to accompany desperately needy people with timely pastoral assistance, consistently giving priority to the most pressing wounds (following the battlefield practice known as triage). For pastors counseling divorced Catholics, this may sometimes mean reconnecting these vulnerable people with the sacraments rather than withholding them. In a footnote (number 351) to chapter 8 of this document, Francis explicitly indicates his support for the pastoral option of (when appropriate) making sacraments available to people fitting this profile, quoting an injunction in his own earlier document *Evangelii Gaudium* that "the Eucharist is not a prize for the perfect, but a powerful medicine and nourishment for the weak."[17]

MERCY FOR REMARRIED CATHOLICS, MERCY FOR ALL THOSE WHO SUFFER

The purpose of the previous discussion is not to make the reader an expert in Roman Catholic sacramental theology or canon law or even to evaluate the advisability of this initiative of Pope Francis for a renewed pastoral practice for certain members of Catholic families. Those topics, important as they are for understanding internal church matters today, are not in themselves central to our study of the social teachings of Francis. But they do in the end have significant bearing on how the church under Francis is dealing with external matters, such as social justice teachings regarding how to help meet the material needs of vulnerable people. By examining how this pontiff prioritizes certain values and concerns regarding family life and marriage, we derive a clearer sense of his commitments to the most marginalized and needy of our neighbors. In short, by observing the actions and value commitments of Francis on matters relating to the family and internal church order, we gain much insight into the very wellsprings of his social teachings.

Precisely what, then, motivates Pope Francis to address the fraught topic of opening a pathway to the Eucharist for divorced and remarried Catholics, even in the face of fierce opposition and at the risk of sowing doctrinal confusion among the faithful? What principle could possibly be worth the political and theological risks involved in "going out on a limb" to propose such a controversial position in this way? The answer can be summarized in a single word: mercy.

It is no coincidence that in the midst of the two-year synod process, Francis proclaimed an Extraordinary Jubilee Year of Mercy (running from December 8, 2015, to November 20, 2016). The April 11, 2015, papal bull of indiction (a document titled *Misericordiae Vultus*, or "The Face of Mercy"[18]) announcing this intention of Francis to call Catholics to a yearlong celebration of mercy includes many words of lyrical praise for this key Christian virtue. It summarizes much of what Francis has said on many occasions (including in a book-length interview appropriately titled *The Name of God Is Mercy*[19]) about this core principle of his ministry. Indeed, mercy sums up the very purpose and mission of the church: to reflect the love of a compassionate and forgiving God to a needy world. Catholics participating in the special prayers and pilgrimages associated with the jubilee year were called to ponder how their own actions might better reflect the divine attribute of mercy. What would a commitment to a fuller exercise of mercy look like in their daily lives?

Mercy is difficult to enact because it requires sacrifice and the overturning of ordinary expectations for how human life proceeds, such as with the perpetuation of petty grudges and automatic punishment for infractions of rules. But mercy is also surprisingly hard to define. In a volume that Pope Francis has identified as one of his favorite works of recent theology, German cardinal Walter Kasper spends well over two hundred scholarly pages developing a full understanding of mercy.[20] In the end, for all he accomplishes, Kasper leaves the reader primarily with an appreciation of the spirit of mercy rather than a precise definition. Since it has proven impossible to pin down mercy as an abstraction, perhaps we will learn more about the quality of mercy from stories that enact it than from textbook generalizations. One of the key scriptural instances of the practice of mercy that Kasper identifies is the Parable of the Prodigal Son (perhaps more appropriately called the Parable of the Merciful Father) in chapter 15 of the gospel of Luke. Here the aggrieved father eagerly pardons the transgressions of his repentant son and lavishly celebrates his reintegration into the family after a time of estrangement and exclusion. But even with this glowing illustration of "mercy in action" (a phrase that serves quite well as the title of this present book), the meaning of mercy remains somehow elusive. It defies exact definition, emerging as something easier to recognize in practice than to define. Kasper joins many previous Christian authors in identifying Jesus Christ as the ultimate exemplar of God's mercy, reflecting as he does the many aspects of the Merciful Father.

If mercy is best understood as a multifaceted reality, then the face of mercy as it is practiced within the realm of family life surely must include tenderness—a quality that Francis praises many times in the course of *Amoris Laetitia*. In paragraph 127, for example, Francis lifts up tenderness ("a sign of a love free of a selfish possessiveness . . . which makes us approach a person with immense respect") as a perfect contrast and remedy to an aggressive and self-aggrandizing "consumerist society." Whether it is family members habitually pardoning offenses and treating each other in gentle ways or outsiders treating a given family with graciousness and understanding in the face of difficult circumstances, the practice of tenderness emerges as a primary requirement and component of healthy family life. This pope who over the years accompanied many families in their genuine struggles for dignity has dedicated his Petrine ministry to the practice of tenderness and mercy toward families and all people. Indeed, the phrase "a revolution of tenderness" was coined to describe what Pope Francis is up to in advocating mercy as the primary principle of all human relations.[21]

Beyond the content of the pope's ethical message, the style of its delivery also demands attention. It would surely be a sign of contradiction if a world leader such as Francis somehow tried to force policies of mercy upon others—for example, by barking orders at individuals or organizations to adopt courses of action contrary to their will in order to do the right thing and behave less selfishly and more ethically. Not only would a coercive or hectoring approach be ineffective, but it would contradict the message of gentle mercy and tenderness itself. Instead, the agenda of Francis has consistently been to make an ardent appeal for mercy, issuing a sincere call for the kind of generous behavior that builds up others. We see this kind of humble approach both in internal church matters (recall the gentle pastoral messages couched within the text of *Amoris Laetitia*) and in the social justice teachings that have emerged under Francis, who so often appeals fervently but respectfully for better treatment of the poor and marginalized.

A mere week after the release of *Amoris Laetitia*, American theologian Richard Gaillardetz summarized the message of the exhortation by saying that here Francis "offers what might be called a preferential option for mercy and inclusion."[22] The word "inclusion"—a face of mercy that demands notice—positively captures the central thrust of the agenda of Pope Francis. Ultimately, the worst treatment we can offer others is to ostracize them—to ignore their requests for inclusion and to relegate them to the ranks of the excluded. Overcoming the forces of exclusion is a key element of how the pope practices "mercy in action."

We close this chapter by considering how this drive for inclusion plays out inside the church and beyond—which invites us to connect the work of Francis in the area of family life with his advocacy for social justice. Within the church, the desire of Francis for ever wider inclusion leads him to extend a welcoming hand of mercy and forgiveness to Catholics whose lives have become messy and whose marital commitments do not measure up to the traditional standards the church has promoted. He begins paragraph 243 of *Amoris Laetitia* with an explicit invitation: "It is important that the divorced who have entered into a new union should be made to feel part of the Church. . . . They should be encouraged to participate in the life of the community." And beyond the ambit of the church, we witness the constant appeals of Francis for the inclusion of all people, no matter where they live or how modest their resources and earning potential, in the fruits of economic prosperity. Chapters 1 to 3 of this volume revealed the pope's deepest social concerns—namely, that neither rampant inequality, nor a constantly churning globalized economy, nor the effects of climate change should be allowed to exclude anyone from access to the material necessities of life. In the next chapter, we will see a further set of appeals by this "pope of inclusion" on behalf of marginalized people such as migrants, refugees, and victims of trafficking.

5

TIRELESS ADVOCACY FOR THE WORLD'S MOST MARGINALIZED PEOPLE

Migrants, Refugees, and the
Victims of Human Trafficking

The last chapter, covering the teachings of Pope Francis on family life, concluded with a treatment of the themes of mercy and inclusion—two guiding lights of the ethical approach of the pope to the full range of social and economic issues. This current chapter describes and assesses what Francis has said and done regarding some of the most marginalized people on earth: those who are separated from their homelands as migrants, refugees, or asylum seekers and those who find themselves victims of human trafficking. Here again, the themes of mercy and inclusion play prominent roles in shaping papal teaching and activism. A few preliminary words about these two themes will help set the stage for this chapter.

When Pope Francis speaks of mercy, he often employs Italian or Spanish cognates of the Latin word *misericordia*. The etymological roots of these words in the Romance languages suggest the image of "one's heart going out to the suffering." Mercy is a key Christian virtue that, among other things, recognizes the value of allowing one's heart to be touched by the plight of the vulnerable, the poor, and the suffering. Few people on earth experience a deeper poverty than refugees, migrants, and those exploited by traffickers for labor or sex. In his appeals for "a culture of mercy" to lift up all these hard-pressed people, Francis is asking that we maintain a heart open to our suffering neighbors, empathize with their needs, and do something substantial to alleviate the hardships they face. Both individual charitable responses and large-scale collective actions (such as organizing church relief efforts and advocating for reforms of public policies) count as important acts of mercy.

Like mercy, inclusion continues to play a key role in our examination of the work of Francis in this area. The pope's thorough commitment to overcoming the forces of exclusion that relegate millions of people to the margins of human society is greatly inspiring. His intention, of course, is to challenge the audiences who hear his words and observe his actions to match his commitment to improving the lot of the suffering and welcome them into communities that will recognize their human dignity and honor their contributions. Looking back over the first four years of the papacy of Francis, the Catholic archbishop of Westminster was moved to declare, "Francis is a genius at creating this sense of belonging for those who feel they are excluded."[1]

By spinning out further implications of these familiar themes, this chapter amplifies the message of our previous chapters regarding the importance of mercy and inclusion. But one departure from the method of our previous study of Francis is that we have now arrived at a topic where Francis has not produced a major document to analyze. Our study of the pope's teachings on the economy, the environment, and family life were well served by a textual analysis of three well-developed documents (each is, for better or worse, among the longest papal writings in history) that contain comprehensive elaborations of his message in these areas. With the topics of migrants, refugees, and trafficked persons, we will rely on shorter writings and public addresses that the pope has offered on a wide variety of occasions. Because these expressions of concern and commitment are somewhat repetitive, the account below features fewer citations to specific statements and less textual analysis of the pope's addresses and documents than previous chapters. Besides producing these scattered words, Francis has shared his message through many rich symbolic actions that express his support for the marginalized, including frequent visits to locations where they dwell. These substantial gestures of solidarity often speak just as eloquently as a well-crafted encyclical or formal address. In order to appreciate his appeals for mercy and inclusion in this crucial arena of human need in our world today, it will be illuminating to examine not only what Francis has said but what he has done and even where he has traveled.

RESPONDING TO THE CONTEMPORARY REFUGEE CRISIS: CONCERN FOR ALL MIGRANTS

The world has never witnessed such large numbers of refugees and migrants as we see today. Over 240 million people currently reside in a nation other than the one of their birth—an astonishing number that testifies to the realities of globalization and enhanced mobility. In a world that is increasingly complex and more densely networked, we observe a proliferation of both "push" and "pull" factors—reasons that motivate people to flee unbearable situations in their homeland as well as inducements that lure them to take up residence in new places. A majority of these émigrés belong to the (somewhat porous) category of economic migrants, or people who cross borders to take advantage of employment opportunities and to pursue a better life in a new setting. Many Americans can easily identify with this narrative of hope for an improved future, since a majority of inhabitants of the United States know of ancestors who trod this same path of voluntary migration to pursue improved economic prospects.

But similarly striking statistics document the dark side of this phenomenon of "people on the move" in the contemporary international scene. There are over 65 million refugees in the world today—people whose dislocation is by and large involuntary.[2] When we disaggregate the staggering numbers of those forced to flee, we identify a range of tragic cases of people displaced from their homes by war, the threat of violence, or political, ethnic, or religious persecution. Some of these involuntarily uprooted persons remain in their home nations and are referred to as internally displaced persons. Others cross into neighboring nations or somehow reach more distant lands, often embarking on arduous and dangerous journeys over land and sea, and formally present themselves as asylum seekers in search of protection and resettlement. International agencies also recognize a newer category of climate change refugees—millions of people who are displaced by adverse environmental conditions and natural disasters such as storms and floods that are traced to the effects of global climate change, including desertification and rising sea levels.

While the suffering and risk taking associated with migration have been evident since the dawn of human history, human rights advocates are correct to call today's situation an unprecedented refugee crisis. Among the hardships witnessed by people on the move today are attitudes of deep hostility and suspicion on the part of citizens of receiving nations. In some parts of the world, the backlash against aspiring immigrants is considerably more intense than in previous generations. With some notable exceptions, there is increasing antagonism toward people fleeing their homelands and seeking welcome in safer places. Even when the human needs are dire and the violations of basic rights driving migration demonstrable, the residents of many receiving nations increasingly display nativism, xenophobia, and exclusionism. Those arriving without permission and full documentation are denigrated as "illegal aliens," whose irregular status is often the basis of contempt and stigmatization.

Further, in an age of terrorism and heightened economic anxiety, newcomers are sometimes perceived as potential threats to national security and the rule of law and demonized as drags on prosperity or as competitors for precious job opportunities. While resettlement efforts surely do require a commitment of resources from host nations, and while careful vetting to screen for security risks is a legitimate part of prudent policy, stereotyping and scapegoating refugees betrays a lack of goodwill. On many occasions, Pope Francis has denounced the anti-immigrant backlash perpetuated by nationalistic political parties and hardliner candidates in certain developed nations.[3] He has emphasized the mutual benefits associated with prudent public policies that would welcome appropriate numbers of migrants and refugees, who have much to contribute if given an opportunity.[4] Still, all too often entry visas, work permits, and grants of asylum status are very difficult to obtain. New arrivals are increasingly likely to face detention, incarceration, and eventual deportation rather than warm welcome, humane treatment, and opportunities to establish a new home.

Besides attitudinal backlash and stricter admissions policies, another barrier to successful resettlement is that international institutions are increasingly overwhelmed by the sheer numbers of migrants. The resources of humanitarian agencies are simply inadequate to the task of accommodating the needs of growing millions of migrants and refugees. After World War II, the office of the United Nations High Commissioner for Refugees was established, and its 1951 "Convention and Protocol Relating to the Status of Refugees" provided steady guidance to national policies for decades, spelling out rights and responsibilities of all parties. But even that constructive framework has been strained to the breaking point by the crush of high demand in recent years. Failing nations such as Somalia, fratricidal conflict zones such as Syria and Afghanistan, and the Sahel and other drought-stricken regions of Africa have generated too many exiles for the overloaded system to handle.

As a result of these worrisome conditions, millions of émigrés are stranded in limbo, languishing in refugee camps, and waiting for their cases to be processed by transit or destination nations during agonizing delays. Heroic international nongovernmental organizations of all stripes assist these people on the move, including exemplary faith-based humanitarian agencies such as Catholic Relief Services. This Baltimore-based international agency assists the poor in dozens of countries around the world, responding to a mandate from the United States Conference of Catholic Bishops to supply relief and development services to the most vulnerable. Tens of millions of people each year benefit from this particular work of collective action that is motivated by the gospel imperative to care for the neediest, including sojourners and migrants seeking immediate shelter, temporary material support, and resettlement assistance.[5]

Into the contemporary refugee crisis stepped Pope Francis. His concern for migrants and refugees has been shaped not only by a keen knowledge of the context described above but also by a distinctive history of Roman Catholic commitment to those separated from their homelands. These few paragraphs can mention only the most obvious theological and organizational resources he inherits.[6] As all people of the Bible are aware, the patriarch Abraham and the entire people of Israel were wanderers and exiles at various points in their history.[7] The Hebrew scriptures are replete with stories of hospitality to sojourners; the act of welcoming a stranger in need is always praised and often handsomely rewarded. The sensibilities of Christians are further influenced by the story of the Holy Family, which joined the ranks of displaced persons when Joseph and Mary fled from Israel to Egypt to protect the infant Jesus from the persecution of the murderous King

Herod (see chapter 3 of the gospel of Matthew). In addition, numerous passages in both the Old and New Testaments (see, for example, Hebrews 13:2) laud the virtue of hospitality.

Recent Catholic teaching documents have developed and applied this theme of the duty to offer pastoral and material care to migrants, though the treatment of these concerns and responsibilities is usually quite brief and general. Obligations to serve migrants and refugees make cameo appearances in several of the social encyclicals, especially those that deal with international political matters. A 1952 Apostolic Constitution of Pope Pius XII ("On Spiritual Care to Migrants," or in Latin *Exsul Familia*, a reference to the Holy Family in exile) was a rare sustained treatment of the topic of migration in papal literature of its era, prompted as it was by the refugee crisis that followed World War II. More frequent in recent decades have been statements of local bishops' conferences about migration concerns in particular regions of the world, such as the 2003 pastoral letter "Strangers No Longer: Together on the Journey of Hope," written collaboratively by the bishops of the United States and Mexico to address mutual concerns regarding the common border.[8]

For decades, popes have issued periodic statements of concern for displaced peoples under the title "Message for World Migration Day." Vatican representatives at the United Nations and other international organizations have advocated relentlessly for more generous treatment of refugees and migrants. On the organizational level, worldwide Catholic relief efforts have long been spearheaded and coordinated by the Pontifical Council for the Pastoral Care of Migrants and Itinerant People. Demonstrating his priority for humanitarian concerns, Pope Francis added this office to the portfolio of the new Dicastery for Promoting Integral Human Development, an enlarged Vatican department formed early in 2017 and headed by Cardinal Peter Turkson, an especially close and trusted advisor to the pope. Through impressive personnel appointments, enhanced resource allocations, and new reporting structures, Francis has sent numerous signals of his strong support and personal interest in the success of this newly reorganized Vatican office for refugees and migrants.[9]

Besides these distinctively religious resources, Pope Francis inherits an international legal framework regarding migration that the Catholic Church has long recognized but with which it has grappled somewhat uneasily. Among the pillars of conventional international law pertaining to migration are two principles that exist in marked tension: first, the right of people to freedom of movement (especially when economic opportunities in their homeland are not readily available), and second, the right of sovereign nations to control and protect their borders. The former right is reflected in pivotal international documents such as the 1948 Universal Declaration of Human Rights, a United Nations document that recognizes the right of people "to freedom of movement and residence" in pursuing the means of a decent life, including conditions favorable for personal development, social advancement, and immunity from political oppression.[10] Indeed, in paragraph 25 of his 1963 social encyclical *Pacem in Terris* ("Peace on Earth"), Pope John XXIII echoed these very same claims and extended them with his contention that "every human being has the right to freedom of movement and of residence within the confines of his own country; and when there are just reasons for it, the right to emigrate to other countries and take up residence there."

But the right of people to free movement is of course not the entire story. The latter principle mentioned just above has the effect of constraining the rights and freedoms of individuals to account for the interests of nation-states and their desire for security and order. The right of territorial states to control their borders, to grant or deny citizenship status, and to restrict entry to noncitizens is a long-standing principle of international law, enshrined prominently in the 1648 Treaty of Westphalia that ended the European Wars of Religion by establishing the modern system of sovereign nation-states.

Nowhere has Pope Francis offered a comprehensive treatment of how best to resolve this tension between the rights of nations and the rights of migrants. But drawing from the way he has addressed migration on many occasions, we can identify several key insights and commitments regarding the principles that should govern migration policy. For example, Francis clearly harbors no expectation that every nation will simply open its borders indiscriminately, with an open-door policy to all potential newcomers. He displays a marked realism in recognizing the continued right of sovereign nations to restrict immigration and to control their borders, as long as policies remain fair, humane, and transparent. Standard Catholic approaches to migration understand very well that every receiving nation will expect new arrivals to abide by legally established frameworks and eligibility standards for immigration status, both temporary and permanent. Francis is also aware that some nations, especially poor nations on the front line of the contemporary refugee crisis, possess a limited capacity to absorb further immigrants.[11] As much as the cosmopolitan vision of Catholic social teaching might include an aspiration for a seamless, borderless world where people facing hardship in one place might easily find haven elsewhere, certain territorially based exclusions will no doubt continue for the foreseeable future.

But Pope Francis also reminds us that these prerogatives of nation-states to adopt and enforce their own laws are not absolute rights; rather, they are political constructs and conventions that may sometimes require prudent adjustments in practice, especially to account for dire human need. His May 24, 2013, plenary address to the Pontifical Council for the Pastoral Care of Migrants and Itinerant People includes an appeal "to leaders and legislators and the entire international community . . . [to come up] with effective projects and new approaches in order to protect their dignity, to improve the quality of their life."[12] The prudent application of civil law must take into consideration a range of values beyond mere formal compliance with statutory law, such as the setting and enforcement of inflexible annual quotas for admitting refugees. The overarching concerns include theological themes such as human dignity, solidarity, and the common good, as well as the rights of migrants and other marginalized people. Our judgments about the content of prudent legislation and the fair application of existing statutory law are subject to deeper commitments, such as our desire to fulfill moral obligations to refugees facing dire situations.

Genuine concern about the well-being of immigrant families is one particularly urgent factor that might call us (as it does Pope Francis) to rethink the unconditional rights of nation-states to demand unwavering compliance with the existing laws. Even well-intentioned civil law often poses a grave threat to families struggling to remain together or to reunite after forced separation. On many occasions, immigrant families desiring to remain intact face formidable obstacles from restrictive provisions of migration law that classify some (but not all) of their members as ineligible to remain in a given country. In the United States, many thousands of young children who enjoy U.S. citizenship by virtue of their place of birth fear the deportation of one or both parents who may be undocumented or subject to deportation for various reasons. Inflexible policies that criminalize a wide range of nonviolent behaviors (for example, undertaking paid employment without proper authorization) account for innumerable hardships, forcing millions of undocumented residents to "live in the shadows" to avoid the risk of detection, prosecution, and deportation.[13]

The U.S. Catholic bishops have accorded a central place in their advocacy for immigration reform to such situations of family hardship, which demand greater sensitivity (such as the opening of a path to eventual citizenship for many categories of immigrants in order not to sunder families) than outmoded U.S. law now reflects. The pro-immigrant stance of the U.S. bishops' conference includes repeated calls for comprehensive immigration policy reform, something that has eluded the U.S. government since 1986.[14] In paragraph 46 of *Amoris Laetitia* and elsewhere, Pope Francis has spoken out similarly to urge nations to adopt more enlightened policies. The mark of compassionate policy is that it serves as a temporary bridge to a more secure future for immigrant families, providing for their protection from undue hardship and placing a priority on keeping them intact whenever possible. By frequently invoking the metaphor of "building bridges rather than walls," the pope is expressing his preference for public policies that (as often as possible) offer a stance of warm welcome rather than harsh judgment and the erection of impossibly high barriers against immigrants.[15]

Besides reflecting this constant Roman Catholic commitment to humane conditions that promote healthy family life, the advocacy of Pope Francis on behalf of migrants and refugees displays the same appreciation for root causes of worldwide problems that we have seen in previous chapters. Just as his analysis of inequality, labor injustice, and other economic problems hopes to help his audience "connect the dots" between sometimes hidden causes and their evident effects, his appeal for improved treatment of migrants hinges on exposing linkages between the deep roots and the visible branches of the refugee crisis. One key to understanding this contemporary problem is to consider the human motivations behind migration. Since people are generally reluctant to leave behind their homelands and familiar ways of life, we can gain a better appreciation of their plight if we consider the economic and political realities that cause them to migrate. In his 2016 apostolic letter

at the close of the Jubilee Year of Mercy, Francis recognizes the plight
of "throngs of people [who] continue to migrate from one country to
another in search of food, work, shelter and peace."[16] Comprehending
and addressing the root causes of these "push" and "pull" factors behind
migration is a major item on the pope's agenda of integral human development.

   One place where he displays his "structural eye" is in paragraph 25
of *Laudato Si'* when he describes the plight of climate refugees. Here
he acknowledges that "many of the poor live in areas particularly affected by phenomena related to warming. . . . Changes in climate . . .
lead them to migrate. There has been a tragic rise in the number of
migrants seeking to flee from the growing poverty caused by environmental degradation." Later in the same paragraph, Francis laments,
"Sadly, there is a widespread indifference to such suffering. . . . Our
lack of response to these tragedies involving our brothers and sisters
points to the loss of that sense of responsibility for our fellow men and
women upon which all civil society is founded." Remarkably, Francis
considers the social cause of the suffering of these climate refugees just
as pernicious as the physical causation associated with global warming
and habitat change. The structural causes of this hardship feature both
material and social aspects—all of which need to be addressed.

   Another major root cause of the refugee crisis is violence, which
forces people to flee their homelands to seek safety. Francis frequently
expresses concern for individuals and families who are in this desperate
situation of seeking a haven from the threat of bloodshed. Turning a
blind eye to the victims of armed conflict, as well as to the needs of
those fleeing all manner of violence, is one of the faces of the "globalization of indifference" that Francis so often laments. By recognizing the
many varieties of violent conflict in the world today, the pope is ahead
of international legal institutions, which have long recognized the needs
of refugees fleeing formally declared wars (such as World War II) but
have been slow to broaden the categories of protection to include those
fleeing other types of violence.

   The global scene today generates millions of refugees fleeing unde-
clared and unofficial wars. These include the types of periodic and
"low-intensity conflict" associated with the operation of paramilitary
insurgents, murderous drug cartels, heavily armed rival gangs, warlords
in lawless regions, bands of modern-day pirates, terrorists, and other

unscrupulous nonstate actors. Some victims are specifically targeted by armed assailants, some are simply caught in the crossfire, and still others suffer the victimhood of profound and prolonged fear of attack. Those fleeing these perilous and disturbing situations are just as much in danger as refugees from the conventional wars of old; they are certainly deserving of protection and shelter. If the concerns of Pope Francis were heeded, they too would be consistently accorded asylum status, eligibility for which is based on a standard international legal formula identifying people "facing a well-founded fear of persecution or in danger of losing life and liberty."

The many words of Francis regarding refugees display a pervasive awareness of the new problems described above (overly restrictive national policies, the category of climate refugees, and those fleeing novel types of violent conflicts) and additional dynamics as well. As an observer of the world scene with an appreciation for structural causes, the pope well knows that migration is often a symptom of deep imbalances in the economy and political systems of nations and regions. Forces rarely seen before are refashioning the profile of people on the move and introducing new hardships that outstrip the ability of the international community to respond to these newly urgent needs.

To offer just one distressing example, there is nothing sadder than the rising tide of unaccompanied minors who have in recent years became refugees when their parents are threatened or even killed by endemic violence in many countries of the world. When violent street gangs or drug lords harm or kill parents, the crime is compounded because it so often sunders families and leaves orphans or abandoned children to flee for their own lives. The southern border of the United States faced a sudden humanitarian emergency fitting this description after a particularly horrific outbreak of gang violence in parts of Central America, just around the time of the 2013 election of Francis, who called attention to this crisis on many occasions.[17] In some cases, even preteens are forced to run away to safety without adult supervision of any sort. These displaced youths then embark on perilous overland journeys; those fortunate enough to survive throw themselves upon the mercy of receiving countries, which often subject them to prolonged detention and inadequate care. Reflecting the profound concerns of Francis for such endangered youths, Archbishop Ivan Jurkovic (the Vatican's observer to United Nations agencies in Geneva) told a June 2017 conference on the subject of unaccompanied migrant children that "the widespread failure to protect the innocent" is an unacceptable "insult to human dignity." The archbishop demonstrated a Francis-like focus on root causes when he declared, "A farsighted approach is urgently needed to tackle the tragic and intolerable situations that drive such a drastic increase in the numbers of children who abandon their lands of birth and search alone for refuge and hope for the future."[18]

Other high-profile humanitarian crises are perhaps more familiar but no less heartbreaking. For example, in 2015 alone 1 million people sought to enter Europe from the Middle East, North Africa, and Asia. Over thirty-five hundred drowned that year alone while attempting sea crossings of the Mediterranean. These refugees uprooted themselves from their homelands (including war zones such as Syria and Iraq) in the type of extreme desperation that leads people to utterly disregard the risks of dangerous traveling conditions. As Pope Francis has remarked, nobody with better options sets out on foot across a desert with no provisions or embarks on a perilous sea crossing on rickety vessels prone to capsizing. The international community owes these casualties of the global political, economic, and climate order better treatment than they have been receiving thus far. The next section further samples the response of Pope Francis to the growing refugee crisis.

SOLIDARITY WITH REFUGEES IN WORDS AND ACTIONS

Francis has certainly taken advantage of the routine opportunities available to a pope to express concern for and commitment to migrants and refugees. Some of these occasions have already been cited: annual messages for the World Day of Migrants and Refugees, regular addresses to the Pontifical Council for the Pastoral Care of Migrants and Itinerant People (and now its successor office in the new dicastery), and brief mentions of this particular concern in encyclicals and other major papal writings. We should add to the list simple occasions such as the homilies he offers at daily Masses and more solemn occasions such as formal addresses to members of the Vatican diplomatic corps, who deal with migration issues as part of their work. True to form in this new age of social media, Francis has also used his Twitter account on many occasions to call attention to the plight of refugees and to propose acts of solidarity and advocacy.[19] When millions of Catholics around the world look up the monthly prayer intentions proposed by the pope, they often find a request for prayers for migrants and refugees. Brief videos promoting these prayer intentions, with voice-overs by Francis himself, are now posted monthly on YouTube, affording unprecedented worldwide attention to the plight of displaced people, among other worthy causes.[20]

Francis further expanded his efforts to publicize the refugee crisis by hosting an especially vibrant high-profile event that grabbed media attention around the world. On the 2016 World Day of Migrants and Refugees (January 17), he welcomed to Saint Peter's Square a diverse group of six thousand refugees and migrants from thirty nations around the world. At that Sunday audience, he spoke fervently to the gathered guests of the inherent dignity they possess—a human quality that transcends the hardships they have endured. He urged the assembled refugees to continue to recognize their own preciousness in the eyes of God and encouraged them to keep alive the hopeful attitude that will lead them and their families to a better life, especially with the benefit of ample assistance throughout a successful resettlement process.[21]

Just over a year later, Francis hosted at the Vatican an International Forum on Migration and Peace that was perhaps less spectacular but afforded an opportunity for deeper and more prolonged reflection by the participants on the specific conference theme: "Integration and Development: From Reaction to Action." The pope's February 21, 2017, address to the delegates was organized into two parts. The first half focused on four key verbs the pontiff proposed as appropriate shared responses to the refugee crisis: "welcome, protect, promote, integrate." The second half of his address treated three types of duties—of justice, of civility, and of solidarity—that all people of the world owe to needy migrants. The major leitmotif of this, among the most developed of the pope's treatments of contemporary migration and the refugee crisis, was the moral obligation of all to promote the authentic human development of those in need. Nobody is to be denied the opportunity to reach his or her full potential, even those separated from their homelands and accustomed ways of life.[22]

Turning now from the words of Francis to the symbolic actions and gestures that have proven just as eloquent, three episodes emerge as particularly emblematic. The first (both in chronological order and in

terms of the world attention it received) unfolded on July 8, 2013. For
the very first voyage of his new papacy beyond the districts of Rome,
Francis chose to visit an unlikely destination: the Mediterranean island
of Lampedusa, which lies along one of the world's deadliest migration
routes. Located in the choppy waters between Sicily and Libya, this
island has witnessed not only the beach landings of many thousands of
refugees seeking a better life in Europe but also the deaths of hundreds
of souls drowned when their boats shipwrecked or capsized, their bodies washed ashore or left adrift.

The introduction to this book mentioned Francis's solemn pilgrimage to this "island of tears" as emblematic of his pastoral concern, as
evidenced by the hours he spent with refugees there—sharing a simple
meal in their makeshift lunchroom and celebrating a public memorial
Mass to mourn their deceased travel companions as well as to encourage the living to maintain hope. The laying of a funerary floral wreath
(featuring the papal colors of white and gold) and the use of an altar and
Eucharistic vessels carved from the wood of shipwrecks were among
the richly symbolic gestures that called further attention to the horrific
conditions and pernicious forces that conspired to produce so many
fatalities. Indeed, the dominant theme of that somber visit was the need
to counter "the globalization of indifference" that contributed to the
tragedies so evident at Lampedusa. The pope deliberately chose liturgical vestments of penitential violet that day to underline the words of his
sermon "begging forgiveness for the indifference of Christians to so
many of our brothers and sisters."[23] Francis made this point so vividly
that many observers agreed this sobering visit was as powerful as any
papal encyclical.

Francis was eager to communicate a similar message of urgent concern for refugees during his visit to Mexico early in 2016. Throughout
the entire itinerary in that stressed nation, the pope chose to spend as
much time as possible with the poor in marginalized neighborhoods
(e.g., in the state of Chiapas and in Morelia), largely eschewing the
corridors of power that most state visits include. On February 17, he
visited the struggling factory town of Ciudad Juárez, which sits just
south of El Paso, Texas, a gateway between Mexico and the United
States. This border town has for decades witnessed great suffering and
horrific violence directed against migrants seeking to cross the border.
Here Mexicans and Central Americans in transit are subject to severe

exploitation by employers, drug traffickers, street gangs, and professional "coyotes" who extract payments for the promise of facilitating passage across the border.[24] Even those who successfully enter the United States often die while traversing the vast deserts just north of the border.

Once again during his Mexican sojourn, Francis eagerly sought to call the world's attention to the plight of a hard-pressed group of desperate people and found fitting symbolic ways to do so. Praying at length beneath a giant wooden cross erected just a few footsteps from the actual border, he struck the pose of a pilgrim visiting a place sanctified by the blood of many victims and tantalizingly close to the intended destination of so many.[25] On this solemn occasion, the cross served as a powerful symbol of both suffering and hope for deliverance. The pope's homily at the Mass at the city fairgrounds that day asked God to give us all "the gift of conversion and the gift of tears . . . to open our hearts . . . to the suffering faces of countless men and women. No more death! No more exploitation!"[26] The call of Francis that day was to both moral reform (to muster the solidarity to care more deeply about migrants in need) and to practical policy reforms, by means of which governments will assume responsibility for the well-being of all migrants. He sought to transform the conscience of the world so that leaders will address the plight of those in desperate need in locations along troubled borders such as the one between the United States and Mexico.

A third instance when Francis backed his words with powerful gestures of solidarity with migrants is once again connected to a papal pilgrimage, this time a 2016 visit to the Greek island of Lesbos. This Aegean island, much like Lampedusa, has served as a stopover point of transit for many thousands of people from the Middle East and parts of Asia on their way to the relative safety of Europe. Hundreds of thousands of people, many of them fleeing the civil strife in Syria, Iraq, and Afghanistan, had reached Lesbos (mostly by boats embarking from Turkey) in the previous year. A substantial percentage of the recent arrivals found themselves stranded there, awaiting deportation unless they should receive a favorable ruling on their asylum application. With the closing of so many European borders to further migrant entry, much of Lesbos had become a de facto detention center. The visit of Francis to the teeming Moria refugee camp on Lesbos on April 16, 2016, was yet

another occasion for papal lament over the regrettable widespread indifference to the plight of the refugees huddled on the island. A photo
of the pope's pastoral visit to Lesbos that sunny day graces the cover of
this volume. Accompanied by Eastern Orthodox Christian church leaders, including his friend Ecumenical Patriarch Bartholomew, Francis
participated in another doleful tour of squalid, overcrowded conditions,
another tearful meal with refugees in their refectory (a converted cargo
container), another sad memorial liturgy, and the casting into the sea of
another laurel wreath to commemorate those lost to drowning and disease along the migrants' way.

But this time, Francis did not return to Rome alone. On his own
initiative, and with adequate lead time to obtain the necessary governmental permissions and to complete the paperwork, the pope invited
twelve refugees to accompany him to Rome, where they were offered
the opportunity of permanent resettlement, facilitated by the Catholic
lay community of Sant'Egidio. The dozen fortunate Syrians were all
Muslims, members of three families (including six children) whose hab-
itations had been bombed and destroyed in the ongoing civil war.[27]
Media outlets around the world rushed to cover this extraordinary gesture of welcome—a demonstration of commitment that was intended to
inspire similar acts of compassion by those in a position to sponsor
refugees or otherwise assist the resettlement of migrants. While not
every refugee can expect to be transported to safety in the papal plane,
the demonstration of a merciful response to people in dire need certainly sent the key signal Francis hoped to share with an apathetic
world. Rescuing a few refugees from danger shined a light on an urgent
crisis, which Francis hopes many will now notice, appreciate, and address. To encourage further such acts, Francis has asked every Catholic
parish and religious congregation in Europe to offer shelter to at least
one refugee family; since that request was extended on September 6,
2016, many have been impressed with the broad and generous compliance throughout the continent.

While the visits to Lampedusa, Ciudad Juárez, and Lesbos occasioned these impressive gestures of solidarity with refugees and migrants, Pope Francis need not travel hundreds or thousands of miles to
express his commitment to these particularly hard-pressed people.
Even within the precincts of Rome, the pope is active in relieving the
burdens of the city's population of homeless and transient people, many

of whom are recent migrants from places far beyond Italy, still in search of adequate resettlement. The head of the Vatican's office of local poor relief, Polish archbishop Konrad Krajewski (who holds the title papal almoner), is kept extremely busy carrying out renewed initiatives that reflect the charitable priorities of Francis.[28] There is now even a church-sponsored laundromat and homeless social service facility named for Pope Francis and dedicated to carrying out his intention to assist impoverished refugees and other indigent people living on the streets of Rome.[29] On numerous occasions, Francis has made pastoral visits to local detention centers, refugee service agencies (such as the Centro Astalli sponsored by the Jesuit Refugee Service), and hospitals and shelters where refugees receive social assistance in the Eternal City. Refugees eking out an existence in Rome are among the many humble people who have been surprised to be invited inside Vatican doors to pray and even on occasion to dine with Pope Francis. While these gestures will not in themselves change the world overnight, they constitute acts of mercy and solidarity that reflect the solid commitment of Francis to witness to a "church of the poor" and to improve the lives of those uprooted from their homelands.

OPPOSING THE SCOURGE OF HUMAN TRAFFICKING

Any complete list of the contemporary world's most marginalized people must include victims of human trafficking. Aptly termed "modern-day slavery," this tragic phenomenon of global trade in forced labor and sex work often remains hidden, as its unscrupulous perpetrators do everything they can to escape media attention, covering their tracks as they take advantage of especially vulnerable people. Its victims—as many as 24 million in any given year—are systematically manipulated and silenced by the criminals and the situations that hold them in bondage, both metaphorically and all too often literally. If, as the saying goes, sunlight is the best disinfectant, then Pope Francis and other brave voices (many of them communities of religious sisters and other advocates within the Catholic Church) are contributing mightily to efforts to expose the scourge of human trafficking and thus to curtail this massive offense against human dignity.

In his most developed treatment of human trafficking, "The Papal Message for the Celebration of World Day of Peace, January 1, 2015," Francis laments "the many faces of slavery yesterday and today." He surveys the shameful history of "man's subjugation by man," including the numerous centuries when chattel slavery was fully recognized by law. In those days, the pope notes, "some people were able or required to be considered property of other people, at their free disposition. A slave could be bought and sold, given away or acquired, as if he or she were a commercial product." Tragically, even the formal legal abolition of the institution of slavery has not removed the scourge of new forms of servitude, in which millions continue to be denied full freedom and "forced to live in conditions akin to slavery."[30] People are still for sale today, as are the services they may unwillingly provide under highly coercive and inhuman conditions.

As Francis notes in this document, human trafficking is enabled by a series of institutional breakdowns. Criminals take advantage of situations where labor regulations are circumvented and laws against coercion are not enforced. Very often the victims are undocumented migrants who are either kidnapped outright or forced under duress to endure horrible working conditions, sometimes lured by false promises of better future employment and disguised under the appearance of supposedly voluntary contracts to which they give consent. The downward spiral from mere exploitation into outright slavery often proceeds because of what Francis calls "a structural dependency of migrant workers on their employers, as, for example, when the legality of their residency is made dependent on their labor contract." The pope next offers a distressing list of the many varieties of victims of trafficking: "persons forced into prostitution, . . . male and female sex slaves, . . . women forced into marriage . . . without any right to withhold their consent, . . . persons made objects of trafficking for the sale of organs, for recruitment as soldiers, for begging, for illegal activities such as the production and sale of narcotics, or for disguised forms of cross-border adoption . . . [and] those kidnapped and held by terrorist groups," including child soldiers.

In this document and on other occasions where Francis has addressed the crisis of trafficking, he combines several roles. Speaking in the voice of a sociologist, he offers a credible description of the disturbing phenomenon—laying out just enough detail regarding human trafficking and its structural causes that his audience appreciates the severity of a problem that so often remains out of sight and in the shadows. At greater length, Francis assumes the role of theologian, attempting to make some sense out of the horror he describes, employing theological categories such as disobedience to God, oppression of neighbor, complicity in sinful corruption, subversion of proper values, and hope of deliverance. Finally, and most enthusiastically, he speaks in the accustomed voice of a pastor of souls, offering an exhortation for the moral improvement that will be required in order to eliminate this scourge. Francis also directs words of consolation and hope to the millions of victims of exploitation, reassuring them that (with adequate assistance) it is possible for them to rise up from servitude, restore their dignity, and assume their rightful places in society.

The final two sections of the document are labeled "A Shared Commitment to Ending Slavery" and "Globalizing Fraternity, Not Slavery or Indifference." By thus devoting to the theme of solidarity the final third of a document on one of the most distressing subjects imaginable, Francis exhibits his support for the specific interventions and far-reaching social changes that will be necessary to redress such injustices and to make true progress, so that the victims can regain their liberty and overcome the trauma they experience. To invoke solidarity is to remind the world that this horror is not a problem belonging to the victims alone but rather a problem for all of humanity to solve together. If broad cooperation replaces indifference, future enslavement can at last be prevented. The pope displays his further commitment to retain a sense of hope and to communicate the basis of that hope to people throughout the world, and especially to victims so desperately in need of all the support that can be offered.

Perhaps most disturbing of all the faces of human exploitation are sex trafficking and forced prostitution. It is hard to imagine the unbearable suffering of young people, primarily teenage girls, who are smuggled across borders to feed the needs of a global sex industry that trades on access to people's bodies and lines the pockets of pimps and drug kingpins. Francis is clearly touched by the profound suffering caused by forced sex slavery, as he mentions it frequently and prominently. He has devoted numerous homilies to what he often refers to as "a plague on humanity" and has frequently made it the subject of prayer intentions he recommends. In addition, the Vatican sponsored symposia in

April 2014 and June 2016 to facilitate mobilization against sex trafficking, encouraging international cooperation and joint law enforcement
efforts.[31]

Further, the pope has repeatedly commended the many congregations of women religious working on the issue, especially those groups
of sisters who have either offered direct material and rehabilitation
assistance to victims or taken on public roles in education and advocacy
to eliminate slave labor in the sex trade. Francis has directed Vatican
departments and church agencies worldwide to participate fully in
interfaith efforts such as the Global Freedom Network to curtail all
forms of trafficking and to rescue and support its victims. The Vatican
has signed the Joint Declaration of Religious Leaders against Slavery,
released in conjunction with the 2014 International Day for the Abolition of Slavery. Francis underlined the importance of such efforts in his
address to the United Nations on September 25, 2015, and in several
paragraphs (75, 210–12) of *Evangelii Gaudium*. Paragraph 211 of that
programmatic papal document testifies, "I have always been distressed
at the lot of those who are victims of various kinds of human trafficking . . . whom you are killing each day in clandestine warehouses, in
rings of prostitution, in children used for begging, in exploiting undocumented labor. Let us not look the other way. There is greater complicity
than we think. The issue involves everyone!"

MERCY TRANSCENDING JUSTICE

This chapter has examined the special concern of Pope Francis for two
groups of people oppressed by especially harsh conditions in our modern world. To the categories of migrants and trafficked persons could
be added many others—for example, persecuted religious minorities,[32]
people addicted to harmful drugs,[33] and people suffering from diseases
that stigmatize them severely,[34] just to mention three groups for whom
the support of Francis is well documented. In words (of homilies, documents, and other public statements) and in actions (such as pastoral
visits to hospitals for the indigent and warm embraces of the suffering
during public events), Francis frequently communicates his solidarity
with and concern for people in these unfortunate situations.

When we inquire into the common characteristics of Pope Francis's social concerns, we begin to gain insight into the central principles informing his social teaching. These various categories of suffering people share, above all, an extremely vulnerable position in society. Indeed, Francis often employs a spatial metaphor to convey their unenviable situation: the poor exist on the margins of society, at the outskirts or on the periphery—far from the powerful people at the center and beyond their ordinary line of sight. Time and again in Francis's writings and addresses, the holders of privilege at the center are described as adhering to a customary "culture of comfort," "culture of waste," or even "throwaway culture"—a selfish (even rapacious) approach that blinds them to the needs of those beyond their immediate circles. Indeed, the sinful callousness of the affluent allows them to treat their needy neighbors as they treat cheap consumer products: as "disposable" or "throwaway people."

The Spanish label *los descartables*, meaning those easily discarded or worthy of being thrown away, best encapsulates this regrettable attitude toward others. In the decade or so before his election to the papacy, Cardinal Jorge Bergoglio invoked this term to describe the scandalous way that a callous Argentinian society (and too often its austerity-minded government) reneged on its obligation to care for its poorest members.[35] Those in dire need were treated, in effect, as nonpersons. Of course, according to a Christian worldview, shaped by scriptural materials such as the parables of the Good Samaritan (Luke 10), the Prodigal Son (Luke 15), the Rich Man and Lazarus (Luke 16), and the Last Judgment (Matthew 25), there can be no throwaway people. The duty to lift up the poor and to care for victims of injustice could not be clearer than it is in the words and deeds of Jesus Christ. To countenance the exclusion of anyone from the mainstream of society is to fail to fulfill one's obligation to care for the well-being of a child of God.

If social exclusion is the root pathology plaguing our world, the remedy is what Pope Francis has taken to calling "a revolution of tenderness." The antidote to selfishness and indifference to the suffering of others is to undergo individual and collective conversion—a radical turnabout that would sensitize us to our struggling neighbors and inspire us to make considerable sacrifices to express our solidarity with those in need. Among the names Francis has coined to describe this renewed social agenda are the "culture of welcome" and the "culture of inclusion," each of which harkens back to the venerable virtue of hospitality, the scriptural roots of which were treated earlier in this chapter. Francis even more frequently employs the phrases "culture of encounter" and "culture of accompaniment"—evocative descriptions of a way of proceeding that is open to others in a radical way. The notion of the culture of encounter (especially when employing the highly resonant Spanish word *encuentro*) is particularly theologically rich because it alludes to the human person's spiritual encounter with God that sets norms for our encounters with other humans. Our relations with mortal neighbors are measured by the loving benevolence we experience in all our encounters with the Divine One, who reaches out to each one of us with the loving hand of mercy (to employ yet another favorite metaphor of the pope).

Commentators have quipped that Pope Francis seems to display a recurring verbal tick when he theologizes: for every laudable and every lamentable quality that exists, there seems to be a "culture" of that thing, which the pope is eager to use as a springboard for his next mini-sermon. While it may be amusing to spoof the pontiff for this trait (and he shows every indication of appreciating some good-natured ribbing over his idiosyncratic choice of phrases), in the end all the "cultures" he describes derive their meaning from a single overarching term: the culture of mercy. All the flawed and sinful cultures are denials of the mercy that God offers to us and prescribes for us. All the noble cultures he describes are mere specifications of the way of mercy that will lead a generous and morally serious person of any background to lighten the burden of the suffering and impoverished among us.

Two questions remain before we conclude this chapter on the tireless efforts of Pope Francis on behalf of the poor. How does the practice of mercy relate (for Francis or for anyone else) to the virtue of justice? And precisely how did Francis acquire his particularly strong emphasis on mercy, especially as it applies to migrants, refugees, trafficked persons, and other groups of the suffering? Each of these questions could easily occupy an entire volume of its own, but it will be helpful to offer the following brief treatments of them.

When Pope Francis urges a generous response to the needs of many suffering people, he tends to rely on a mix of two discourses that ethicists have long employed to describe how people are moved to action: the language of love and mercy, on one hand, and the language of justice, rights, and obligations, on the other hand. Both are valuable elements we inherit from Christian ethics and moral philosophy, and they have long worked hand in hand in the tradition of Western moral reflection. A discourse favoring justice is especially eager to justify particular courses of action as congruent with respect for the rights of others—"rendering to each what is due," in the classic formulation traced back to Aristotle and Cicero and adopted by Thomas Aquinas and modern Catholic social teaching. Following this path will lead us to ask precisely what we rightfully owe to others in dire need, including refugees and trafficked persons. How do our obligations to strangers, even distant strangers we will never meet, relate to our duties to family, close friends, or fellow countrymen, especially when the finitude of our resources forces us to limit the assistance we can offer? What is the relationship between our special obligations (what we owe to our own family and immediate neighbors) and our commitment to the universal common good, which embraces the widest circles of humankind?[36]

Neither in this chapter nor elsewhere in this book have we seen Pope Francis wrestle with such pointed questions and dilemmas in any detail. While he occasionally uses the terms "justice," "rights," and "obligations," the pope shows a rather marked preference for the language of mercy and love. This does not mean that he in any way rejects an analysis that hinges on the concept of justice. Rather, he prefers to focus his teaching ministry as pope on the task of motivating people throughout the world to undertake works of mercy to benefit their neighbors in need. While Francis does not hesitate to challenge and even criticize those who shirk their obligations toward others, he is more likely to recommend practicing the traditional corporal works of mercy (feed the hungry, shelter the homeless, etc.) than to appeal to the contents of international legal instruments enumerating specific rights and duties. After all, a sincere readiness to welcome migrants and to make the considerable sacrifices required to facilitate their successful resettlement must be motivated by something stronger than a desire to comply with the dictates of an abstract moral law or even the strictures of international law. Pastors like Francis are well positioned to appeal to deeper religious narratives, such as the powerful Christian story of humankind's common creation, redemption, and destiny, all of which are bound up with a compassionate God who calls us to follow the path of love and mercy.

A further part of the explanation for this has to do with the pope's expectations regarding what he can hope to accomplish in his specific role. Like previous popes, Francis is well aware of the limits of his office as Universal Pastor, a clergyman whose words are heard simultaneously in diverse contexts and settings throughout the globe. In local circumstances, it might be appropriate for a religious leader to spell out the detailed channels (that is, the specific demands of distributive or commutative justice) through which the love and mercy he advocates might flow. Indeed, works of love and mercy require a good dose of structure and specification in order to be effective; even efforts with the best of intentions still need to be operationalized and to find proper policy instruments to exert their intended effects. The language of justice will always fill this important role in social ethics.

Given these constraints, Francis deliberately opts for a strategy of articulating only quite general principles and appealing to the noblest of motives that humans share: showing mercy to those in need and lifting the burden of the suffering. He leaves it to others to work out the details of calculating optimal strategies for relief efforts and precise allocations of resources, satisfied to focus his appeals on inspiring emotional and affective commitment to the well-being of others and the alleviation of suffering. While he clearly favors more generous treatment of refugees and freely shares his opinion that the developed world is shirking some of its responsibility, Francis does not venture to calculate appropriate increases in the quotas that affluent nations adopt for new admissions. When asked to specify what type of debt we owe our neighbors, he is more likely to cite a story from the Bible or the lives of the saints illustrating the importance of generosity or responsibility than to enumerate a list of human rights or to specify precisely what level of financial obligations we might have to our neighbors in need.[37]

The pope's way of proceeding in social teaching is not simply a matter of personal style but actually one of theological method. Because he displays greater interest in concrete human needs than in more abstract questions such as procedures for determining the demands of justice, Francis has sometimes been called a personalist—a label applied to a loose school of advocates for the well-being of persons. Personalists may be secular or religious in background, but they all exhibit a commitment to fostering favorable conditions for human thriving and opposing threats to human dignity. It is undeniable that Pope Francis

supports such a person-centered agenda, both in his appeals for a charitable individual response to human needs and his prescriptions for
large-scale structural changes that would advance integral human development. Indeed, one article appearing on the first anniversary of his
election took note of these features of the pope's moral teachings and
summarized the ethical approach of Francis in its succinct title: "See
the Person."[38]

Further, theologians tend to classify the ethical method of Francis as
"inductive," a label that means giving priority to actual human experience rather than starting with abstract first principles, as would a predominantly "deductive" method. The preference of Francis for this type
of "bottom-up" rather than "top-down" approach has led many to speculate about the influence on his thought of a school of theology called
teologia del pueblo, or theology of the people. Theologians employing
this approach turn to the actual religious practices of faithful church
people, including their sense of popular religiosity and pious devotions,
as a primary source of theology, so they clearly have much in common
with the inductive and "bottom-up" pastoral approach of Francis. Because it is a distinctively Argentinian variant of Latin American liberation theology, and because some of the Jesuit teachers and associates of
the future pope are counted among the founders of this school, that the
social teaching of Francis reflects elements of this approach is hardly
surprising.[39]

For present purposes, the most significant thing about Francis's
theological method is that it leads him to emphasize mercy in a way that
complements and in some ways transcends justice. Of course, the pope
is careful to in no way undercut the importance of justice—a cornerstone of modern Catholic social teaching. He is very forthright in stating
that "justice should [never] be devalued or rendered superfluous." Indeed, he makes this claim in two particularly pivotal paragraphs of his
2015 document announcing the Jubilee Year of Mercy (*Misericordiae
Vultus*, or "The Face of Mercy"). Here Francis deliberately inserts a
careful reflection on "the relationship between mercy and justice,"
which he holds up as "not two contradictory realities, but two dimensions of a single reality that unfolds progressively until it culminates in
the fullness of love." Francis cites the example of Jesus, who "goes
beyond the law" in showing love to sinners and those in need and thus
"makes us realize the depth of his mercy." Francis continues, "Mercy is

not opposed to justice but rather expresses God's way of reaching out to the sinner." Left to their own devices, "humans beings [tend to] ask merely that the law be respected. But mere justice is not enough. Experience shows that an appeal to justice alone is not enough."[40]

Here Francis is revealing the wellspring of his theology, his spirituality, and indeed his own sense of Christian vocation. With his friend Cardinal Walter Kasper (whose reflections on the supreme importance of mercy we glimpsed at the end of chapter 4), Francis identifies mercy as the absolute core of the gospel. He agrees particularly strongly with Kasper's point that we must reject the notion that, compared with the virtue of justice, with its "hard edge" of inalienable rights and measurable requirements, mercy is merely romantic or sentimental. For the pope, there is nothing "soft" or ethereal about mercy; indeed, it is not only demanding in its own way but also the very lifeline that each one of us depends upon for salvation. As Francis says in *Misericordiae Vultus*, an appeal to justice alone comes up short for every one of us, whether we are materially poor on the periphery of society or among the fortunate affluent. We are all the beneficiaries of undeserved gifts, graces, and acts of mercy. Whether our need is for redemption from our many sins or simply for the means to stave off the hunger of today, we simply cannot rely with assurance on justice to deliver us from our insecure position. Without God's mercy, every sinner would stand condemned by the righteous judgments of a Lord acting strictly according to the dictates of divine justice. In a similar way, the earthly lives of millions of people have been preserved by acts of mercy (such as philanthropy, advocacy, and volunteer work to benefit the marginalized) that go beyond the demands of strict justice. When any person "goes beyond the call of duty" and exceeds the narrow demands of justice to show mercy (such as to a migrant seeking refuge and asylum), for Francis that person reflects the face of God.

This brings us to the final question of this chapter. Why does the social teaching of Pope Francis feature mercy so prominently? What factors motivate Francis to be so empathetic toward the poorest and so eager to adopt this message of mercy, especially regarding migrants, refugees, and trafficked persons? Where does all this come from?

Anybody watching the pope's trips to refugee camps on the islands of Lampedusa and Lesbos could easily detect the emotional investment Francis made in these sober visits. On these and other occasions when he interacts with migrants and those in need, he exhibits a special bond he shares with suffering people. Some Vatican watchers attributed his natural empathy on these occasions to his previous experience of ministering to thousands of displaced people in the city of Buenos Aires, the Argentine city of his birth and decades of ministry, which has long been a haven for desperate refugees from Bolivia, Paraguay, and other parts of South America. As we have seen, the future pope was strongly drawn to the shantytown neighborhoods where he could exercise a warm pastoral ministry to the humble migrants who settled there. While this insight surely contains much truth, a further biographical angle on the pope's close identification with refugees surfaced in April 2017, when Pope Francis video-recorded and released an eighteen-minute TED talk. He thus became the first pope in history to deliver this particular genre of address (albeit not in the usual in-person format) in the long-running series featuring a focus on "technology, entertainment and design." Besides making the expected appeal for social responsibility to his privileged audience, to whom he appealed to foster "more equality and social inclusion," Francis chose this moment to reveal something important about his motivations in advocating for displaced people.

Francis spoke of his boyhood memories regarding the vulnerabilities of his own family of origin, whose members had migrated from a life of great poverty and insecurity in Italy to the promise of a new and more prosperous life in Argentina. His forebears had arrived around the onset of the Great Depression, just a few years before his birth in 1936. He reminisced, "I myself was born in a family of migrants. My father, my grandparents, like many other Italians, left for Argentina and met the fate of those who are left with nothing. I could have very well ended up among today's discarded people. And that's why I always ask myself deep in my heart, 'Why them and not me?'"[41] Francis need not make much of a mental leap to share the suffering of today's migrants. Based on his own family history and childhood memories, he readily identifies with their anxieties about being relegated to a status among *los descartables*—discardable people—who often depend upon the mercy of others for their continued existence.

If the migrant Bergoglio family (in the 1930s) received the mercy of others, the adult Father Bergoglio (in the early 1990s) also came to a painfully acquired consciousness of being humbled, of relying upon and ultimately receiving the unmerited loving mercy of God. All the major biographies of Pope Francis document a particularly difficult time in his priestly career when his earlier efforts to lead the Jesuit community through Argentina's Dirty War were repudiated and his reputation undermined. He found himself suddenly ostracized, stripped of his distinguished professional positions, and sent by his new superiors across the country into virtual exile in the smaller city of Córdoba. After experiencing great desolation and anguish for many months, he somehow emerged from this period of deep reflection and spiritual purification more bighearted and gregarious than ever before—with a new eagerness to minister directly to the poor and marginalized. Close friends remarked in wonder at the rejuvenation of a suddenly warm-smiling Bergoglio. One biographer interprets this episode as the single most pivotal experience in the life of the future pope, attributing the turnaround to a profound encounter in prayer with God's mercy and love.[42] In interviews, the pope himself speaks somewhat cryptically of coming during those months to a new awareness of human fragility and dependence on God and resolving to reflect to the needy poor of the world the same mercy he experienced at the most vulnerable juncture of his own life.[43]

A final influence on the pope's special dedication to migrants involves not some subtle point of his biography but an institution sponsored by his own religious congregation. This is an inspiring story with a definite hero: a Spanish Jesuit named Arrupe. As a young Jesuit, Jorge Mario Bergoglio much admired the Jesuit superior general Pedro Arrupe. During his studies in Argentina in the 1960s, the future pope even wrote a heartfelt letter to Rome asking to be assigned to mission lands, in particular to Japan, where Arrupe himself had once worked among the small native Catholic community as well as among migrants and expatriates. Bergoglio's request was denied, perhaps because his health had been seriously compromised by delicate surgery on his lung (an episode that gave the young man an early experience of dependence on God's mercy). The two men crossed paths frequently in the 1970s, when Bergoglio served as provincial superior and as, in his last years as superior general, Arrupe considered plans to launch the Jesuit Refugee Service (JRS). This agency, sponsored by the Society of Jesus but serving and employing people from all faiths and walks of life, coordinates an impressive worldwide response to the refugee crisis of our era. Starting with service to the needs of the boat people of Southeast Asia in the early 1980s and continuing to support people displaced by wars and famines today, the JRS approaches its fortieth anniversary with impressive vitality, continuing to rededicate itself to the task of serving migrants not reached by other relief agencies.

Since its inception as the brainchild of Arrupe, the JRS has relied on three pillars that define its mission: service, accompaniment, and advocacy. The middle term is a sine qua non of its operation, which thrives on a continual practice of "walking with refugees" in ways of companionship that require staff and volunteers to share in the struggles and stories of the people seeking uplift. In each of the forty-five nations where it operates, JRS attempts to combine all three of these elements, whether in large-scale refugee camps or in urban settings where recent migrants receive vital assistance in their efforts to resettle. It is no mere coincidence that, when the subject of people on the move arises, the first Jesuit pope speaks so often of the "culture of accompaniment." With its unique focus on providing educational, health-care, and psychosocial services to forcibly displaced persons, JRS provides a model of how practical interventions conducted in an atmosphere of respectful collaboration and empowerment can lift up some of the poorest people on earth with a hand of healing and mercy. A key to this success is the spirit of accompaniment, which deliberately steers clear of self-defeating paternalism and even distinguishes itself from a noblesse oblige approach, which sometimes includes a sense of false superiority.

Pope Francis thinks so highly of JRS that he has paid special visits to its Astalli Center for Refugees as well as its central administrative offices in Rome. His fraternal remarks on these occasions demonstrate his particular appreciation for the enormous promise of a series of creative educational initiatives being developed by JRS. These include the revolutionary network called Jesuit Worldwide Learning and the ambitious Global Educational Initiative started in 2015. On November 14, 2015, Francis offered these words of praise to the JRS: "All your projects have this ultimate aim: to help refugees to grow in self-confidence, to realize their highest inherent potential, and to be able to defend their rights as individuals and communities."[44]

During another meeting with JRS staff the following year, Pope Francis affirmed his support for the launch of a campaign to fund new educational projects by saying, "To give a child a seat at school is the finest gift you can give." Francis was commenting on ambitious plans to extend educational outreach to an additional hundred thousand refugees around the globe, considerably expanding course offerings at all levels. When it came time for JRS planners to select a name for this campaign (to commence during the Jubilee Year of Mercy that Francis had designated), they chose the phrase "Mercy in Motion." Clearly, the admiration and lines of influence between the remarkable Jesuit agency and the first Jesuit pope are mutual. After all, if Pope Francis can lift the notion of accompaniment from the mission statement of JRS, then borrowing a signature phrase from the pope should be fair game.

6

THE MISSION TO PEACEMAKING AND CONFLICT TRANSFORMATION IN OUR TIME

As in the previous chapter, we have come to a topic where Pope Francis has published no comprehensive document that we might analyze to produce a straightforward summary of his teachings on this theme. But peacemaking, like the plight of refugees and other suffering people, has been the subject of innumerable papal statements, gestures, and efforts since Francis took office. While the pope does not frequently address matters pertaining specifically to armed warfare and peace treaties, he does engage in many efforts to foster peaceful resolution of conflicts, both on the international scene and in other arenas where parties are sharply divided. This chapter presents the major teachings of Francis, reflected once again in both his words and actions, regarding peacemaking.

It is especially appropriate these days to enter such an investigation with a broad understanding of the pope's mission to peacemaking, since the field of peace studies has widened its scope in recent years. While we of course still witness far too many conventional wars, most violent conflicts today differ in nature, scope, and cause from those of previous centuries. Only a small fraction of violence today consists of armed conflict between nations on well-defined battlefields. Not satisfied to "respond to the last war," scholars of peace have adopted more flexible terminology to capture the contemporary challenges and constructed broader frameworks to describe the task of peacemaking amid the new complexities we face. In an age when most violent conflict involves dangerous nonstate actors (such as terrorists, bands of ethnic militia, armed drug cartels, modern-day pirates, and organized crime syndicates), terms such as "peacebuilding," "conflict prevention," and "conflict transformation" have come into prominence.

This new paradigm emphasizes prevention over mere reaction to violence. It recommends adopting a wider view of what can be done to create the conditions for peace, beyond merely avoiding imminent violence and limiting its extent and destructive effects. Anyone serious about the vital task of resolving the deep ethnic grievances, political rivalries, and festering disputes over land and resources that all too often flare up into open armed conflict will be eager to address the historical roots and structural factors that account for conflict situations. Defusing these potential sources of armed hostility is the goal of preventive diplomacy and related strategies for the long haul. Pope Francis is one leader on the international stage whose words and actions reflect an awareness of these new realities and the priorities required to support a broad agenda of reconciliation that has a real chance of succeeding.[1]

Indeed, the broad term "reconciliation" might be the single best word we could use to capture the efforts of Pope Francis on every topic treated within Catholic social teaching. His efforts described in each chapter of this book are accurately portrayed as a ministry of reconciliation (in tandem, of course, with the related concept of mercy). Whether the subject at hand is economic justice, ecological sustainability, or any other matter of social concern, Francis's agenda is solidly dedicated to reconciling diverse parties with their competing claims so that they might heal divisions, come to mutual respect, and forge a new dedication to work together constructively. To reconcile is to mend fractured relationships and set them on a proper basis going forward. Sometimes this involves persuading people to put down literal weapons; on other occasions, the task of reconciliation is subtler and more complex, as this chapter on the peacebuilding efforts of Pope Francis attests.

WORDS OF ADVOCACY FOR THE MANY WAYS OF PEACE

The most obvious opportunity for any pope to propose priorities for forging a more peaceful world is in the papal message for the World Day of Peace that is celebrated each year on January 1. Pope Francis has certainly taken advantage of this built-in annual opportunity to promote peace and to expand the agenda of peacemaking, as we shall see below. Because peace is a multidimensional reality, these annual statements have covered an astonishing number of specific topics over the years—by no means restricting themselves to halting armed conflicts of the moment. For example, in his 1990 message John Paul II focused on themes relating to ecology, arguing that sustainability has become a key to good global order and right relations among people and their fellow creatures. As we saw in the previous chapter, Pope Francis dedicated his 2015 message to ending the scourge of human trafficking, again displaying a holistic view of the importance of forging a more peaceful order in human society by eliminating an especially horrific violation of human rights.

These two examples demonstrate the recurring affirmation of recent Catholic teaching that "peace is not merely the absence of war."[2] Rather, it is something positive, a substantive good unto itself—one that requires hard work in establishing the justice upon which lasting peace is built. When in the 1960s Pope Paul VI employed the phrases "If you want peace, work for justice" and "Development is the new name for peace,"[3] he was tapping into a rich scriptural heritage of associating peace with a thoroughgoing social harmony (indicated by the richly resonant Hebrew word *shalom*) that involves every aspect of human life. The meaning of peace is not exhausted by specific efforts "to get the shooting to stop" or even to maintain a fragile balance of power between enemies. Despite the truncated imagination indicated by the casual way peace is invoked in popular parlance, for Christians true peace is an all-encompassing gift of God that reshapes every human relationship and involves the totality of life in society.

As of this writing, Pope Francis has published three other messages for World Day of Peace observances. His first, released (as is the custom[4]) about three weeks in advance of January 1, 2014, consists of an extended reflection on the virtue of solidarity, which he proposes as the basis of all efforts "to build a just society and a solid and lasting peace."

In the course of this brief document, solidarity emerges as a vital (but often tragically absent) component of social harmony, indeed as the perfect antidote to "a globalization of indifference which makes us slowly inured to the suffering of others and closed in on ourselves." Francis takes advantage of this high-profile opportunity not so much to lay out an agenda for the urgent resolution of specific conflicts or to describe preferred strategies to advance peace but rather to articulate his diagnosis regarding the greatest overarching hindrance to true peace: a widespread lack of commitment to true brotherhood and sisterhood.

In a passage at the very center of that 2014 document, in the course of paying homage to the social teachings of his most recent predecessors on the Chair of Peter, Francis refers to peace as *opus solidaritatis*, or a work of solidarity. The most dramatic appeal for peace comes in a section labeled (quite strikingly) "Fraternity extinguishes war": "I appeal forcefully to all those who sow violence and death by force of arms: in the person you today see simply as an enemy to be beaten, discover rather your brother or sister, and hold back your hand! Give up the way of arms and go to meet the other in dialogue, pardon and reconciliation, in order to rebuild justice, trust and hope around you!"[5] Francis follows up these emotional words by mentioning a very specific cause that he hopes will be advanced by a "conversion of heart" to change an intolerable situation—namely, ending the global arms trade. The pope offers a heartfelt plea "for the nonproliferation of arms and for disarmament of all parties, beginning with nuclear and chemical weapons disarmament." As with so many of the items (including the environment and human trafficking) that he mentions rather briefly in this, his first annual message on peace, he would return to the topic with substantial elaboration in subsequent years.

In examining the commitment of Francis to ending human trafficking, the previous chapter already examined the pope's 2015 message for the World Day of Peace, which bears the title "No Longer Slaves, but Brothers and Sisters." Recall the eagerness of Francis to place the horrors of sex and labor trafficking within the wider social contexts of increased migration and the persistence of armed conflict, as criminals so often take advantage of powerless people on the move and weak or distracted governments to prey on the victims they exploit. The 2016 message, true to its title, "Overcome Indifference and Win Peace," presents a stark and systematic description of the vice of indifference.

With sections on indifference to God, indifference to our neighbors, and indifference to the natural environment, this document affords Francis an opportunity to apply the themes of the Jubilee Year of Mercy (during which this document was released) to practical world matters that involve the dynamics of peacemaking.

Like many social teaching documents, this 2016 papal message moves from a sobering assessment of many contemporary world problems to a hope-filled exhortation. It begins with a litany of challenges to peace, which include "war and terrorism, accompanied by kidnapping, ethnic or religious persecution and the misuse of power . . . [that] have become so common as to constitute a real 'third world war fought piecemeal.'"[6] Midway through the document, the tone pivots from one of lamenting these problems caused by the many faces of indifference to one of hope in the power of "the conversion of hearts" to overcome indifference and thus reverse the course of these threats to peace. Through the efforts of public officials, charitable and nongovernmental organizations, journalists, teachers, and families, hope for a better world can indeed be nourished. If peace is to dawn, it will be "the fruit of a culture of solidarity, mercy and compassion." Francis closes by offering "some examples of praiseworthy commitment" and expressing the hope that the cause of expanding solidarity and the practice of mercy will gain momentum in our time.

The 2017 message for the World Day of Peace represents a noteworthy departure for Pope Francis. Perhaps because it marks the fiftieth occasion when a pope has promulgated a document for this occasion, Francis uses the opportunity of this landmark to step back and provide some long-view considerations about the very nature of peacemaking. Bearing the title "Nonviolence: A Style of Politics for Peace," the document revisits the most long-standing tension in Christian approaches to peace and war: the question of whether the call of Christ to be peacemakers is best lived out by the practice of creedal and exceptionless nonviolence (sometimes called pacifism). Christians have been debating for many centuries whether the use of some coercive force can be justified as a legitimate interpretation of the command of Jesus "to love your neighbor." Francis does not, of course, settle the entire matter in the seven pages of this document. Because the debate between adherents of nonviolence and supporters of the just-war approach (the major alternative in Christian thought) is so complex and has been raging for so many centuries, it will resist such easy resolution. But by reviewing the many admonitions of Jesus to eschew violence and by heaping words of praise upon recent practitioners of the school of "active nonviolence" (Mahatma Gandhi, Martin Luther King Jr., and Mother Teresa), Francis uses this document to put a most appealing face upon the stance of nonviolence—constituting perhaps the most enthusiastic advocacy any pope has yet offered for such a position.

Especially moving is a passage early in this document where Francis considers highly favorably the nonviolent witness of "victims of violence [who] are able to resist the temptation to retaliate . . . [and] become the most credible promoters of nonviolent peacemaking."[7] The clear preference of Francis for the peaceful resolution of conflicts is most evident in his plea for "an ethics of fraternity and peaceful coexistence between individuals and among peoples," which will include "disarmament and the prohibition and abolition of nuclear weapons." Francis is eager to drive home two further points about the significance of nonviolence. First, it should never be reduced to a simple prohibition of the use of force—it is not just a no to something we ought to avoid but a yes to following the nonviolent way of Christ. Second, the pope states, "Nonviolence is sometimes taken to mean surrender, lack of involvement, and passivity, but this is not the case." He hastens to identify it as an engaging lifestyle that is both principled and effective. By using terms throughout the document like "peacebuilding," "peacemaking," and "active and creative nonviolence" rather than pacifism or passive resistance, Francis displays his intention to present the nonviolent option as a viable and highly attractive one for contemporary Christians.

Still, the document leaves us with as many questions as firm answers. Some of the questions are supplied by Francis himself. Early in the document, he asks, "Can violence achieve any goal of lasting value? Or does it merely lead to retaliation and a cycle of deadly conflicts that benefit only a few 'warlords'?" The implied answers clearly indicate the support of Francis for exploring the way of creedal pacifism, perhaps even to the point of suggesting that Catholics should designate their church "a peace church," joining the ranks of such Protestant denominations as the Anabaptists, Quakers, and Mennonites, which reject all resort to violent means. But further questions implicit throughout this document raise a caution about embracing perfectionistic codes of behavior such as an ethic of absolute nonviolence. Seeing Francis grapple with matters of practicality has a countervailing effect, supplying a sobering check on the straightforward idealism that would renounce the resort to violence under any circumstance.

For example, on several occasions in this document Francis employs the word "responsibilities." Invoking this word reminds the reader familiar with past debates over the viability of nonviolence of a major principled objection to pure pacifism—one captured by the phrase "responsibility to protect" often used to justify humanitarian interventions backed by military force. While a stance of nonviolence succeeds in keeping one's own hands clean, it does not advance all the values that a socially responsible Christian should hold or ensure outcomes that are acceptable to loving persons. In an imperfect and insecure world, anybody possessing the power to prevent atrocities and preserve human life faces hard decisions. Many of these involve choosing, at least on rare occasions, to rely upon the use of force to practice social responsibility, particularly the duty to protect innocent people from harm at the hands of imminent attackers. While nobody inspired by the gospel would deliberately set out to inflict violence on another without serious cause and as a last resort, history has not afforded us the luxury of operating in the ideal world of our choosing—characterized by guarantees of lasting justice and security for all.

The mainstream of Christian political thought has justified the occasional use of force to defend the innocent from harm under strict conditions. These are the traditional *jus ad bellum* and *jus in bello* criteria that constitute just-war theory—an approach aimed at limiting the incidence and extent of warfare even as it accepts its potential justification. Not to be confused with supporters of crusade (or "holy war" unlimited in scope), just-war thinkers appeal to the virtue of prudence to identify those rare instances when the undeniable damage caused by war may be justified by potential objectives promoted by military action, such as the protection of endangered lives and the removal of stubborn obstacles to eventual peace. The just-war approach seeks to reconcile, however uneasily, the obligation to shield the innocent from harm with the demands of Christian discipleship to love even the enemy. Further, certain theorists have appealed to Christian-inspired values to defend the use of force not only in emergencies like humanitarian interventions (e.g., preventing genocide) but even in pursuit of broad principles like national sovereignty and self-determination (e.g., when President

George H. W. Bush cited just-war principles to justify the liberation of
Kuwait from Iraqi forces in 1991).

The best of recent Catholic teaching on war and peace has invited
closer scrutiny in the application of these just-war norms and reaf-
firmed the (sometimes overlooked) presumption against the use of
force.[8] However prudent it might be to reserve the option of a last-
resort reliance on armed strength, for most real-world problems a lasting military solution is indeed illusory. Still, while just-war theory can
surely be manipulated for cynical purposes (to uncritically endorse or
rationalize rather than to prevent or limit actual wars), it remains a
formidable achievement of Christian ethical reflection and a potentially
constructive framework for prudent responses to armed aggression.
Notwithstanding the challenging questions raised by Pope Francis,
Catholic teaching has not repudiated the principle that, in some cases,
the socially responsible thing to do is to take up arms in defense of
innocents, at least as a genuine last resort to prevent greater harm.

Where does Pope Francis really stand on these age-old questions of
war and peace? Are there any conditions under which he would ap-
prove of armed intervention? The indications he has offered so far
remain somewhat ambiguous; the remainder of this section examines
the most obvious evidence that will help us locate his commitments and
identify his ultimate stance regarding nonviolence and the just-war approach.

On one hand, months before he produced this document full of
praise for the principle of nonviolence, he had arranged for the Vatican
to host a conference of more than eighty scholars and practitioners of
peace from every continent to deliberate on the topic "Nonviolence and
Just Peace." Held from April 11 to 13, 2016, and cosponsored by the
Pontifical Council for Justice and Peace and Pax Christi International,
the conference reflected on the promise of new paradigms for peacemaking (such as the "just-peace" approach[9]) that, if adopted, would
distance the Catholic Church considerably from the just-war framework. The delegates produced a two-page "Appeal to the Catholic
Church to Re-commit to the Centrality of Gospel Non-violence." Besides summarizing its support for alternatives to the just-war framework, this document "calls upon Pope Francis to share with the world
an encyclical on nonviolence and Just Peace," further committing the
church to a stance of "creative and active nonviolence."[10] While the

prospect of new formal papal teachings on nonviolence remains merely a matter of speculation, by all accounts Francis welcomed the contribution of this landmark conference.[11]

On the other hand, there is ample evidence that Francis, however ardently he yearns for a world free of the scourge of war, does not consider himself an absolute pacifist or adherent of complete nonviolence. While he clearly desires to subject the resort to military force to closer ethical scrutiny and is eager to affirm that voices advocating peaceful resolution of conflicts hold the moral high ground, he stops short of embracing absolute nonviolence. Indeed, on occasion he has defended the legitimacy of using force to stop unjust aggressors. For example, in one of his customary airborne press conferences (on his return flight to Rome from South Korea in August 2014), he voiced no disapproval of the use of an air bombing campaign by the United States to stop the Islamic State in Iraq. A journalist inquired whether the ongoing airstrikes to prevent further incursions by the terrorist group into Kurdish-held territory could be justified. The pope's words of explanation echoed the classic texts of just-war theory: "It is legitimate to stop an unjust aggressor."[12] While hastening to offer qualifications regarding the conditions under which such a use of force would be justifiable (United Nations authorization and maximum precautions against civilian casualties), Francis nevertheless reflected a stance often struck by his recent papal predecessors, who consistently expressed hatred of war and urged military restraint but did not automatically condemn all armed interventions.[13] Departures from the lofty principles of nonviolence are to be interpreted as a matter of moral necessity in line with prudence, not as capitulation to expedience or accommodation to self-serving agendas. As religious rather than political leaders, popes are understandably hesitant to question the prerogatives of sovereign nations to determine considered courses of action in promoting self-defense, protecting their citizens, and conducting wider security operations. For better or worse, this tradition of deference to policy decisions of world powers continues to this day.[14]

Of course, nobody would interpret the occasional cautious acquiescence of Francis to the projection of military power in this instance or on other occasions as an unmixed enthusiasm for military solutions to complex world problems, even when a response to brutal aggression may be necessary. To acknowledge that military action may be permissible under certain narrowly defined circumstances in no way erodes the fervent desire for the abolition of war in our time. The pope's innumerable utterances about international conflicts feature repeated calls for patient restraint against aggression and the de-escalation of hostilities and saber rattling (for example, on the Korean Peninsula). They also favor the prudent deployment of "soft power" (such as diplomacy and dialogue) over traditional "hard power" (such as military force and threats of retaliation).

In the search for ways to resolve differences, diplomatic negotiations are infinitely preferable to bloodshed. This has always been true from an ethical perspective, and lovers of peace hope to confirm the practicality of relying on soft power to resolve conflicts. Though we still live in a blood-stained world, there are indeed numerous occasions when diplomacy effectively defuses international tensions and influences the behavior of rogue nations and dictators more effectively than the hard power of guns and bombs. Francis is one such lover of peace who never tires of advocating the ways of diplomacy. Characteristically, the frequent appeals of Francis for peaceful resolution of conflicts (and especially for a renunciation of terrorism) often lift up the agonizing plight of defenseless civilians caught in the crossfire of armed conflict—innocent children of God who deserve protection in a dangerous world. While not an absolute pacifist, Francis frequently expresses his clear preference for nonviolent solutions to tensions wherever possible. He displays an ardent desire for reconciliation and peaceful resolution of differences in every tense situation within the global arena.

PURSUING PEACE IN GESTURES AND DEEDS

The World Day of Peace messages represent just one annual opportunity for Francis to advocate for peace. The section above could easily have examined other important genres of papal writings and regular addresses where peacemaking is a frequent focus of attention, such as speeches to the Vatican diplomatic corps, addresses to gatherings of diplomats (from approximately 190 nations) that are accredited to the Holy See, and the annual *Urbi et Orbi*[15] messages. In fact, there are numerous occasions in the course of any year when the pope enjoys the opportunity to give voice to his commitment to work for peace, to help resolve conflicts, and to foster reconciliation across the globe. Even if the message on all these occasions may at times grow somewhat repetitious, it is a credit to Pope Francis that he never appears to grow weary of reaffirming this vital commitment.

Beyond these routine occasions, Francis has seized some exceptional opportunities to promote peacemaking on the world stage. Two of the most prominent instances unfolded during the pope's visit to the United States in 2015: his speech to a joint session of the U.S. Congress on September 24 (the first such occasion for any pope) and his address to the General Assembly of the United Nations on September 25 (only the fifth such papal address in history). Including these two events in this section of the chapter (on "gestures and deeds") rather than the previous section (on "words of advocacy") calls attention to the power of the pope's presence and performance on these remarkable consecutive days. Francis was extending a gesture of personal witness that transcended the words he spoke. By entering the hallowed halls of arguably the two most influential seats of political power in the world today, the pope was deliberately bringing his insistent appeal for peace into the glow of the brightest spotlight available. Although he said many memorable things in each address, the peace-related content in each instance focused especially on the urgency of curtailing the global arms trade and halting the proliferation of deadly weapons throughout the world.

Speaking bravely in labored English (never one of his strongest languages), Francis packed one of the opening paragraphs of his speech to Congress with three noteworthy phrases with great ethical import: "social responsibility," "the common good," and "the vocation of a political society." He proceeded to unravel the ethical implications of these key concepts for wise public policies regarding several social justice issues close to his heart: a more generous response to migrants and refugees, the defense of human life at every moment (including an appeal for a principled rejection of abortion and capital punishment), a commitment to the fight against poverty and escalating economic inequality, and protection of the natural environment. The final quarter of the address treats how the three ethical concepts apply to America's duty to promote global peace—though the topic of globally responsible behavior emerges as anything but an afterthought in this fervent speech. The

pope's paragraph on the obligation to stop armed conflict, in particular
by ending the weapons trade, reads in full as follows:

> Being at the service of dialogue and peace also means being truly
> determined to minimize and, in the long term, to end the many
> armed conflicts throughout our world. Here we have to ask our-
> selves: Why are deadly weapons being sold to those who plan to
> inflict untold suffering on individuals and society? Sadly, the answer,
> as we all know, is simply for money: money that is drenched in blood,
> often innocent blood. In the face of this shameful and culpable si-
> lence, it is our duty to confront the problem and to stop the arms
> trade.[16]

In his delivery, Francis did not pause to document the extent of the
global arms trade or dwell on U.S. responsibility for it, perhaps because
there was no need for his primary audience to hear the familiar facts.
Members of Congress well know that the primary exporter of weapons
around the globe (to the tune of $40 billion each year) is the United
States, which has unique power to change the dreadful situation whereby munitions flow so easily into the wrong hands. Small arms and major
weapons systems produced by the American defense industry and sold
abroad with the approval of governmental officials (many of them sit-
ting in the House chamber with Pope Francis that day) account for
untold casualties each year. Indiscriminate use of U.S.-manufactured
weapons, both by U.S. allies and other parties who may surreptitiously
acquire them, is the source of many atrocities as well as much political
instability. The money spent on arms by developing nations is often
diverted from investments in health, education, nutrition, and social
services—indirectly robbing the poor of precious resources. Halting
this profitable trade would save many lives each year.

Calling attention to the economic dimension of this global arms supply chain brings further insight to the matter, as Francis exposed the
financial incentives that perpetuate this lethal and endemic problem.
This was not a brand-new message for Francis or church leadership;
fifty years earlier Vatican II had characterized the arms race as "an
utterly treacherous trap for humanity,"[17] and Pope Benedict XVI had
strongly denounced arms sales in his 2006 World Day of Peace message. The U.S. bishops have repeatedly condemned as a moral scandal
the sale of American-manufactured weapons systems to nations with

dubious human rights records. But on the occasion of this historic address to Congress, Francis cut to the chase of this issue. He employed his accustomed structuralist lens to identify greed for profit as a root cause driving many armed conflicts around the world. Putting guns and advanced weapons systems into global circulation escalates and prolongs deadly conflicts, rendering the sellers of arms complicit in the ultimate harm done. Francis directly challenged those legislators with the most power to reform the situation to strike at the root of the problem.

The next day at the United Nations in New York, Francis again gave prominent attention in his address to his deep concern about threats to peace. The pope began by recounting the list of accomplishments for which the United Nations could be proud as it celebrated its seventieth anniversary. Many of these praiseworthy achievements pertained to advancing peace: "the resolution of numerous conflicts, operations of peacekeeping and reconciliation." The pope's address touched upon all the major topics treated in this book (with especially ample attention to poverty, economic justice, the environment, family life, migrants, and trafficked people), so no one topic could dominate his limited time before the General Assembly. But Francis did seem especially eager to highlight the dangers of war and the global arms trade. He mentioned them at several junctures as occupying a place among the most urgent issues facing the global community. After all, Francis proclaimed, "war is the negation of all rights and a dramatic assault on the environment. If we want true integral human development for all, we must work tirelessly to avoid war between nations and between peoples."[18]

Taking full advantage of this high-profile opportunity to promote peace, Francis paused in his discussion of a rapid succession of topics to decry "the proliferation of arms, especially weapons of mass destruction, such as nuclear weapons. . . . There is urgent need to work for a world free of nuclear weapons." Among his appeals for enhanced peacebuilding efforts, he specifically advocated greater multilateral efforts to restrain the global arms trade. Early in this UN address, the pope lamented how the "weapons trade . . . [exacts a] toll in innocent lives." Later he included the arms trade (alongside the illicit narcotics trade, money laundering, and trade in trafficked persons) among the most disturbing signs of corruption in our globalized world—deep threats to integral human development. Although Francis made no specific mention of a new UN initiative in this area, it is no coincidence that restricting the global availability of conventional arms is the subject of a groundbreaking UN-sponsored treaty (the UN Arms Trade Treaty of 2014). As was the case when Francis spoke in 2015, this multilateral agreement is still in search of signatory parties and ratification by major players in the global arms bazaar, such as the United States.[19] Francis was evidently signaling his ardent support for ongoing efforts of UN officials to fulfill the organization's charter, which (to cite an excerpt from the Charter preamble that Francis cited in his address) includes a mandate for "saving succeeding generations from the scourge of war."

Appearing at the United Nations and before the U.S. Congress allowed the pope to share a message that transcends even the highly substantive words he uttered. His very presence in Washington and New York, including his eager sharing of time with fellow world leaders charged with the task of reconciliation, spoke volumes of his commitment to peace. These visits remain among his most significant gestures in support of peacemaking. Any attempt to compile a complete list of the pope's gestures and initiatives to build peace will fall short, as practically all his travels and efforts contain a peacemaking component—an observation in line with the papal title Francis most relishes: *pontifex maximus* (or great bridge builder). Nevertheless, it will be instructive to recall at least the following five peace-themed episodes from his papacy so far, some of which include especially rich symbolic gestures capable of inspiring peacemakers to greater efforts. This selection proceeds in chronological order.

First, in his very first months as pope, Francis resolved to do whatever he could to prevent escalation of the already brutal multiparty fighting in Syria. In August 2013, Western leaders were preparing to respond with a massive bombing campaign to punish President Bashar al-Assad's regime for using deadly sarin gas in chemical weapons attacks that summer against civilians. Out of deep concern for further civilian casualties from Western airstrikes and the dangerous instability that would accompany any further weakening of the embattled Assad's hold on power, Pope Francis appealed for restraint. Mustering all the "soft power" available to him, he mobilized a campaign of spiritual resistance against an escalation of the Syrian conflict.

Francis announced a day of prayer and fasting for peace (September 7) and organized an impressive five-hour outdoor prayer vigil that evening in Saint Peter's Square, over which he personally presided. The penitential spirit of that prayer service reflected the seriousness with which the pope takes war—the ultimate fruit of human sin. Hundreds of millions of Catholics around the world either watched the Vatican events on live television or attended parallel vigils in their own parishes. The Twitter hashtag established for this purpose (#PrayForPeace) became a global sensation and has since been employed for many papal initiatives to respond to conflict situations. In the end, the sincerity of these gestures, combined with Francis's savvy communication strategy, appeared to have played a major role in persuading Western leaders to call off the intended airstrikes. While President Barack Obama and his Western allies also surely had their eyes on political considerations in their respective contexts, worldwide religious advocacy played an important role. The spectacle of a popular pope leading from the moral high ground helped stave off their plans to pursue "peace through war" yet again. It is important to add that the world will never know whether the planned airstrikes would have accomplished more harm than good, however such ratios are calculated. Though Syria would remain a fratricidal disaster for years afterward, Pope Francis had at least contributed to a lull in the ongoing storm and, in the short run, helped prevent numerous innocent lives from becoming further collateral damage of war.[20]

Second, the following year witnessed Francis again placing some of his political capital on the line to promote peace and forestall further conflict. The region of concern was again the Middle East, this time the bitterly divided Holy Land. During his May 2014 visit to that site of endemic political conflict, the pope invited Israeli president Shimon Peres and Palestinian president Mahmoud Abbas to join him the following month in Rome for a day of prayer. Francis had been outspoken in his support for full Palestinian statehood and expressed solidarity with Palestinians suffering from Israeli policies, so there was no certainty that any Israeli politician would jump at such an opportunity. The key to the success of this invitation was probably its modest agenda: there would be no attempt at mediation, merely an opportunity for meditation together, with no expectation of political engagement or deal making. The two leaders did wind up spending some quiet hours in the Vatican gardens, participating in a joint interfaith prayer service for

peace, sharing some brief exchanges of pleasantries, and posing together for the obligatory photographs.

Official accounts emphasize that Peres and Abbas were not "praying
together" but rather "coming together to pray," each according to his
own tradition.[21] Regardless, they were joined that day (June 8) not only
by Pope Francis but also by Orthodox patriarch Bartholomew of Con-
stantinople, whose church maintains an important presence in strategic
locations within the Holy Land. The low-key prayer event did nothing
to change any geopolitical equations but perhaps succeeded in putting a
human face on the players in a tense competition between rivals who
will eventually need to enter into delicate negotiations. The constructive event led many to a deeper appreciation of Francis's priorities, and
his hosting of the prayer opportunity sent the unambiguous signal that
he is willing to lend the full power of his papacy to coax even the
smallest step forward toward peace—in the Holy Land or anywhere
else. Francis will indeed go anywhere and talk to anyone—with no
preconditions—to advance the cause of reconciliation.

Cuba is certainly one of those places where reconciliation is long
overdue, and the efforts of Pope Francis for a diplomatic breakthrough
between Cuba and the United States constitutes a third key example of
papal efforts to heal strained relationships. As the first pope from Latin
America, Francis has a keen understanding of the damage springing
from over a half century of enmity, mutual denunciations, and trade
embargos between these two rivals. Even the end of the Cold War
could not break the logjam that has sundered families and generated
needless antagonism. Not wanting to miss an opportunity to make a
distinctive contribution to peace, sometime in 2014 Francis signaled his
willingness to act as a broker or back channel for communication between the estranged governments. He reportedly started the diplomatic
momentum by writing private letters to leaders of both nations offering
his services to explore possible terms for a rapprochement.

While the full details may never enter the public domain, through
the good offices of the pope and the Vatican diplomatic staff, the outlines of a process that might result in a normalization of commercial and
political ties between Cuba and the United States gradually emerged.
In a December 2014 agreement that included provisions for the release
of political prisoners held in Cuba, the two nations pledged cooperation
to reestablish full diplomatic relations. Presidents Barack Obama and

Raúl Castro each publicly acknowledged the personal intervention of Pope Francis as indispensable to the progress. Although subsequent developments have presented certain setbacks to the easing of trade sanctions and travel restrictions between Cuba and the United States, the initiative of the pope in brokering such a dramatic diplomatic breakthrough in this long-standing stalemate demonstrates the potentially constructive role of religious leaders in working for peace.[22]

A fourth example of the pope's commitment to peacemaking involves one of the poorest and remotest corners of the world: the war-ravaged Central African Republic. When Francis announced his intention to arrange a November 2015 visit to this struggling landlocked nation following his visits to Kenya and Uganda, many scoffed at the proposal. Did the pope not realize that the entire nation, including its ethnically and religiously divided capital Bangui, was an active war zone? Francis would be the first pope ever to enter such a dangerous area of civil strife and armed conflict, featuring almost daily sectarian attacks and acts of terrorism. What purposes could possibly justify the security risks entailed by such a visit? Francis waved off the well-intended advice, including the countersuggestion to conduct a merely perfunctory stopover at the nation's main airport. Only a substantial papal visit, featuring some of his customary pastoral encounters in low-income neighborhoods to mix with the ordinary people of humble estate, would succeed in expressing Francis's deep solidarity with their suffering and call adequate international attention to this needy nation.

And so, putting the considerable security concerns aside and trusting in the goodwill of his hosts (and some armed UN peacekeepers), Francis landed in the Central African Republic and proceeded with his well-planned three-day visit. The pope deliberately selected an itinerary that would allow him to express solidarity with those who live with great insecurity each day, including in local camps for those displaced by the endemic national violence. In meetings with diverse parties, he expressed his hopes for a peaceful resolution of political differences that have sharply divided the population of nearly 5 million since a coup in 2013—divisions exacerbated by the growth of an armed insurgency that has splintered into rival offshoots. The deadly political disputes feature an overlay of religious and ethnic divisions, with Christians and Muslims sequestered into warring enclaves, living in constant fear of deadly raids, ambushes, and kidnappings.

So local observers were astonished when Francis ventured out of the relative safety of territory controlled by the majority Christian population into an Islamic neighborhood, where he mingled with people on an impressive interfaith mission. His visit to the main mosque in Bangui captured worldwide attention. Journalists reported on his utter fearlessness and resolve to spread his message of reconciliation, as when he boldly urged militia members to put down their deadly weapons. Wherever he was invited to speak, Francis underlined his hope for a renewed local commitment to toleration and dialogue that would lead to a peaceful resolution of grievances, beginning with a negotiated settlement between the government and rebel forces.[23] In the months immediately after this historic visit, the nation witnessed a modicum of progress toward peace (negotiated cease-fires, steps toward a new constitution and fair elections), but eruptions of deadly armed clashes eventually resumed.[24] History may look back upon the pope's visit as merely a brief respite from that nation's "descent into hell," as its president described the prolonged national crisis to Francis. Or perhaps the witness to the power of reconciliation provided by a visiting emissary of peace will inspire the warring parties to turn the corner at last toward a peaceful resolution of differences.

A fifth and even more recent peace effort of Pope Francis also involved a nation on the African continent with a recent history of political turbulence, this time a much more populous and influential one with a heavy Muslim majority. A papal visit to Egypt from April 28 to 29, 2017, afforded Francis the opportunity to offer both words of peace (especially at a major interfaith Cairo conference on opposing violent religious extremism) and gestures of peace (warm embraces of Coptic Orthodox pope Tawadros II and Sheikh Ahmed el-Tayeb, the grand imam of Al-Azhar Mosque, the highest seat of learning for Sunni Islam). Once again, Francis received broad admiration merely for daring to set foot in a dangerous environment, as a Palm Sunday suicide bombing at a Coptic Christian church (part of an Islamic State campaign against the small Christian minority in Egypt) had killed forty-seven people just weeks earlier.[25] The visit to the heart of the Islamic world not only sent a message of support to local Christians anxious about violent attacks and religious persecution but also reached out to Islam in new ways—encouraging peace-loving Muslims that terrorists will not have the final say.

The pope's many words and deeds in Egypt constituted an articulate rebuke of any effort to justify hatred and violence in the name of religious belief. He quite deliberately shared public appearances with a range of Egyptian leaders who challenged the moral legitimacy of Islamic fundamentalists who support terrorism. Negotiating the considerable tensions within Egyptian political circles, Francis agreed to meet cordially with President Abdel Fattah el-Sisi (a strongman who came to power in a 2013 military coup) but also took advantage of the opportunity to put him on notice that the violent tactics and human rights violations with which he is frequently charged have not gone unnoticed. In an outwardly genial joint appearance before media representatives, Francis walked a fine line in reprimanding his host for hypocrisy on civil liberties but simultaneously standing with him in a show of unity against terrorism and extremism. One journalist present that day shared an observation that accurately summarizes all five of the papal episodes described above: "The pope . . . [has] repeatedly made the case that he will meet anyone, anywhere to establish dialogue and deliver his inclusive message."[26]

SETTING OUT ALONG THE PATH OF PEACE

In his pursuit of peace, Francis follows a path trod by many courageous popes before him. Indeed, Catholic leaders for centuries and at all levels have raised their voices to advocate for peaceful solutions to political and religious conflicts—sometimes engaging in successful diplomatic efforts to ease global tensions and persuade rivals to settle differences at the bargaining table rather than on the battlefield. Pope Francis stands in strong continuity with this constructive tradition.

But observers have also noted some distinctive qualities in the peace activism of this particular pope—a style, an urgency, an unwavering commitment that makes Francis stand out in his dedication to peace and reconciliation. The five episodes treated above provide vivid testimony of the personal witness to peacemaking that sets Francis apart. An instructive way to conclude this chapter is to explore these two questions: How did Pope Francis acquire these qualities and commitments? What features of his personal background and experience provided the motivations and skills that have made him such a dedicated and successful peacemaker?

One obvious place to look is in Francis's Jesuit background and experience. From its very founding in the sixteenth century, the Society of Jesus has been dedicated to a ministry of reconciliation—both in the narrow sense of sacramental reconciliation from the effects of personal sin and in the broader social (and even formal political) reconciliation between rivals. Jesuit historian John O'Malley reports that the earliest generations of Jesuits time and again attempted to play the role of peacemakers wherever they served—both in mission lands where they brought the gospel anew and especially in parts of Christian Europe where familiarity with the words and deeds of Jesus did not consistently prevent fierce hatreds. Inspired by elements of Ignatian spirituality, they "effected reconciliation among warring factions" divided by fierce vendettas, making great efforts to "convince villagers to renounce the bloody feuds that had raged for years."[27] Jesuits serving as parish priests and spiritual directors took up this specialized ministry of reconciliation that involved preaching a message of forgiveness and delicate interparty mediation. Another account attests, "From the earliest days of the Society of Jesus, the ministry of reconciliation emerged as a defining characteristic of the Jesuit charism."[28] Encouraging people to "soften their hearts," extend a hand of forgiveness, and make peace with rivals is a true work of mercy that is part of the spiritual DNA of anyone emerging from the long program of Jesuit priestly formation. Pope Francis, with his emphasis on the practice of mercy and pardon, exhibits an especially keen appreciation of this mission to reconciliation and an instinctive ability to persuade parties to bury the hatchet. His ministry as provincial superior of the Jesuits in Argentina during the fierce Dirty War surely instructed him further in the urgency of peacemaking and in the skills required to mend frayed relationships.

As noted in the introduction, the Jesuit spirituality of the pope is complemented by his deep appreciation of Franciscan spirituality. Saint Francis of Assisi is remembered for, among other qualities, an extraordinary dedication to peace, and his famous "peace prayer" (which begins "Make me an instrument of your peace") has deeply inspired millions, including the first pope ever to select this particular namesake. Most strikingly, Saint Francis pioneered the heroic journey in pursuit of peace when, in 1219, he set out from Italy with a single companion to try to end the bloody Fifth Crusade. His quixotic sojourn brought him across the Mediterranean to the court of Sultan Malik al-Kamel in Damietta, Egypt, where a sultan and a future saint spent three weeks engaged in a "culture of encounter"—an impressive early instance of respectful interreligious dialogue. During his own peace venture to Egypt eight hundred years later, Pope Francis explicitly acknowledged the historical parallelism of two men named Francis reaching out during times of mass violence to break down barriers between Christianity and Islam. The greatest spiritual revolutionary in Western Christianity has indeed inspired a latter-day admirer to overcome obstacles of both geography and human suspicion to reconcile estranged peoples.

We may never fully understand the deep sources of motivation that give Pope Francis his incomparable energy to work for peace. Surely the vision of a promising future characterized by amity and harmony accounts for much of his dedication. Conversely, his oft-expressed revulsion at fratricidal violence also appears to be a powerful motivator of his tireless work for peace. As noted above, the future pope caught a prolonged glimpse of the horrific effects of a nationwide breakdown of trust and decency when he endured the prolonged civil strife of Argentina's Dirty War. A further personal experience of suffering and trauma due to conflict, on a much smaller scale but still clearly significant, was brought to light by the recent release of a 2015 letter the pope wrote to a priest he knows. In this personally revealing reflection, Francis laments a painful childhood memory of bickering that disturbs him still:

> In my family, there was a long history of disagreement and quarrels. Uncles and cousins quarreled and separated. As a child, when one of these fights was discussed or when we could see a new incident was about to take place, I cried a great deal, in secret, and sometimes I offered a sacrifice or a penance so that such events might not occur. I was very affected. . . . These events left a deep mark on me in my childhood and created a desire in my heart for people to not fight, to remain united. And if they fight, that they return to better feelings.[29]

Traumatic experiences at an impressionable age may certainly exert a powerful influence on the psychology of any person. Simply being a survivor of chronic family bickering may not set every person on a lifelong quest for peace and harmony, but (with the benefit of a good dose of hindsight) Francis shows every sign of having turned this experience of pain and conflict into positive energy in his eventual ministry of reconciliation, which has now gone worldwide.[30] His extraordinary emphasis on mercy is likely informed by such profound experiences of bitterness and festering wounds. Whatever he knew as a child, the adult Jorge Bergoglio has long exhibited a burning passion for peace as well as an ardent desire that no person be forced to endure the suffering that accompanies prolonged unresolved conflict.

Finally, appreciating the factors that motivate the pope's commitment to peace sheds much light on his preferred style of peacemaking. Since all the "why" factors that set him on the path of peace boil down to concern for concrete persons and their urgent needs, it makes sense that the "how" questions relating to his pursuit of peace involve concrete persons as well.[31] Peacebuilding is never something abstract for Francis. There is even a (somewhat ironic) shorthand phrase for the pope's preferred brand of diplomacy that displays these priorities: the Francis Doctrine. One papal observer calls this one-on-one style an "artisanal approach [that] runs through the pope's peace efforts."[32] Francis displays a particular knack for cultivating warm personal relationships with world leaders, forging a bond of immediate connection with political and religious leaders alike, and deftly parlaying his good rapport into breakthroughs for peace. Of course, the freewheeling flexibility exhibited in how Francis conducts himself in the presence of world leaders cannot be captured by anything described as a "doctrine" in the usual sense of that word. The pope evidently subscribes to the notion that peace is the by-product of many trusting personal relationships. As this chapter suggests, leaders on every continent will readily confirm that Francis has helped overcome all manner of human estrangements and contributed to the transformation of numerous conflicts as part of his ambitious agenda for peace.

CONCLUSION

As noted at the outset, this volume examines only a fraction of the overall agenda of Pope Francis. We have focused specifically on how Francis has advanced Catholic social teaching, which concerns matters of social order beyond the boundaries of the church. For this reason, each of the six foregoing chapters has surveyed the pope's words and deeds on a particular topic with social, political, and economic import for all people—not just Catholic believers. Regardless of one's faith convictions or religious practice, everyone on earth is affected by the topics treated in this volume: economic inequality, worker justice, environmental degradation, the health of family life, the well-being of refugees and other displaced people, and the advancement of peace.

Only a much longer book could include what has been deliberately left out. Some readers might be eager for chapters on additional social issues, including bioethics (treating hot-button issues such as abortion and end-of-life decisions), criminal justice (law enforcement policies, capital punishment, etc.), or respect for religious freedom around the world. Other readers might yearn for coverage of internal justice issues within the Catholic Church, to examine how Pope Francis applies principles of fairness and mercy in complex management decisions. Relevant here would be the church's policies toward women, its treatment of members of the LGBTQ community, and its handling of the clergy sex-abuse scandal. It would be the rare observer who found the leadership of Pope Francis flawless on all these sensitive matters or who had no suggestions for improved handling of the internal church reforms

Francis has undertaken, such as the reorganization of the entrenched Roman Curia or the scandal-ridden Vatican Bank.

It is safe to say that the agenda of Pope Francis (at least as we approach the five-year mark of his papacy, as this book goes to press) is still unfinished. While no human could expect unqualified success on all these simultaneous fronts, the most astute Vatican observers keep a sharp eye out not just for a long list of papal accomplishments but above all for ethical consistency in how a given pope carries out his agenda. After all, we live in an age that has developed a particular sensitivity to instances of hypocrisy. Civil and religious leaders are judged (and rightly so) on how the words and actions they direct toward others are applied to their own internal affairs. The credibility of one's message depends on first setting one's own house in order. For a pope, this means that his teachings on social justice issues will be thoroughly scrutinized for their consonance with the internal administration of the Catholic Church. Do the inner workings of the church under Francis reflect his insistence on key values like mercy, inclusion, dialogue, and reconciliation? Has the pope been successful in institutionalizing within the organization he leads the same standards of justice he proposes for the wider society? In the words of the 1971 church document "Justice in the World," cited in chapter 3, "While the church is bound to give witness to justice, she recognizes that anyone who ventures to speak to people about justice must first be just in their eyes."[1]

Every reader will judge for him- or herself how successfully Pope Francis witnesses to the values he professes—in other words, whether "he walks his own talk" in an exemplary way. But notably, the chapters above (admittedly written by an appreciative observer) have included descriptions both of substantive church policies and symbolic gestures of the pope that suggest a sincere respect for all people and a commitment to treating even the least powerful with fairness and respect. Large and small efforts alike can be significant. Pausing a motorcade to embrace a sick child or reaching out to offer pastoral consolation to someone in evident distress may not in themselves prove that a pope is unfailingly consistent in his dedication to justice principles, but such gestures do indicate a likely commitment to commendable values and social priorities. When Pope Francis engages in vivid actions that communicate mercy, inclusion, and reconciliation, the rich symbolism often

speaks as eloquently as his spoken and written words appealing to principles of social concern.

Every pope enjoys numerous daily opportunities to communicate his
priorities and social vision in the way he guides the church. Already in
print are numerous books about the ecclesiology of Pope Francis—that
is, his understanding of the church, its proper functioning, and its role
in the world. Clearly, this is a pope who has encouraged the development of a more open and inclusive church, one featuring ministers
dedicated to practicing pastoral care with an emphasis on flexibility and
responsiveness rather than rigid adherence to set hidebound procedures. Francis repeatedly challenges pastors to "smell like the sheep"
and to "go out to the periphery" on joyful missions of love and mercy.[2]

The connection of ecclesiology to social teachings is obvious. There
is an intimate association between one's vision of the church's identity
and the church's mission in the wider world. Placing a priority on pastoral service and solidarity with the most vulnerable, as Francis clearly
does, naturally orients the church's economic and political stances in a
prophetic direction. In this context, the word "prophetic" refers to one
particular aspect of the overall mission of the Old Testament prophets—namely, exposing the harsh social injustices of their time, which
exacerbated the split between rich and poor. Contemporary prophets,
for their part, denounce global economic structures that in our day trap
millions in poverty and frustrate their efforts to attain a life of dignity.
The three addresses of Francis to the World Meetings of Popular
Movements contain the clearest expression of these themes. But even
in these highly challenging speeches where his prophetic style is on full
display, Francis repeatedly emphasizes the more positive message delivered by prophets through the ages, such as the joy associated with a
close relationship to God and hope for a better future. Just as the
Hebrew prophets pointed to an eventual fulfillment of God's loving
plans for the people of Israel, contemporary popes often remind us of
the consolation of the gospel, which promises an era of reconciliation
and justice. While Francis is fully capable of speaking sharply and con-
fronting injustice with great conviction, nobody would confuse him with
a humorless scold who relishes prolonged finger wagging. Even when
the pope is being especially firm, he never leaves behind his instinctive
gentleness of manner. His preferred style of discourse uses soft, nonad-

versarial speech to encourage and invite all parties to engage in partnerships for constructive social change.

This fresh vision of a Catholic Church that reaches out with greater energy and dedication to the needy has been warmly welcomed by many but has also been criticized by some. It has hardly been a tranquil papacy in this regard. Among the pope's harshest critics are those wary of departures from doctrinal purity and eager to maintain consistent application of customary church disciplines. As we saw in chapter 4, the pope's document on family life, *Amoris Laetitia*, especially worries certain traditionalists, who interpret his willingness to lift burdens from people currently separated from the sacraments as a slide into laxness or relativism. The eagerness of Francis to adjust received norms to the concrete needs of people today has given rise to detractors who wish to put the brakes on what they perceive to be overly rapid change. Some portray him as a reckless and bumbling theological lightweight; others, as an autocratic schemer threatening a disastrous rupture from accustomed church practices.[3]

While words like "rupture" and even "revolution" are tossed around cavalierly at times, it is far more likely that future historians will apply the more moderate (and equally alliterative) words "reform" and "renewal" to the papacy of Francis. It is wise to take Francis exactly at his word: that his overriding desire is to breathe new life into a church that needs to revive its power to "warm the hearts" of the faithful. There is nothing doctrinally dangerous about an initiative as sincere as this. And if there is any demurral about this characterization, the doubt certainly does not arise in the area of social teachings. All six chapters of this study have documented a great preponderance of continuity with previous church stances on social and economic issues. In those areas where Francis has modified the message of recent popes, such as John Paul II and Benedict XVI (for example, on care for the environment and concern for refugees), the innovation has involved little more than an elaboration of previously articulated Catholic principles in light of new societal problems. Francis has supplemented established social teachings with notes of enhanced urgency and deepened church commitment to safeguarding values that the Catholic tradition has long identified as worthy of protection.

Still, some Vatican watchers and media outlets are hungry for controversy, even if they have to invent it out of whole cloth. If we wish to maintain a helpful sense of perspective, we might start by recalling the detailed analysis of the previous six chapters. It is hard to identify any-thing Francis has subtracted from the church's tradition of social teach-ings. His additions (a deeper commitment to dialogue and consultation, a broader notion of solidarity, a more consistent care for creation) turn out to be extremely valuable. They represent renewed strategies for effecting the type of positive social change that the Catholic Church has been advocating for many decades. Obviously, the pursuit of integral human development and a healthy society are tasks that require con-stant updating; Pope Francis has worked hard to extend the church's social concerns to ever wider circles in our globalized age.

Francis is by no means the first pope to dedicate himself to promot-ing worldly change. He is, however, the pope who has most strongly linked effecting social change to the task of evangelization. A folksy phrase Francis has repeated on many occasions, that "you cannot call yourself a Christian without living like a Christian," identifies social responsibility as a key behavioral mark of a faith-filled person. Further, for him, an essential part of the spread of the Christian gospel is en-gagement in important struggles for justice in the secular arena, where we have daily opportunities to put our values into practice. Pope Fran-cis repeatedly affirms that Christians must indeed meddle in politics, that business is a noble vocation,[4] and that the service of faith necessari-ly includes the promotion of social justice. All parts of our lives matter to the faith we profess, and all spheres of human endeavor present opportunities to live out our deepest principles of love, mercy, and justice. Listening to the pope time and time again describe the urgency of economic and social reform confirms that in his view there is no place for apathy or complacency among followers of Jesus Christ. Fran-cis preaches against indifference extraordinarily often. A person who is motivated by religious principles to improve society will be eager to engage anyone, adherents of any faith or none at all, in a genuine dialogue to discern the optimal course of action.

Living lives of ethical consistency has never been an easy task, and it is particularly challenging in the increasingly complex world we inhabit. In paragraph 189 of *Laudato Si'*, Francis calls us "to develop a new economy, more attentive to ethical principles." But even a person with a sincere wish to respond to this appeal still requires considerable further guidance on how to direct his or her efforts. Today, it is especially difficult to pinpoint the causes of the vast unmet needs and the endemic human suffering we encounter. The keen desire of Pope Francis for reform of the global economy to serve people better is matched with a frank acknowledgment that assisting the marginalized will require more than good intentions and a generous heart. This study has referred often to structural evil that traps people in poverty through the operation of malevolent impersonal forces. It has also described Pope Francis as exhibiting a structuralist perspective—a keen eye for diagnosing social ills such as inequality, unemployment, and exclusion by paying close attention to sometimes hidden mechanisms at work and linkages among issues and causal factors. It is not enough to practice kindness and personal generosity. Effective interventions rely upon reform of structures, systems, and the large organizations that inhabit them.

A stellar example of Pope Francis's advocacy for systemic remedies for structural evils involves the topic of labor injustice. Chapter 2 examined the pope's deep concern for the range of problems that workers face in this global economy, including unemployment, poor working conditions, and the exploitation associated with inadequate wages. At the root of these injustices is a sharp imbalance of power. Transnational firms with increasing ability to shift production overseas in search of lower-cost labor and fewer regulations enjoy the upper hand in labor negotiations wherever they operate. The threat of capital flight renders workers timid to advocate for their own rights, especially where the labor force is not organized. For Francis, the decline of labor unions is an important factor in disadvantaging workers, causing poverty and exacerbating inequality. In a June 28, 2017, address to a delegation from Italy's Confederation of Trade Unions (an umbrella organization similar in function to the AFL-CIO), Francis declared, "The labor union . . . gives voice to those who do not have it . . . [and] denounces and unmasks the powerful that trample the rights of the most frail workers. . . . There is no good society without a good labor union."[5]

The point here is not that Pope Francis is urging his hearers to take sides in the complex maneuverings of industrial relations. Rather, he is inviting all to join him in engaging in a more sophisticated diagnosis of worker injustice than religious communities customarily encourage. The legitimate role of labor unions is to empower the vulnerable to protect themselves, taking advantage of collective bargaining in contract negotiations to lift themselves up by their own efforts. By parlaying strength in numbers into countervailing power in labor markets, workers win concessions that allow them to improve their lives and provide for their families. While labor unions have been operating this way for centuries, and Catholic social teaching has officially supported them since 1891, noting this pope's endorsement of trade unions on this occasion is a particularly fine way to conclude this study of the social teaching of Francis. This instance illustrates very clearly his preferred strategy for the alleviation and prevention of poverty: not a paternalistic approach (doing something for the poor) but an empowerment approach (creating favorable conditions for the vulnerable to overcome their disadvantages). The social reforms for mutual benefit that he advocates are indeed described very well by his signature phrases: "the culture of accompaniment," "the culture of inclusion," and "the culture of encounter." If we wish to change the world in a way that reflects the approach of Francis, these phrases provide important clues to the style we should adopt.

For Francis, our poorest neighbors deserve every effort we might make to forge a more inclusive society and create the structures that allow all to flourish. In paragraph 198 of *Evangelii Gaudium*, he affirms the importance of the recently formulated theological principle of "the option for the poor." In an especially lyrical passage, he yearns once again for "a church which is poor and for the poor" and adds that the poor "have much to teach us. . . . We need to let ourselves be evangelized by them. . . . We are called to find Christ in them, to lend our voice to their causes, but also to be their friends, to listen to them, to speak for them and to embrace the mysterious wisdom which God wishes to share with us through them." We can indeed advance this objective of mutual enrichment under the right conditions, but we must be extremely careful how we enact these good intentions. The only truly sustainable solutions to problems such as low incomes and labor exploitation are approaches that put power in the hands of the marginalized, that foster their moral agency and allow them to become subjects of their own history—not mere objects of charity. While philanthropic strategies that offer freewill gifts to the powerless are to be commended as far as they go, charity without justice is incomplete and unsustainable.

Eager to emphasize the importance of work for structural justice, Francis here reveals a marvelous instance of what he has been doing throughout his ministry: advocating for social change by encouraging structural reforms that will benefit those on the periphery. Whether the excluded are refugees seeking resettlement, workers organizing to obtain a fair contract, or struggling farmers displaced by climate change, Francis lends his voice to worthy causes on many occasions. By now, the world is familiar with his customary communication strategy: he uses the global media's spotlight on the papacy to highlight suffering, to appeal to the consciences of people around the world to address it, and to move them to effective action.

In the final section of the *Spiritual Exercises*, Saint Ignatius of Loyola shares the insight that love ought to show itself in deeds more than in words. From his decades as a Jesuit following this venerable guide to spiritual discernment and prayer, Francis is thoroughly familiar with this sentiment. As this study has shown, he truly is a man of action and bold deeds that express his concern for those in special need. But he also knows the power of well-placed words to instruct and encourage people to greater involvement in works of mercy and projects of justice. In both powerful words and inspiring actions, Pope Francis has appealed to the moral imagination of Christians and all people of goodwill to picture a world of greater social justice and reconciliation. It is up to the many millions of his hearers to follow his lead and put into action the mercy he extols.

NOTES

INTRODUCTION

1. For details of this occasion, see Austen Ivereigh, *The Great Reformer: Francis and the Making of a Radical Pope* (New York: Henry Holt and Company, 2014), 45–46. Francis was speaking to Argentinian pilgrims in Rio de Janeiro when he lapsed into the local Spanish slang of his homeland. The phrase *hacer lío* literally means to make a ruckus or create havoc, as when Argentinians follow the custom of rushing into the streets on certain occasions and banging pots to express passion for a cause. In the context of World Youth Day, this obviously constituted a call for expressing enthusiasm in spreading the gospel, even if it meant relaxing the norms of orderly behavior.

2. For an overview of the political history of twentieth-century Argentina, see the early chapters of Ivereigh, *The Great Reformer*. For coverage of the deeper theological and intellectual influences on Pope Francis, see Thomas R. Rourke, *The Roots of Pope Francis's Social and Political Thought: From Argentina to the Vatican* (Lanham, MD: Rowman & Littlefield, 2016).

3. On church-state relations in recent Argentinian governments, see Elisabetta Pique, *Pope Francis: Life and Revolution: A Biography of Jorge Bergoglio* (Chicago: Loyola Press, 2013), 137–42.

4. A further motivation to press this line of inquiry pertains to the juridical standing of a Jesuit who is serving the church as a bishop or even as pope. Like all members of religious congregations who assume high ecclesiastical office, Jesuits who become bishops are released from their specifically Jesuit vows (which include a vow of obedience to local and provincial superiors), as it would be a serious conflict of interest for a bishop to be under obedience to a

religious superior other than the pope. Electing a pope from a religious order is rare; the most recent was Gregory XVI, a Benedictine elected in 1831.

5. Cited in Philip Endean, "Writings on Jesuit Spirituality by Jorge Mario Bergoglio, S.J.," *Studies in the Spirituality of Jesuits* 45, no. 3 (autumn 2013): 2.

6. From the "Principle and Foundation" as found in Joseph Richaby, SJ, *The Spiritual Exercises of St. Ignatius Loyola: Spanish and English with a Continuous Commentary*, 2nd ed. (London: Burns, Oates and Washbourne, Ltd., 1913), 18. I retain the non-gender-inclusive language only to preserve the sense of the original Spanish text and its translation into English over a century ago.

7. See, for example, "A Good Catholic Meddles in Politics," *Vatican Insider*, September 16, 2013, http://www.lastampa.it/2013/09/16/vaticaninsider/eng/the-vatican/francis-a-good-catholic-meddles-in-politics-zItEROwIDaSRq8k3OHYmTI/pagina.html. Bergoglio had been using this aphorism for at least a decade, dating to his leadership of the archdiocese of Buenos Aires during some fierce church-state controversies in Argentina.

8. This phrase forms the subtitle of Decree Four ("Our Mission Today: The Service of Faith and the Promotion of Justice") of General Congregation 32, promulgated May 8, 1975, and appearing in English translation in *Documents of the 31st and 32nd General Congregations of the Society of Jesus* (Saint Louis, MO: Institute of Jesuit Sources, 1977), 411–38.

9. Especially impressive is the 2016 document "Justice in the Global Economy: Building Sustainable and Inclusive Communities," a thirty-five-page report from a task force on the economy commissioned by the Social Justice and Ecology Secretariat that the Society of Jesus maintains as part of its central curia in Rome. The report appears in the online Jesuit publication *Promotio Justitiae* (issue no. 121 for January 2016): 1–35. Accessible at http://www.sjweb.info/sjs/PJ/index.cfm?PubTextId=15696.

10. Ivereigh, *The Great Reformer*, esp. 58–65.

11. Rourke, *The Roots*, esp. 15–40.

I. ECONOMIC JUSTICE

1. The Latin and English titles will be used interchangeably here. Several print editions are readily available, and the full text in several languages is available on the website of the Holy See at http://w2.vatican.va/content/francesco/en/apost_exhortations/documents/papa-francesco_esortazione-ap_20131124_evangelii-gaudium.html.

2. Paragraph 184 of *Evangelii Gaudium* explains, "This Exhortation is not a social document" and will not "examine in detail the many grave social questions affecting today's world." Nevertheless, valuable advances in social teaching do unfold in the course of this long document and are hardly peripheral to its primary purpose.

3. Paragraph 14 of *Evangelii Gaudium* explains the occasion for writing. The Synod of Bishops meets every three years in Rome and focuses on a predesignated topic. The topic for the October 2012 session was "The New Evangelization for the Transmission of the Christian Faith." Pope Benedict XVI presided over the deliberations of the body of over two hundred selected bishops and others, but his resignation and departure in February 2013 left to Pope Francis the task of issuing the customary postsynodal exhortation (in this case, some thirteen months later) summarizing the deliberations and providing his own theological interpretation to point the way forward.

4. It is easy to find instances where phrases and entire sentences contained in *Evangelii Gaudium* appear in previous published works or addresses given by Bergoglio (see his contributions to the 2007 Aparecida deliberations of the Conference of Latin American Bishops, for example) or, after his papal election, by Francis (see the texts of his many addresses at general audiences and similar public occasions).

5. A careful reading of New Testament texts that treat the topic of wealth reveals that possessions are portrayed as both a sign of God's blessing and a source of obligation to others in need. Commentators who overlook the dangers or perils of holding great wealth ignore the close identification of Jesus with the poor, as well as major parts of (in particular) Luke's gospel, including the parable of Lazarus and Dives in Luke 16.

6. Address of Archbishop Jorge Mario Bergoglio to the Fifth Conference of Latin American Bishops, Aparecida, Brazil, May 21, 2007.

7. See Andrea Tornielli and Giacomo Galeazzi, *This Economy Kills: Pope Francis on Capitalism and Social Justice* (Collegeville, MN: Liturgical Press, 2015). See also Andrew Ross, "A Few Words from the Pope on the Economy," *San Francisco Chronicle*, November 28, 2013, C1, C5.

8. The predecessor of Francis, Pope Benedict XVI, devoted major sections of his social encyclical *Caritas in Veritate* to a theological analysis of the financial crisis of 2008. In fact, Benedict delayed its release several months, until July 2009, in order to include in the document his own description of what had gone wrong with the world's economy in recent years and how a return to proper values and ethical practices could address some of the core problems.

9. Pope John XXIII used this phrase in an official radio message of September 11, 1962, precisely a month before he presided over the opening of the Second Vatican Council. John was especially interested in embracing the grow-

ing church in the developing world, which was struggling with poverty just as many nations had gained independence from the European powers that had exerted colonial control over them.

10. The close identification of the church with the poor goes back, of course, to the teachings of Jesus (for example in the Beatitudes) and the very earliest days of Christianity (see St. Paul's Letter to the Galatians 2:9 and Acts of the Apostles 4:34). Several documents of the Second Vatican Council reflect the renewal of this orientation, such as the opening paragraph of *Gaudium et Spes* ("Pastoral Constitution of the Church in the Modern World").

11. The English transcription of the interview appears as chapter 15 in Tornielli and Galeazzi, *This Economy Kills*. This quote appears on page 151.

12. *Gaudium et Spes* makes this point in paragraph 69, which bears the customary name of this Christian theological principle, "The Common Purpose of Created Things." It is also sometimes called "The Universal Destination of Created Goods." Pope Paul VI treats it in *Populorum Progressio*, paragraph 22. Pope Francis paraphrases this set of beliefs in paragraphs 190 and 192 of *Evangelii Gaudium*.

13. In paragraph 79 of the 1961 social encyclical *Mater et Magistra*, Pope John XXIII covers this same ground with great insight by listing some core economic goals of any modern nation and relating them to pursuit of "the common good on the national level." The goals cited by Pope John include "to make accessible the goods and services for a better life to as many persons as possible; either to eliminate or to keep within bounds the inequalities that exist between different sectors of the economy . . . ; to balance properly any increases in output with advances in services provided to citizens, especially by public authorities."

14. Drew Christiansen, SJ, "On Relative Equality: Catholic Egalitarianism after Vatican II," *Theological Studies* 45 (1984): 651–75, at 674.

15. *Populorum Progressio*, paragraph 8.

16. See chapter 4 ("Private Property and the Universal Destination of Material Goods") in his 1991 social encyclical *Centesimus Annus*, esp. paragraphs 40 and 42.

17. Named for the Italian statistician Corrado Gini (1884–1965), who developed this commonly used measure of income distribution.

18. Thomas Piketty, *Capital in the Twenty-First Century*, trans. Arthur Goldhammer (Cambridge, MA: Harvard University Press, 2014).

19. Joseph E. Stiglitz, *The Great Divide: Unequal Societies and What We Can Do about Them* (New York: W. W. Norton, 2015); Joseph E. Stiglitz, *The Price of Inequality: How Today's Divided Society Endangers Our Future* (New York: W. W. Norton, 2012); Anthony B. Atkinson, *Inequality: What Can Be Done?* (Cambridge, MA: Harvard University Press, 2015).

20. See, for example, Richard Wilkinson and Kate Pickett, *The Spirit Level: Why Greater Equality Makes Societies Stronger* (London: Bloomsbury Press, 2009). The authors are British public health researchers who draw startling conclusions using cross-national data comparisons.

2. PROMOTING LABOR JUSTICE IN A GLOBALIZED ECONOMIC ORDER

1. Chapter 4 of *Evangelii Gaudium* contains a section with three paragraphs (231–33) labeled "Realities are more important than ideas." This is the third of four axioms that are listed and treated here and which reflect a trope Bergoglio had used often in addresses and writings over the span of decades. The other three axioms are "Time is greater than space," "Unity prevails over conflict," and "The whole is greater than the part."

2. Regarding gender injustices in global labor markets, see Christine Firer Hinze, *Glass Ceilings and Dirt Floors: Women, Work, and the Global Economy* (New York: Paulist Press, 2015).

3. All the quoted words in this paragraph come from the official English translation of the pope's remarks at his "Meeting with Workers" in Largo Cargo Felice, Cagliari, Sardinia, on September 22, 2013. Available at http://w2.vatican.va/content/francesco/en/speeches/2013/september/documents/papa-francesco_20130922_lavoratori-cagliari.html.

4. From the English translation of the pope's address at the "Meeting with the People and Various Social Categories of the Scampia Neighborhood," Piazza Giovanni Paolo II, Naples, Italy, March 21, 2015. Available at http://w2.vatican.va/content/francesco/en/speeches/2015/march/documents/papa-francesco_20150321_napoli-pompei-popolazione-scampia.html.

5. Details and quotes appear in "Legitimate Redistribution of Wealth Needed, Pope Says," *San Francisco Chronicle*, May 10, 2014, A5.

6. The quotation and account of this event appear in "South Korea: Pope Implores Youths to Reject Materialism," *San Francisco Chronicle*, August 15, 2014, A4.

7. This is a paraphrase of a key passage in the encyclical *Laborem Exercens* ("On Human Labor"), published in 1981 by Pope John Paul II. The official English translation of paragraph 9 includes the phrase "Work is a good thing for man." Paragraph 6 includes the similar sentiment "In the first place, work is 'for man' and not man 'for work.'" In the interest of accuracy, I have retained the non-gender-inclusivity of these phrases in the original.

8. The original Spanish version of the text also uses three alliterative words, in this case beginning with the letter *t*: *tierra* (land), *techo* (housing or lodging), and *trabajo* (work or labor).

9. All quoted phrases in this paragraph come from "Address of Pope Francis to the Participants in the World Meeting of Popular Movements," held at Old Synod Hall in Vatican City, October 28, 2014. Available at http://w2.vatican.va/content/francesco/en/speeches/2014/october/documents/papa-francesco_20141028_incontro-mondiale-movimenti-popolari.html.

10. Jim Yardley and Binyamin Applebaum, "In Fiery Speeches, Francis Excoriates Global Capitalism," *New York Times*, July 12, 2015, 12.

11. Direct quotations here and in the next paragraph come from "Address of Pope Francis to the Participants at the Second World Meeting of Popular Movements," held at Expo Fería Exposition Center in Santa Cruz de la Sierra, Bolivia, July 9, 2015. Available at http://w2.vatican.va/content/francesco/en/speeches/2015/july/documents/papa-francesco_20150709_bolivia-movimenti-popolari.html.

12. Quotations in this paragraph and the next come from "Address of Pope Francis to the Participants in the Third World Meeting of Popular Movements," held at the Paul VI Audience Hall in Vatican City, November 5, 2016. Available at http://w2.vatican.va/content/francesco/en/speeches/2016/november/documents/papa-francesco_20161105_movimenti-popolari.html.

13. In an apostolic letter issued by Francis on August 17, 2016 (and taking effect on January 1, 2017), this more inclusive name was established when the duties of the Pontifical Council for Justice and Peace were merged with those of three other entities, including the Pontifical Council for the Pastoral Care of Migrants and Itinerant People. See http://w2.vatican.va/content/francesco/en/motu_proprio/documents/papa-francesco-motu-proprio_20160817_humanam-progressionem.html.

14. For coverage of this gathering, see Jim McDermott, SJ, "San Diego Bishop McElroy Encourages Catholics to Be Hope-Filled 'Disrupters,'" *America*, March 20, 2017, 16.

15. Quotations in this paragraph and the next come from "Address of Pope Francis to Participants in the Plenary of the Pontifical Council for Justice and Peace," held at Clementine Hall in Vatican City, October 2, 2014. Available at http://w2.vatican.va/content/francesco/en/speeches/2014/october/documents/papa-francesco_20141002_pont-consiglio-giustizia-e-pace.html.

16. Bishop Thomas Dabre, "Not Just Admiration but Taking Steps unto Imitation," in *Unto the Margins: Pope Francis and His Challenges*, ed. John Chathanatt, SJ (Bangalore, India: Claretian Publications, 2013), 55–60, at 56.

17. "Pope Francis: It's a Grave Sin to Lay People Off Carelessly," Catholic News Agency, March 15, 2017, https://www.catholicnewsagency.com/news/pope-francis-its-a-grave-sin-to-lay-people-off-carelessly-20523.

18. The poignant prayer of Francis on this occasion is reproduced in Kevin Cotter, ed., *A Year of Mercy with Pope Francis: Daily Reflections* (Huntington, IN: Our Sunday Visitor Publishing Division, 2014), 173.

19. "Visit to the Community of Varghina," Rio de Janeiro, Brazil, July 25, 2013. Available at http://w2.vatican.va/content/francesco/en/speeches/2013/july/documents/papa-francesco_20130725_gmg-comunita-varginha.html.

20. Joshua J. McElwee, "Pope Lambastes Poor Treatment of Workers," *National Catholic Reporter*, February 26–March 10, 2016, 5.

21. "Address of Pope Francis to Participants in the 38th Conference of the Food and Agriculture Organization of the United Nations," given at Clementine Hall in Vatican City, June 20, 2013. Available at http://w2.vatican.va/content/francesco/en/speeches/2013/june/documents/papa-francesco_20130620_38-sessione-fao.html.

22. Cardinal Walter Kasper, *Pope Francis' Revolution of Tenderness and Love: Theological and Pastoral Perspectives* (New York: Paulist Press, 2015), 81.

23. Both these quoted phrases recur in the Bolivia address of July 9, 2015; see note 11 of this chapter for details.

3. A BOLD CALL FOR INTEGRAL ECOLOGY

1. In 2013, Francis unveiled another encyclical letter, *Lumen Fidei*, or "The Light of Faith." As Francis noted at the time, that encyclical was "the work of four hands," two of which belonged to Pope Benedict XVI. Textual analysis reveals that the vast majority of this text was indeed produced by Benedict, who did not have time to complete the work before his resignation went into effect in February 2013. Further, it is clear that "The Light of Faith" is the third in a trilogy of encyclicals planned early in the pontificate of Benedict, one on each of the theological virtues of faith, hope, and love. See his 2005 encyclical *Deus Caritas Est* ("God Is Love") and his 2007 encyclical *Spe Salvi* ("Saved in Hope") for comparison. An encyclical is a teaching letter written by a pope (generally with assistance) and intended to be circulated among bishops and eventually all the faithful. It invokes the highest level of teaching authority belonging to a pope (as opposed to the even higher authority of documents of an ecumenical church council). The phrase "social encyclicals" describes the fraction of these writings that deal primarily with social relations, including political, economic, and cultural matters. Apostolic exhor-

tations are papal documents similar in form to encyclicals but are proposed with a somewhat lower level of doctrinal authority.

2. In paragraph 10 of *Laudato Si'*, Pope Francis holds up Saint Francis of Assisi as "the example par excellence of care for the vulnerable and of integral ecology. . . . He is the patron saint of all who study and work in the area of ecology. . . . He was a mystic and a pilgrim who lived in simplicity and in wonderful harmony with God, with others, with nature and with himself. He shows us just how inseparable the bond is between concern for nature, justice for the poor, commitment to society, and interior peace."

3. "Homily of Pope Francis for the Inaugural Papal Mass," at Saint Peter's Square, Vatican City, March 19, 2013. Available at http://w2.vatican.va/ content/francesco/en/homilies/2013/documents/papa-francesco_20130319_ omelia-inizio-pontificato.html.

4. His second tweet (also falling on March 19, 2013) urged all to exercise care to be "loving custodians of creation." His many tweets on creation and ecology are treated in Martin J. O'Loughlin, *The Tweetable Pope: A Spiritual Revolution in 140 Characters* (New York: HarperCollins Publishers, 2015), esp. chapter 7 ("Creation"), 93–106. The author notes that the single most dramatic "Twitterbomb" emanating from Pope Francis to date was a rapid series of over sixty messages on ecology immediately upon the release of *Laudato Si'* on June 18, 2015.

5. See paragraph 9 of "Message of His Holiness Francis for the Celebration of the World Day of Peace," Holy See, January 1, 2014, http://w2.vatican. va/content/francesco/en/messages/peace/documents/papa-francesco_ 20131208_messaggio-xlvii-giornata-mondiale-pace-2014.html.

6. See the 1971 apostolic letter of Paul VI, *Octogesima Adveniens* ("The Coming Eightieth"), especially paragraph 21, with its mention of the "ill-considered exploitation of nature" by which man "risks destroying it and becoming in his turn the victim of this degradation."

7. The 1971 Worldwide Synod of Bishops published a short but influential document, *Justitia in Mundo* ("Justice in the World"), that includes a warning about "high rates of consumption and pollution," which raise "the danger of destroying the very physical foundations of life on earth . . . the destruction of the heritage which we are obliged to share."

8. This citation appears in paragraph 8 of Pope John Paul II, "Peace with God the Creator, Peace with all of Creation," Holy See, http://w2.vatican.va/ content/john-paul-ii/en/messages/peace/documents/hf_jp-ii_mes_19891208_ xxiii-world-day-for-peace.html.

9. Pope John Paul II, *Centesimus Annus*, paragraph 37.

10. The text of this document, along with many helpful essays expanding upon its themes, is found in Drew Christiansen and Walter Grazer, eds., *"And*

God Saw That It Was Good": Catholic Theology and the Environment (Washington, DC: United States Conference of Catholic Bishops Publishing Services, 1994).

11. The official English version of the text appears at "Encyclical Letter Laudato Si' of the Holy Father Francis on Care for Our Common Home," Holy See, http://w2.vatican.va/content/francesco/en/encyclicals/documents/papa-francesco_20150524_enciclica-laudato-si.html.

12. Francis is eager to indicate his reliance upon the environmental contributions of his two predecessors and to acknowledge his debt of gratitude. Among the 172 footnotes in *Laudato Si'*, John Paul is cited thirty-seven times and Benedict thirty times.

13. Even before he began writing *Laudato Si'*, Francis provided hints that he wished to recast the sharp separation of human ecology and natural ecology that we find in John Paul II (see his 1979 encyclical *Redemptor Hominis*, paragraph 8, and *Centesimus Annus*, paragraph 38) and Benedict XVI (see *Caritas in Veritate*, paragraphs 48–51). In *Evangelii Gaudium*, Francis links human and natural ecology more closely (see, especially, paragraphs 215–16).

14. For a sample of these occasions, see paragraphs 113, 204, 206, 209, and 215.

15. Although he is not cited explicitly in the encyclical, this phrase is associated with Leonardo Boff, a former Franciscan priest and Brazilian missionary whose book *Cry of the Earth, Cry of the Poor* (Maryknoll, NY: Orbis Books, 1997) is widely considered to have influenced the thinking of Pope Francis on this topic. A liberation theologian, Boff himself offered ample praise for the early ecological activism of Pope Francis in *Francis of Rome and Francis of Assisi: A New Springtime for the Church*, trans. Dinah Livingstone (Maryknoll, NY: Orbis Books, 2014).

16. Even a brief survey of newspaper headlines from the week of its release in June 2015 reveals that *Laudato Si'* was received in less than optimal ways in the public media, representing a missed opportunity for more profound instruction and more constructive attention. For example, on the day of its release, a front-page headline in the *San Francisco Chronicle* read "Pope Blasts State Cap-and-Trade System" (news article by David R. Baker on page A1 of the June 19, 2015, issue). Besides this undue fixation on relatively minor aspects of the encyclical and their rather local implications, some news coverage focused on speculations regarding partisan political ramifications of the encyclical. See, for example, this story on the content of the encyclical (which was responding to a partial version of the document that had been leaked three days in advance of the official release): Coral Davenport, "Pope's Views Press G.O.P. on Climate: Echoing Message in Key Election States," *New York Times*, June 16, 2015, A1, A6. Even more disheartening was the poor reception

accorded to the encyclical by *Washington Post* columnist George F. Will, who, on September 17, 2015, decided to sprinkle a widely syndicated vitriolic column titled "On Pope Francis' Fact-Free Flamboyance and Medieval World View" with a string of scurrilous insults to the pontiff.

17. See the text, sidebars, and numerous charts accompanying Laura Whitaker, "Who Cares? We Do: *U.S. Catholic* Readers Say Pope Francis' Encyclical *Laudato Si'* Has Inspired Them to Care for Our Common Home," *U.S. Catholic*, April 2016, 32–36.

18. Edward Mailbach et al., *The Francis Effect: How Pope Francis Changed the Conversation about Global Warning* (Fairfax, VA: George Mason University Center for Climate Change Communications, 1995).

19. Center for Applied Research in the Apostolate, *"Laudato Si'*: Catholic Attitudes about Climate Change," Nineteen Sixty-Four, June 16, 2016, http://nineteensixty-four.blogspot.com/2016/06/laudato-si-catholic-attitudes-about.html.

20. Pope Francis, "Letter for the Establishment of the World Day of Prayer for the Care of Creation," Holy See, August 6, 2015, http://w2.vatican.va/content/francesco/en/letters/2015/documents/papa-francesco_20150806_lettera-giornata-cura-creato.html.

21. Some previous popes, especially John Paul II and Benedict XVI, expressed serious reservations about affirming the teaching authority of documents emanating from national episcopal conferences and so rarely cited them in Vatican documents that appeared during their papacies. In 1998, John Paul II promulgated the *motu proprio* document *Apostolos Suos*, which restricted the invocation of doctrinal authority pertaining to such documents.

22. See the website of Catholic Climate Covenant at http://www.catholicclimatecovenant.org.

23. Donal Dorr, *Option for the Poor and for the Earth: From Leo XIII to Pope Francis*, rev. ed. (Maryknoll, NY: Orbis Books, 2016), 448.

4. PROMOTING HEALTHY FAMILY LIFE IN CHALLENGING TIMES

1. The address of Francis at the close of the Synod of Bishops on October 25, 2015, included this insight: "Cultures are in fact quite diverse, and each general principle needs to be inculturated if it is to be respected and applied." His next sentence cites wording from the Final Relatio (or report) of the 1985 Synod, which "spoke of inculturation as 'the intimate transformation of authentic cultural values through their integration into Christianity, and the taking root of Christianity in the various human cultures.'" In the eighth and final footnote that accompanied the text version of this spoken address (available on

the website of Vatican Radio), Francis provides a shorthand formula for his purpose in calling the synod on this particular topic, linking his intention closely to the task of inculturation: "inventing renewed programs of pastoral care for the family based on the Gospel and respectful of cultural differences."

2. Accompanying this development was the problematic identification of women with the private sphere and men with the public sphere. This, of course, was an error not limited to Roman Catholic thought. On this point, see Jean Bethke Elshtain, *Public Man, Private Woman: Women in Social and Political Thought* (Princeton, NJ: Princeton University Press, 1993).

3. See Lisa Sowle Cahill, *Family: A Christian Social Perspective* (Philadelphia: Fortress Press, 2000); Julie Hanlon Rubio, *Family Ethics: Practices for Christians* (Washington, DC: Georgetown University Press, 2010); Florence Caffrey Bourg, *Where Two or Three Are Gathered: Christian Families as Domestic Church* (Notre Dame, IN: Notre Dame University Press, 2004). All three of these exemplary works by Catholic feminist scholars emphasize the nurturing of children in social virtues such as hospitality, generosity, and service for less fortunate members of society. Each underlines the social dimensions of numerous family practices. The Vatican's own *Compendium of the Social Doctrine of the Church* (see, especially, paragraphs 248–54), published by the Pontifical Council for Justice and Peace in 2004, treats many social aspects and functions of family life.

4. "Charter of the Rights of the Family" of the Holy See, released November 24, 1983, and printed in *Origins* 13, no. 27 (December 15, 1983): 461–64.

5. See Paola Dal Toso, ed., *Pope Francis and the Family* (Washington, DC: United States Conference of Catholic Bishops, 2014) for the texts of these family-themed homilies from March to August 2013. See *Pope Francis on the Family* (San Francisco: Ignatius Press, 2015) for the texts of the general audience addresses on this theme from December 17, 2014, to September 16, 2015.

6. These particular points regarding the nature and purpose of Christian marriage are also treated quite comprehensively in the most recent document on this subject by the U.S. bishops. See "Marriage: Love and Life in the Divine Plan," United States Conference of Catholic Bishops, November 17, 2009, http://www.usccb.org/issues-and-action/marriage-and-family/marriage/love-and-life/upload/pastoral-letter-marriage-love-and-life-in-the-divine-plan.pdf.

7. The ban on artificial contraception is a central teaching of Pope Paul VI's 1968 encyclical *Humanae Vitae*.

8. An early appearance of the phrase "domestic church" is in paragraph 11 of *Lumen Gentium* ("Light of the Nations"), Vatican II's Dogmatic Constitution on the Church. Francis cites it prominently in paragraphs 67 and 86.

9. The notion of family as "the first cell of society" appears in paragraph 11 of Vatican II's Decree on the Apostolate of the Laity, which coined the term "the first and vital cell of society." Subsequent church documents offer variants of this phrase. *The Compendium of the Social Doctrine of the Church*, a 2004 reference work from the Pontifical Council for Justice and Peace, dedicates an entire long chapter (one of just twelve chapters summarizing all aspects of social teaching) to family themes and titles this chapter "Family: The Vital Cell of Society."

10. In paragraph 69, Francis acknowledges his debt to John Paul II, who employed this phrase in *Gratissimam Sane* (his 1994 letter to families) and in his 1981 apostolic exhortation *Familiaris Consortio*.

11. For a reliable explanation of the changes in canon law that enacted this initiative of Pope Francis in 2015, see Cindy Woodson, "Pope Simplifies Annulment Process, Asks That It Be Free of Charge," Catholic News Service, September 8, 2015, http://www.catholicnews.com/services/englishnews/2015/pope-simplifies-annulment-process-asks-that-it-be-free-of-charge.cfm.

12. The law of gradualism was discussed at the 1980 Synod of Bishops (when the topic of family life was being considered), and the phrase appears in the 1981 postsynodal exhortation *Familiaris Consortio* of John Paul II. In the year or so after the publication of *Amoris Laetitia*, some of the most insightful theological assessments of what Francis achieves in this exhortation appeared in the Jesuit-sponsored journal *Theological Studies*. See, for example, James Keenan, SJ, "Receiving *Amoris Laetitia*," *Theological Studies* 78, no. 1 (March 2017): 193–212; Gerald O'Collins, SJ, "The Joy of Love (*Amoris Laetitia*): The Papal Exhortation in Its Context," *Theological Studies* 77, no. 4 (December 2016): 905–21.

13. The pope had said in 2014, "What I didn't like was, what some people, within the church as well, said about the purpose of the synod: that it intends to allow remarried divorcees to take communion, as if the entire issue boils down to a case. . . . I wouldn't like us to fall into this question: Will it be possible for communion to be administered or not? The pastoral problem regarding the family is vast. Each case needs to be looked at separately." From "Interview of Pope Francis with Journalists during the Return Flight from the Holy Land," May 27, 2014, reprinted from the Vatican website in "Pastoral Challenges Regarding the Family," *C21 Resources* (spring 2015): 16.

14. Conor M. Kelly, "The Role of the Moral Theologian in the Church: A Proposal in Light of *Amoris Laetitia*," *Theological Studies* 77, no. 4 (December 2016): 922–48, at 925.

15. Perhaps the strongest statement of dissatisfaction with Francis on this count in the popular media appears in a column by conservative Catholic layman Ross Douthat, "His Holiness Declines to Answer," *New York Times*,

Sunday Review, November 27, 2016, 11. The author complains that *Amoris Laetitia* "essentially talked around the controversy, implying in various ways that communion might be given case by case, but never coming out and saying so directly." While this characterization is accurate enough, Douthat makes the mistake of casting the pope's approach as a cynical political dodge rather than as a sincere pastoral approach. At the end of this column, Douthat claims that Francis was trying to win favor from both liberals and conservatives, and so "avoiding clarity seemed intended as a compromise, a hedge." Douthat's column uses the word "Machiavellian" but never mentions the notion of mercy. For him, a pope is assuredly a rule maker and arbiter of law but not so clearly a pastor of souls—with responsibility to offer guidance to people who live messy lives.

16. One moral theologian, reprising what was said earlier in this chapter about the agenda of inculturation of the church's teachings on family life, interprets *Amoris Laetitia* as extending a key message of Francis's: the importance of the local church. Not only does Francis cite nine different statements of local bishops' conferences in his document on family life, but he noticeably leaves the determination of key pastoral matters to the local level. See Thomas A. Shannon, "The Lasting Legacy of *Amoris Laetitia*," Catholic Theological Ethics in the World Church, March 30, 2017, http://www.catholicethics.com/forum-submissions/-the-lasting-legacy-of-amoris-laetitia.

17. It is worth pointing out that this stance of Francis's, while an evident departure from official policy outlined in John Paul's 1981 *Familiaris Consortio* and elsewhere, does not represent a major rupture with actual pastoral practice. Catholics around the world have long resorted to "internal forum" solutions to work out with their pastors and confessors a confidential understanding that allows them to return to the sacraments despite living in "irregular situations." The archdiocese of Vienna, led by Cardinal Christoph Schönborn, a high-profile confidant of Pope Francis, has for years sponsored a local program of discernment and penitential practice to facilitate such a pathway to the sacraments. South African bishops in particular quickly expressed great delight with this proposal of Francis's, indicating an openness to address the long-standing "disconnect" between official church regulatory disciplines and certain pastoral realities in that region as well as others.

18. Pope Francis, "Misericordiae Vultus," Holy See, http://w2.vatican.va/content/francesco/en/apost_letters/documents/papa-francesco_bolla_20150411_misericordiae-vultus.html. A similarly themed document marking the end of the Jubilee of Mercy is "Misericordia et Misera," Holy See, November 20, 2016, https://w2.vatican.va/content/francesco/en/apost_letters/documents/papa-francesco-lettera-ap_20161120_misericordia-et-misera.html.

19. Pope Francis, *The Name of God Is Mercy: A Conversation with Andrea Tornielli*, trans. Oonagh Stransky (New York: Random House, 2016).

20. Cardinal Walter Kasper, *Mercy: The Essence of the Gospel and the Key to Christian Life*, trans. William Madges (New York: Paulist Press, 2013).

21. When Cardinal Kasper produced a follow-up book to his 2012 volume *Mercy*, cited in the previous note, a 2015 publication that described the major developments in the papacy of Francis thus far, he called it *Pope Francis' Revolution of Tenderness and Love: Theological and Pastoral Perspectives* (New York: Paulist Press, 2015). Francis subsequently embraced the phrase "a revolution of tenderness" as the goal that his Jubilee Year of Mercy hoped to advance.

22. Richard R. Gaillardetz, "In the Service of the People," *Tablet: The International Catholic Weekly*, April 16, 2016, 6–8, at 8.

5. TIRELESS ADVOCACY FOR THE WORLD'S MOST MARGINALIZED PEOPLE

1. Cardinal Vincent Nichols, "Understanding Francis," *Tablet: The International Catholic Weekly*, February 18, 2017, 4–5.

2. Statistical data from the United Nations refugee agency's annual "Global Trends Report" appears in Rick Gladstone, "Displaced Population Hit Record in '16, U.N. Says," *New York Times*, June 19, 2017, A5.

3. One of these occasions was in the letter Francis sent to the U.S. Regional World Meeting of Popular Movements, which met in Modesto, California. Cardinal Turkson read the text of the letter to the delegates on February 16, 2017. The letter called on all to renounce "hate and xenophobia" and to resist the temptation to demonize immigrants. See coverage at Michael J. O'Loughlin, "Pope Francis to activists: Stand with migrants, do not deny climate science, there is no such thing as 'Islamic terrorism,'" *American Magazine*, February 17, 2017, https://www.americamagazine.org/politics-society/2017/02/17/pope-francis-activists-stand-migrants-do-not-deny-climate-science-there.

4. Noteworthy too have been many acts of resistance against these anti-immigration sentiments. For example, anti-immigrant executive orders proposing strict travel bans shortly after the inauguration of President Donald Trump were met with massive public demonstrations and other acts of protest. Pro-immigrant sentiment was frequently expressed in popular culture, such as in the genre of protest music. For example, in April 2017 recording artist Bruce Springsteen lent vocals to a song written and performed by musician Joe Grushecky titled "That's What Makes Us Great." The song includes the lyrics

"Some wanna slam the door / Instead of opening the gate . . . Aw, let's turn this thing around / Before it gets too late."

5. The Catholic Relief Services website (www.crs.org) describes all facets of the ongoing work of this premiere humanitarian relief organization, including the grounding of its work in the principles of Catholic social teaching.

6. For further theological analysis of the Catholic commitments in this area, see Kristin E. Heyer, *Kinship across Borders: A Christian Ethic of Immigration* (Washington, DC: Georgetown University Press, 2012); Donald Kerwin and Jill Marie Gerschutz, eds., *And You Welcomed Me: Migration and Catholic Social Teaching* (Lanham, MD: Rowman & Littlefield, 2009); Elizabeth W. Collier and Charles R. Strain, *Global Migration: What's Happening, Why, and a Just Response* (Winona, MN: Anselm Academic, 2017). The analysis of this chapter draws upon concepts developed in each.

7. Biblical scholars count at least three dozen occasions in which the Old Testament enjoins the welcoming of strangers and travelers from other lands and the generous treatment of resident aliens. See Exodus 23:9 and Leviticus 19:33, among others.

8. See "Strangers No Longer: Together on the Journey of Hope," United States Conference of Catholic Bishops, January 22, 2003, http://www.usccb.org/issues-and-action/human-life-and-dignity/immigration/strangers-no-longer-together-on-the-journey-of-hope.cfm.

9. For details, see "Signs of the Times: Refugee Office," *America*, January 2, 2017, 10.

10. Three articles of that landmark 1948 document directly treat issues of migration, albeit with considerable open-endedness. Article 13 affirms the right of all to freedom of movement; Article 14 guarantees "the right to seek and to enjoy in other countries asylum from persecution"; Article 15 guarantees "the right to a nationality" and "the right to change nationality."

11. A good example is the North African nation of Chad, one of the poorest nations on earth, which currently hosts 300,000 refugees from Sudan who are fleeing drought, famine, and civil strife.

12. Pope Francis, "Address to the Participants in the Plenary of the Pontifical Council for the Pastoral Care of Migrants and Itinerant People, May 24, 2013," reprinted in *The Church of Mercy: A Vision for the Church* (Chicago: Loyola Press, 2014), 105.

13. Concerns about fair and adequately flexible applications of existing federal laws have led a growing number of cities and municipalities in the United States to declare themselves "sanctuary cities," where local law enforcement and other civic agencies deliberately do not cooperate with federal authorities on immigration enforcement. The concept of sanctuary is of course based on long-standing religious principles and practices, whereby church buildings

serve as inviolable sites of safe refuge for the persecuted. Although many U.S. congregations have adopted a sanctuary stance to shield migrants from federal immigration enforcement, such protection is necessarily a short-term option requiring more permanent arrangements and strategies.

14. For a succinct account of this impressive advocacy over the past century, see Julia G. Young, "Still Welcoming the Stranger: The U.S. Bishops and Immigration," *Commonweal*, March 10, 2017, 9–10.

15. Pope Francis most famously employed this metaphor on February 18, 2016. In a wide-ranging exchange with reporters aboard his return flight to Rome after his visit to Mexico, he was asked to respond to the proposal of then candidate Donald Trump to build a border wall between Mexico and the United States. Without mentioning the name of Trump, the pope identified the Christian path as the one that builds and embraces bridges to others rather than constructing walls against them. His exact words were "A person who thinks only about building walls, wherever they may be, and not building bridges, is not Christian. This is not in the Gospel." See coverage of this controversy in Patrick Healy, "Trump Fires Back at Sharp Rebuke by Pope Francis: A Clash on Immigrants," *New York Times*, February 19, 2016, A1, A20. The dispute did not prevent Francis from hosting President Trump's visit to the Vatican on May 24, 2017, where the two met cordially. Francis offered as a gift to the president copies of the three major papal writings treated in this volume.

16. Paragraph 18 of Pope Francis, "Misericordia et Misera," Holy See, November 20, 2016, https://w2.vatican.va/content/francesco/en/apost_letters/documents/papa-francesco-lettera-ap_20161120_misericordia-et-misera.html.

17. Francis wrote a strongly worded July 2014 letter decrying this situation and calling for an urgent response by Mexican and U.S. officials. The letter was delivered by the pope's top diplomat Cardinal Pietro Parolin (the Vatican's secretary of state) to the Colloquium on Migration and Development, which included abundant Mexican representation.

18. Archbishop Jurkovic spoke on June 9, 2017, to the conference "Unaccompanied Migrant Children and Adolescents and Human Rights" convened by the United Nations Human Rights Council in Geneva. See coverage in Junno Arocho Esteves, "Not Protecting Child Migrants Is an 'Insult to Human Dignity,' Vatican Says," *American Magazine*, June 12, 2017, https://www.americamagazine.org/politics-society/2017/06/12/not-protecting-child-migrants-insult-human-dignity-vatican-says?utm_source=Newletters&utm_campaign=083fb4a723-EMAIL_CAMPAIGN_2017_06_08&utm_medium=email&utm_term=0_0fe8ed70be-083fb4a723-57441285.

19. For an engaging account of the skillful use of the Twitter account of Pope Francis for this purpose, see Martin J. O'Loughlin, "Immigration," chap-

ter 14 of *The Tweetable Pope: A Spiritual Revolution in 140 Characters* (Chicago: Loyola Press, 2015), 85–196.

20. These short monthly videos are easily located on YouTube or atwww.thepopevideo.org.

21. Insightful coverage of this event appears in a "Newsroom" posting by Jacquelyn Pavilon, "Global: Opening the Doors, World Day of Migrants and Refugees," Jesuit Refugee Service, January 16, 2016, http://en.jrs.net/news_detail?TN=NEWS-20160118055435.

22. For the full text of this address, see "The Protection of Migrants Is a Moral Duty," Vatican Radio, February 21, 2017, http://en.radiovaticana.va/news/2017/02/21/pope_francis_the_protection_of_migrants_is_a_moral_duty/1293921#.

23. For the full text of the homily at the Mass in the sports field on Lampedusa, see "Visit to Lampedusa, Homily of Holy Father Francis," Holy See, July 8, 2013, https://w2.vatican.va/content/francesco/en/homilies/2013/documents/papa-francesco_20130708_omelia-lampedusa.html.

24. For a description of the fierce violence endemic to this border region (often directed especially against women), see Nancy Pineda-Madrid, *Suffering and Salvation in Ciudad Juárez* (Philadelphia: Fortress Press, 2011).

25. A rather complete account of the Mexican itinerary of Francis is found in Jim Yardley and Azam Ahned, "Francis, at Border, Weighs in on American Debate over Immigration: Offers a Prayer for Compassion," *New York Times*, February 18, 2016, A6.

26. The full text of the homily at the Ciudad Juárez Fair Grounds on February 17, 2016, appears at http://w2.vatican.va/content/francesco/en/homilies/2016/documents/papa-francesco_20160217_omelia-messico-ciudad-jaurez.html.

27. An informative account of the pope's visit to Lesbos appears in Jim Yardley, "12 Syrians Get Gift of Refuge from the Pope," *New York Times*, April 17, 2016, A1, A4.

28. For some revealing details of the Vatican's local charitable activities, see Christopher Lamb, "View from Rome," *Tablet: The International Catholic Weekly*, January 14, 2017, 26.

29. See the brief video covering the opening of this facility sponsored by the Sant'Egidio Community, at "Pope Francis Opens a Laundromat," *America Magazine*, April 11, 2017, http://www.americamagazine.org/faith/2017/04/11/pope-francis-opens-laundromat.

30. Pope Francis, "Message for the Celebration of World Day of Peace, January 1, 2015," Holy See, http://w2.vatican.va/content/francesco/en/messages/peace/documents/papa-francesco_20141208_messaggio-xlviii-

giornata-mondiale-pace-2015.html. The message bears the title "No Longer Slaves, but Brothers and Sisters."

31. "Human Trafficking: Pope Francis: 'A Crime against Humanity,'" *America*, April 28–May 5, 2014, 9; "Hope against Human Trafficking," *America*, June 20–27, 2016, 11.

32. Francis has repeatedly advocated for the rights of persecuted religious minorities, including (besides Christians in Muslim-dominated lands) the Rohingya, a small Muslim minority in the predominantly Buddhist nation of Myanmar. See Kimiko de Freytas-Tamura, "Pope Rebukes Myanmar for Abuse of Rohingya," *New York Times*, February 9, 2017, A6.

33. See "Defeating the Darkness of Drug Dependency: Address to the Staff and Patients at the St. Francis Hospital," delivered July 23, 2013 in Rio de Janeiro and appearing in John Chathanatt, SJ, ed., *Unto the Margins: Pope Francis and His Challenges* (Bangalore, India: Claretian Publications, 2013), 313–16.

34. At his May 18, 2017, audience, Francis blessed, greeted, and embraced 150 sufferers of a highly stigmatizing genetic disorder called Huntington's disease. See Nicole Winfield, "Huntington's Disease: Pope Reaches Out to Sufferers to End Its Stigma," *San Francisco Chronicle*, May 19, 2017, A4.

35. On this history, see Austin Ivereigh, *The Great Reformer: Francis and The Making of a Radical Pope* (New York: Henry Holt and Company, 2014), esp. 313–14.

36. An influential recent resource is the collection of essays in David Hollenbach, SJ, ed., *Refugee Rights: Ethics, Advocacy and Africa* (Washington, DC: Georgetown University Press, 2008). See, especially, William O'Neill, SJ, "What We Owe to Refugees and IDPs: An Inquiry into the Rights of the Forcibly Displaced," 27–49.

37. One scriptural passage Francis frequently cites to inspire social commitment is the encounter between God and the murderous Cain, who attempts to cover his guilt by asking, "Am I my brother's keeper?" (Genesis 4:9). He invoked this, for example, at Lampedusa to support care for refugees and also in paragraph 211 of *Evangelii Gaudium* to justify concern for trafficked persons.

38. John Langan, SJ, "See the Person: Understanding Pope Francis' Statements on Homosexuality," *America*, March 10, 2014, 13–16.

39. On these points, see an influential article by an Argentinian Jesuit who was a teacher of the future pope: Juan Carlos Scannone, SJ, "Pope Francis and the Theology of the People," *Theological Studies* 77, no. 1 (March 2016): 118–35. See also Rafael Luciani, *Pope Francis and the Theology of the People*, trans. Phillip Berryman (Maryknoll, NY: Orbis Books, 2017).

40. All citations in this paragraph are from paragraphs 20–21 of *Misericordi-ae Vultus* (or "The Face of Mercy"), which is the April 11, 2015, Bull of Injunction of the Extraordinary Jubilee of Mercy. It appears at http://w2.vatican.va/content/francesco/en/apost_letters/documents/papa-francesco_bolla_20150411_misericordiae-vultus.html.

41. The transcription is contained in Russell Goldman, "Pope Tells Technology Leaders to Nurture Ties with Others," *New York Times*, April 27, 2017, A4.

42. Paul Vallely, *Pope Francis: Untying the Knots: The Struggle for the Soul of Catholicism* (New York: Bloomsbury, 2015). Other biographies of Francis render similar accounts of the pope's months in Córdoba.

43. See Antonio Spadaro, SJ, "A Big Heart Open to God: The Exclusive Interview with Pope Francis," *America*, September 30, 2013, 14–38.

44. From the 2015 annual report of Jesuit Refugee Services (JRS)/USA, 8. Annual reports and many other materials on JRS/USA are available at www.jrsusa.org; seewww.jrs.netfor materials on the worldwide organization with offices in Rome.

6. THE MISSION TO PEACEMAKING AND CONFLICT TRANSFORMATION IN OUR TIME

1. One impressive resource documenting these recent trends in Catholic approaches to peace (and published shortly before the election of Pope Francis) is Robert J. Schreiter, R. Scott Appleby, and Gerard F. Powers, eds., *Peacebuilding: Catholic Theology, Ethics and Praxis* (Maryknoll, NY: Orbis Books, 2010).

2. *Gaudium et Spes*, paragraph 78.

3. *Populorum Progressio*, paragraphs 76–78 and 87. Note the deliberate contrast to the ancient slogan "If you want peace, prepare for war."

4. In the Catholic liturgical calendar, December 8 marks the Solemnity of the Immaculate Conception of the Blessed Virgin Mary, who is considered the Queen of Peace, so popes have appropriately often released these annual messages on this major Marian feast.

5. Pope Francis, "Fraternity: The Foundation and Pathway to Peace: Message for the Celebration of World Day of Peace, 1 January 2014," Holy See, December 8, 2013, http://w2.vatican.va/content/francesco/en/messages/peace/documents/papa-francesco_20131208_messaggio-xlvii-giornata-mondiale-pace-2014.html.

6. "Message of His Holiness Pope Francis for the Celebration of the XLIX World Day of Peace, 1 January 2016," Holy See, December 8, 2015, http://w2.vatican.va/content/francesco/en/messages/peace/documents/papa-francesco_20151208_messaggio-xlix-giornata-mondiale-pace-2016.html.

7. "Message of His Holiness Pope Francis for the Celebration of the Fiftieth World Day of Peace, 1 January 2017, Holy See, December 8, 2016, http://w2.vatican.va/content/francesco/en/messages/peace/documents/papa-francesco_20161208_messaggio-l-giornata-mondiale-pace-2017.html.

8. Many statements of national bishops' conferences, both during and after the Cold War, invited closer scrutiny in applying just-war criteria. In 1983, the U.S. bishops published the pastoral letter "The Challenge of Peace: God's Promise and Our Response," calling into question several pillars (such as the doctrine of deterrence that includes mutually assured destruction and the targeting of civilians) of American military policy during the Ronald Reagan years.

9. The best introduction to this approach is a volume edited by a noted late American Baptist scholar who compiled essays primarily from Protestant scholars: Glen Stassen, ed., *Just Peacemaking: Ten Practices for Abolishing War*, 2nd ed. (Cleveland, OH: Pilgrim Press, 1998).

10. The English text of the two-page April 2016 statement appears at "An Appeal to the Catholic Church to Re-commit to the Centrality of Gospel Nonviolence," Catholic Nonviolence Initiative, https://nonviolencejustpeace.net/final-statement-an-appeal-to-the-catholic-church-to-re-commit-to-the-centrality-of-gospel-nonviolence.

11. See two illuminating articles on this Vatican conference that appear in the June 15, 2017, issue of *Commonweal*: Gerald W. Schlabach, "Just War: Enough Already?" (11–14) and Peter Steinfels, "The War against Just War: Enough Already" (15–20).

12. This account is supplied in John L. Allen Jr., *The Francis Miracle: Inside the Transformation of the Pope and the Church* (New York: Time Books, 2015), 85.

13. For example, John Paul II, despite his many pleas for peace amid global antagonisms throughout his reign as pope, did not issue words of disapproval when North Atlantic Treaty Organization forces intervened with force to protect Kosovars, Bosnians, and other ethnic minorities threatened by Serbian aggression after the breakup of Yugoslavia in the 1990s. In 1991, the Polish pope forthrightly declared, "We are not pacifists, we do not want peace at any cost." In the following decade, John Paul objected strenuously to the American-led invasion of Iraq in 2003 but not to the earlier military incursion into Afghanistan to hunt down al-Qaeda terrorists. Pope Benedict XVI justified the use of force by supporting the principle of "responsibility to protect," which implies a willingness to employ even lethal military force to protect

civilian lives. But recent popes have also on occasion scolded world powers for illegitimate or premature reliance on the force of arms, such as when they needlessly militarize efforts to contain terrorism.

14. *Gaudium et Spes* acknowledges that "governments cannot be denied the right to legitimate defense once every means of peaceful settlement has been exhausted," though its notes of realism were not unmixed. The hopeful tone of that Vatican II document is reflected in its idealistic expectation that someday war will be "rooted out of human affairs" and that we will eventually reach "the time when all war can be completely outlawed by international consent" through "the establishment of some universal public authority" (paragraphs 79, 82).

15. The Latin phrase means "to the City [i.e., Rome] and to the World." This traditional Easter Sunday address often includes substantive reflections on the pope's aspirations for the church and wider world. It is thematically most appropriate to include an appeal for peace in ushering in a season of hope and new life and presenting the pope's Eastertide blessing over the crowds gathered in Saint Peter's Square.

16. The full text of the address to Congress is at "Visit to the Joint Session of the United States Congress, Address of the Holy Father, United States Capitol, Washington, D.C.," Holy See, September 24, 2015, http://w2.vatican.va/content/francesco/en/speeches/2015/september/documents/papa-francesco_20150924_usa-us-congress.html.

17. *Gaudium et Spes*, paragraph 81.

18. Citations in this paragraph and the next are from the English text of the pope's UN address at "Apostolic Journey of His Holiness Pope Francis to Cuba, to the United States of America and Visit to the United Nations Headquarters (19–28 September 2015)," Holy See, http://w2.vatican.va/content/francesco/en/speeches/2015/september/documents/papa-francesco_20150925_onu-visita.html.

19. The UN Arms Trade Treaty was adopted by the General Assembly on April 2, 2013, and went into force on December 24, 2014. As of this writing, ninety-one nations have ratified it, and forty-two other nations have signed but not ratified it, including the United States.

20. Some details in this account of 2013 events regarding Syria are taken from Allen, *The Francis Miracle*, 78–81.

21. Allen, *The Francis Miracle*, 84.

22. An additional benefit of this episode was a warming relationship between Francis and Raúl Castro, who has since met with and expressed great esteem for the pope. When Francis was looking for a neutral location for a meeting with Patriarch Kirill of the Russian Orthodox Church, Castro volunteered to host the historic encounter at the Havana airport, when Francis was

passing through the Caribbean on his way to his February 2016 visit to Mexico. See Jim Yardley, "Pope and Russian Orthodox Leader Meet in Historic Step to Heal Rift: Talk in Cuba Is First since East-West Split," *New York Times*, February 13, 2016, A4.

23. Certain of these details of the pope's visit to the Central African Republic appear in Chris Stein and Somini Sengupta, "In Africa, Pope Makes First Visit to a War Zone," *New York Times*, November 30, 2015, A6.

24. Hippolyte Marboua, "Central African Republic: 100 Dead in Armed Clashes in Wake of Peace Pact," *San Francisco Chronicle*, June 22, 2017, A5.

25. Certain details of the pope's visit to Egypt in this paragraph appear in Molly Hennessy-Fiskel, "Pope Delivers Antiterrorism, Unity Message," *San Francisco Chronicle*, April 29, 2017, A2. Others appear in Christopher Lamb, "The Pope in Egypt: Pilgrim for Peace," *Tablet: The International Catholic Weekly*, May 6, 2017, 4–5.

26. Jason Horowitz, "Pope Francis, in Egypt, Delivers a Blunt Message on Violence and Religion," *New York Times*, April 29, 2017, A6.

27. John W. O'Malley, SJ, *The First Jesuits* (Cambridge, MA: Harvard University Press, 1993), 169. Vivid accounts of this early Jesuit ministry of reconciliation appear on 169–71.

28. William C. Woody, SJ, "'So We Are Ambassadors of Christ': The Jesuit Ministry of Reconciliation," *Studies in the Spirituality of Jesuits* 49, no. 1 (spring 2017): 1–41, at 1.

29. Excerpt from a 2013 letter of Pope Francis to Reverend Alexandre Awi, released publicly in 2015 and appearing in Mark K. Shriver, *Pilgrimage: My Search for the Real Pope Francis* (New York: Random House, 2016), 13–14.

30. The sole inhabited continent not mentioned so far in this chapter is the pope's homeland of South America. A worthy additional case study in the peacemaking efforts of Francis is his September 2017 visit to Colombia, where he used every opportunity to promote the recently signed peace accords aimed at ending a half century of civil conflict in that bitterly divided nation. See Gerald O'Connell, "Pope Francis Tells Colombians, 'Be Slaves of Peace,'" *America*, October 2, 2007, 15.

31. The entire second half of chapter 4 of *Evangelii Gaudium* (paragraphs 217–57) deals with dialogue, the common good, and peace in society. In explaining his maxims "unity prevails over conflict" and "realities are more important than ideas," Francis displays his preference for the concrete over abstractions and his emphasis on persons over principles.

32. Allen, *The Francis Miracle*, 86.

CONCLUSION

1. "Justice in the World," Second General Assembly of the Synod of Bishops (1971).

2. A fine collection of many writings and addresses of Pope Francis on his vision of the church and exemplary pastoral leadership is Giuseppe Merola, ed., *With the Smell of the Sheep: The Pope Speaks to Priests, Bishops, and Other Shepherds* (Maryknoll, NY: Orbis Books, 2017). The two phrases in quotation marks recur frequently in this collection.

3. Among the most dramatic portrayals of these controversies is Marco Politi, *Pope Francis among the Wolves: The Inside Story of a Revolution* (New York: Columbia University Press, 2014). Politi provides lengthy descriptions of opposition to many of Francis's initiatives among officials of the Roman Curia.

4. Paragraph 129 of *Laudato Si'*.

5. This address was given to a delegation from the CISL (the Italian acronym for the Confederation of Workers' Unions) that had been invited to the pope's general audience on June 28, 2017. Besides affirming the constant support of Catholic social teaching (since *Rerum Novarum* in 1891) for labor unions, the address includes statements of concern about economic corruption, unemployment, and violations of the rights of women in the workplace. An English translation of the entire address appears at "Work Is a Form of Civil Love," ZENIT, June 28, 2017, https://zenit.org/articles/work-is-a-form-of-civil-love.

SELECTED BIBLIOGRAPHY

Allen, John L., Jr. *The Francis Miracle: Inside the Transformation of the Pope and the Church*. New York: Times Books, 2015.

Boff, Leonardo. *Francis of Rome and Francis of Assisi: A New Springtime for the Church*. Translated by Dinah Livingstone. Maryknoll, NY: Orbis Books, 2014.

Chathanatt, John, SJ. *Unto the Margins: Pope Francis and His Challenges*. Bangalore, India: Claretian Publications, 2013.

Christiansen, Drew, SJ. "On Relative Equality: Catholic Egalitarianism after Vatican II." *Theological Studies* 45 (1984): 651–75.

D'Ambrosio, Rocco. *Will Pope Francis Pull It Off? The Challenge of Church Reform*. Collegeville, MN: Liturgical Press, 2017.

Dal Toso, Paola. *Pope Francis and the Family*. Washington, DC: United States Conference of Catholic Bishops, 2014.

Deck, Allan, SJ. *Francis: Bishop of Rome: The Gospel for the Third Millennium*. New York: Paulist Press, 2016.

Dorr, Donal. *Option for the Poor and for the Earth: From Leo XIII to Pope Francis*. Maryknoll, NY: Orbis Books, 2016.

Faggioli, Massimo. *Pope Francis: Tradition in Transition*. New York: Paulist Press, 2015.

Francis, Pope. *The Name of God Is Mercy: A Conversation with Andrea Tornielli*. Translated by Oonagh Stransky. New York: Random House, 2016.

Gehring, John. *The Francis Effect: A Radical Pope's Challenge to the American Catholic Church*. Lanham, MD: Rowman & Littlefield, 2015.

Irwin, Kevin W. *A Commentary on* Laudato Si': *Examining the Background, Contributions, Implementation, and Future of Pope Francis's Encyclical*. New York: Paulist Press, 2016.

Ivereigh, Austen. *The Great Reformer: Francis and the Making of a Radical Pope*. New York: Henry Holt and Company, 2014.

Kasper, Cardinal Walter. *Mercy: The Essence of the Gospel and the Key to Christian Life*. Translated by William Madges. New York: Paulist Press, 2013.

———. *Pope Francis' Revolution of Tenderness and Love: Theological and Pastoral Perspectives*. New York: Paulist Press, 2015.

Keenan, James F., SJ. "Receiving *Amoris Laetitia*." *Theological Studies* 78, no. 1 (March 2017): 193–212.

Kelly, Conor M. "The Role of the Moral Theologian in the Church: A Proposal in Light of *Amoris Laetitia*." *Theological Studies* 77, no. 4 (December 2016): 922–48.

Luciani, Rafael. *Pope Francis and the Theology of the People*. Maryknoll, NY: Orbis Books, 2017.

Merola, Giuseppe, ed. *With the Smell of the Sheep: The Pope Speaks to Priests, Bishops, and Other Shepherds*. Maryknoll, NY: Orbis Books, 2017.

O'Collins, Gerald, SJ. "The Joy of Love (*Amoris Laetitia*): The Papal Exhortation in Its Context." *Theological Studies* 77, no. 4 (December 2016): 905–21.

O'Loughlin, Martin J. *The Tweetable Pope: A Spiritual Revolution in 140 Characters*. New York: HarperCollins Publishers, 2015.

O'Malley, John W., SJ. *The First Jesuits*. Cambridge, MA: Harvard University Press, 1993.

Piketty, Thomas. *Capital in the Twenty-First Century*. Translated by Arthur Goldhammer. Cambridge, MA: Harvard University Press, 2014.

Pique, Elisabetta. *Pope Francis: Life and Revolution: A Biography of Jorge Bergoglio*. Chicago: Loyola Press, 2013.

Politi, Marco. *Francis among the Wolves: The Inside Story of a Revolution*. New York: Columbia University Press, 2015.

Pontifical Council for Justice and Peace. *Compendium of the Social Doctrine of the Church*. Washington, DC: United States Conference of Catholic Bishops, 2004.

Rourke, Thomas R. *The Roots of Pope Francis's Social and Political Thought: From Argentina to the Vatican*. Lanham, MD: Rowman & Littlefield, 2016.

Scannone, Juan Carlos, SJ. "Pope Francis and the Theology of the People." *Theological Studies* 77, no. 1 (March 2016): 118–35.

Schreiter, Robert J., R. Scott Appleby, and Gerard F. Powers, eds. *Peacebuilding: Catholic Theology, Ethics and Praxis*. Maryknoll, NY: Orbis Books, 2010.

Sedmak, Clemens. *A Church of the Poor: Pope Francis and the Transformation of Orthodoxy*. Maryknoll, NY: Orbis Books, 2016.

Shriver, Mark K. *Pilgrimage: My Search for the Real Pope Francis*. New York: Random House, 2016.

Spadaro, Antonio, SJ. "A Big Heart Open to God: The Exclusive Interview with Pope Francis." *America*, September 30, 2013, 14–38.

Stassen, Glen, ed. *Just Peacemaking: Ten Practices for Abolishing War*. 2nd ed. Cleveland, OH: Pilgrim Press, 1998.

Tornielli, Andrea, and Giacomo Galeazzi. *This Economy Kills: Pope Francis on Capitalism and Social Justice*. Collegeville, MN: Liturgical Press, 2015.

Vallely, Paul. *Pope Francis: Untying the Knots: The Struggle for the Soul of Catholicism*. New York: Bloomsbury, 2015.

INDEX

abortion, 107, 159, 171
Albania, 49
Amoris Laetitia ("On Love in the Family"), viii, 70, 97–98, 103, 104–114, 116–117, 127, 174, 190n12
Aparecida, 26, 181n4
Argentina, v, 8, 16, 31, 49, 53, 66, 101, 139, 143, 145–146, 168, 169, 179n2–179n4
arms trade, 152, 154, 159–162
Arrupe, Pedro, 146

Bangladesh, 59
Bartholomew, Patriarch. *See* Orthodox Christian Churches
Bellarmine, St. Robert, 16
Benedict XVI, Pope, v, 19, 29, 75, 80–86, 160, 174, 181n3, 181n8, 185n1, 187n12–187n13, 188n21, 198n13
Bergoglio family, 4–6, 145–146, 169–170
Bible. *See* scripture
Bishops' Conferences, 74–75, 92, 93, 102, 124, 188n21, 191n16, 198n8. *See also* USCCB and CELAM
Bolivia, 6, 55, 57, 65, 145, 184n12
Buenos Aires, 4–6, 8, 66, 67, 110, 145

Caritas in Veritate ("Charity in Truth"), 76, 187n13
cartoneros (garbage pickers), 6, 66

Catholic Church: global mission of, 1; internal reforms of, 3; as "a poor church for the poor", 2, 31–32, 55, 135, 177; teachings on environment before Francis, 72–76; teachings on inequality before Francis, 33–39; teachings on refugee rights (before Francis), 124
Catholic Relief Services, x, 123, 193n5
Catholic social teaching: continuity and change in, vi; defined, vi, 24; development of, 17–19; on the environment, 72–74; and *Evangelii Gaudium*, 33–39; Francis develops, 23; as offering only general principles, 65; and Peronism, 7; positions on economic production, 62; topics within, viii, 98; vehicles of, 1
CELAM (Spanish acronym for Latin American Conference of Bishops), 32, 181n4
Centesimus Annus ("On the Hundredth Anniversary of *Rerum Novarum*"), 74, 187n13
Central African Republic, 165–85, 200n23–200n24
charity and justice (as related), 18, 30, 35, 177
children, 56, 60, 101, 108, 109, 126–127, 129–130, 134, 194n18